DEMOLISHING DETROIT

DEMOLISHING DETROIT

HOW STRUCTURAL RACISM ENDURES

NICHOLAS L. CAVERLY

STANFORD UNIVERSITY PRESS
Stanford, California

Stanford University Press
Stanford, California

This book has been published with the assistance of the Office of the Vice Chancellor for Research and Engagement, University of Massachusetts Amherst.

Library of Congress Cataloging-in-Publication Data
Names: Caverly, Nicholas L., author.
Title: Demolishing Detroit : how structural racism endures / Nicholas L. Caverly.
Description: Stanford, California : Stanford University Press, [2026] | Includes bibliographical references and index.
Identifiers: LCCN 2025026349 (print) | LCCN 2025026350 (ebook) | ISBN 9781503640252 (cloth) | ISBN 9781503644687 (ebook)
Subjects: LCSH: Abandoned buildings—Michigan—Detroit. | Wrecking—Social aspects—Michigan—Detroit. | White supremacy (Social structure)—Michigan—Detroit. | Detroit (Mich.)—Buildings, structures, etc. | Detroit (Mich.)—Economic conditions. | Detroit (Mich.)—Social conditions.
Classification: LCC F574.D48 A2485 2026 (print) | LCC F574.D48 (ebook) | DDC 307.309774/34—dc23/eng/20250603
LC record available at https://lccn.loc.gov/2025026349
LC ebook record available at https://lccn.loc.gov/2025026350

Cover design: Jason Anscomb
Front cover art: Charles McGee, *Urban Extract II* (1979), mixed media, Detroit Institute of Arts; © Detroit Institute of Arts / Bridgeman Images; back cover art: photo by the author

The authorized representative in the EU for product safety and compliance is: Mare Nostrum Group B.V. | Mauritskade 21D | 1091 GC Amsterdam | The Netherlands | Email address: gpsr@mare-nostrum.co.uk | KVK chamber of commerce number: 96249943

CONTENTS

MAP. Detroit and surrounding region.

Credit: Erin Greb Cartography.

ACKNOWLEDGMENTS

I will never be able to adequately thank the people and places who made this book possible—especially people in Detroit, Ann Arbor, New York, and Massachusetts. But I will try. Maria Galano has lived with this book for as long as I have. I would not have made it without her supportive reminders that the point of writing a book is for other people to read it.

Alongside Maria, this book would literally not exist without the people in Detroit who welcomed me onto their porches and into their homes, offices, workplaces, and lives. Their analyses of their city, its buildings, and its demolitions were my starting points. Detroiters' careful generosity and critiques over more than a decade made my work better. The people I call Rayshawn, Kenyetta, Dorothy, Daisy, Sam, Jay, Billy, and Joel were especially key over the years. If they're reading this, they know who they are. Patient staff in libraries and special collections at the Detroit Public Library, the University of Michigan, Wayne State University, and the Library of Michigan helped me find indexed files, as well as unindexed ones. Employees in the Wayne County Clerk's Office taught me how any administrative office can be an archive with the right FOIA request. Staff in the Detroit City Clerk's Office, the Detroit Land Bank Authority, and the Michigan Department of Environmental Quality (subsequently Department of Environment, Great Lakes, and Energy) also helped with such requests.

Academic institutions that made this book possible are settler colonial projects built from stolen Indigenous lands. This includes the forced taking of Bodwewademi, Odawa, and Ojibwe lands to establish the endowment of the University of Michigan. It also includes the lands of at least eighty-two Indigenous nations across the continent that state actors stole and sold as part of the Morrill Land Grant Act to establish what is now the University of Massachusetts. I have benefited from these institutions—including through the compound interest of university research trusts. Acknowledging how our places of learning and scholarship are propped up on the collateralized violence of racial capitalism is important. But it is not justice. Justice requires institutional actions that return stolen lands to their peoples. As a settler descendent, I am grateful to coworkers, neighbors, and students who are teaching me how to fight for actual justice in our classrooms and workplaces.

At the University of Michigan, the Science, Technology, and Society Program, the Institute for the Humanities, and the Department of Anthropology provided supportive structures for grappling with a messed-up world and struggles to make it otherwise. Andrew Shryock showed me the promise of ethnography and encouraged me to let my interlocutors speak on their own terms. Eric Mueggler modeled writing through experiences that are embodied and emplaced, as well as the importance of historical analysis. Liz Roberts's insistence that everything is complicated, so being specific matters has shaped the trajectory of my work. Will Glover was always there when I needed to be reminded that cities are physical landscapes as much as conceptual ones. Gabrielle Hecht is an inspiration for so many reasons, especially her refusal to take disciplines too seriously, commitments to keeping politics in view, and always making time for rest.

I landed in Western Massachusetts during the end of the world as I knew it. Thank you to the members of 413 Pandemic Social Club for helping me find safe ground in a new home. I also owe gratitude to my coworkers at the University of Massachusetts, especially in the Department of Anthropology, for opening the door for me when I needed it. Julie Hemment, Beverly Morrison, Maureen Perry-Jenkins, Grace Rock, and Jackie Urla worked miracles large and small at crucial junctures. Krista Harper and Kiran Asher are the best senior colleagues an assistant professor could have. They helped me find pleasure in being, as Kiran puts it, "a bastard child of disciplines." Krista, Kiran, Maria Galano, Juniper Katz, Sarah Roelker, Denise Pope, Sonia Rupcic, and Julia McDougal-Ronconi have kept me accountable to my writing.

I am fortunate to have had people to think with whose insights made this book richer, more precise, and just plain better. Audiences at the Five College Crossroads Institute for Studies of the Americas, Bentley University, Georgetown University, James Madison University, Smith College, and a Zube Lecture in Landscape Architecture and Regional Planning at the University of Massachusetts improved my ideas and arguments. So did participants in various meetings of the American Anthropological Association, Association of American Geographers, the Society for the Social Studies of Science, and the University of Michigan–Wits University Sugarman workshops. Individual conversations also shifted the course of this book. They include ones with Chloe Ahmann, Jamie Lee Andreson, Kiran Asher, Anne Berg, Katie Berringer, Christine Chalifoux, Sharad Chari, Carey Clouse, Henry Cowles, Robyn d'Avignon, Kevin Donovan, Jatin Dua, Sarah Ensor, Kriszti Fehervary, Cassie Fennell, Maria Galano, Claudia Gastrow, Will Glover, Brady G'Sell, Pamila Gupta, Krista Harper, Zehra Hashmi, Gabrielle Hecht, Colin Hoag, Joel Howell, Geoffrey Hughes, Matt Hull, RJ Koscielniak, Ali Kenner, Erik Mueggler, Emma Park, Damani Partridge, Dilshaine Perera, Vyjayanthi Rao, Josh Reno, Liz Roberts, Josh Roth, Sonia Rupcic, Shira Schwartz, Perrin Selcer, Andrew Shryock, Shreyas Sreenath, Marisa Solomon, Bettina Stoetzer, Nishita Trisal, Antina von Schnitzler, Kirsten Weis, Daniel Williford, and two anonymous readers. I apologize to everyone I've missed here. Kiran, Krista, Maria, Marisa, Sonia, and those two anonymous readers warrant extra special thanks.

Fellowships from the Rackham Program in Public Scholarship, the Graham Institute for Sustainability, the Institute for the Humanities, and the Department of Anthropology—all at the University of Michigan—supported early stages of research that laid the groundwork for this book. Grants from the Social Science Research Council, the National Science Foundation (Cultural Anthropology #1628096), and the Wenner-Gren Foundation (#9326) were key to remaining in Detroit for years at a time. Support from Bentley University's Valente Center for Arts and Sciences helped me reframe chapter 6. I would not have completed a full manuscript on schedule without the precious leave afforded by a Hunt Fellowship from the Wenner-Gren Foundation (#10553). Financial support for manuscript production was provided by the Office of the Vice Chancellor for Research and Engagement, University of Massachusetts Amherst.

Research and writing are work. I had the opportunity to become a researcher only because generations of Graduate Employees' Organization (AFT #3550, AFL-CIO) members imagined, argued, and struck to win contracts that made the University of Michigan accessible to people without independent wealth. GEO members taught me how power works and what solidarity looks like. They also protected the insurance that got me through fieldwork whole. Similar thanks to my fellow faculty and librarians in the Massachusetts Society of Professors (MTA/NEA), who strive for the University of Massachusetts that our students, coworkers, and commonwealth deserve.

At Stanford University Press, Dylan Kyung-lim White saw promise in this project and helped me remember why I was writing it. I am lucky to have worked with an editor who thinks carefully about what university press books can be and how they can matter in the world. SUP staff, especially Dylan, Austin Araujo, and Justine Sargent, facilitated the review process. Chris Peterson guided the manuscript through production. Barbara Armentrout's careful copyediting made this book readable. Celia Braves's index made it easier to find what you're looking for. Melissa Jauregui Chavez was key to getting the completed book into readers' hands. I am also grateful to the estate of Charles McGee and the Detroit Institute of Arts for permission to use "Urban Extract II," as well as to Jason Anscomb for incorporating it on the cover.

Finally, I would not be here without the care of the people who have raised and sheltered me. Mary, Ed, and Jordan have cheered for me at every turn. My confidence to say what I mean is thanks to them. Maria, Nancy, Fidel, Elena, Fidel, Christine, and Brittany have all made space in their lives for me to have a home. My life is better with them in it.

I'm grateful for all of you. This book is thanks to you. Except the faults—those are mine.

INTRODUCTION

FROM DESTRUCTION

This book is about structural racism. Specifically, it is about how racially unequal landscapes of power, resources, privileges, and harms endure in the absence of deliberately racist ideologies and policies. My approach to understanding the ongoing reality of structural racism comes by way of empty-building demolitions in Detroit. Since the middle of the twentieth century, crews have leveled hundreds of thousands of buildings in Detroit, totaling more than half of the structures ever built there. The more than 30,000 buildings demolished in the past decade include warehouses, factories, office towers, apartment blocks, and thousands upon thousands of homes. If you know Detroit, you know those empty buildings are the products of racist disinvestment from the city, especially white flight, capital abandonment, and antiblack dispossession. For city residents, public officials, and onlookers, transforming empty buildings into grassy lots appeared to create economic opportunities and environmental uplift for Detroit's majority-Black, working-class populace. And yet, demolitions also produced unstable housing, hazardous working conditions, and other difficulties for city residents. When demolitions created profit and benefits, they mostly ended up going to wealthier, typically whiter people elsewhere. Thus, projects that many hoped would result in a more equitable city further engrained white supremacy and intersecting conditions of injustice. Alone, destruction does not even out racist landscapes of power, resources, privileges, and harms. Doing so demands strategically reconfiguring systems to make those landscapes work differently.

Here is an example of what I mean. Early on a summer morning, excavator operators unloaded heavy machinery on an otherwise quiet street in the northern reaches of Detroit's east side. A hundred or so people lived on the block at that point. Their one- and two-story dwellings wrapped in various colors of vinyl and aluminum siding sat side by side with nearly identical buildings whose missing windows and doors, drooping rooflines, and collapsed porches signaled that nobody had lived there for a while. Workers connected hoses to fire hydrants and began soaking six empty buildings with water. High-pitched hydraulic whines, the thunder of diesel engines, and the forceful pounding of metal treads as an excavator trundled off a trailer drew people who lived on the block onto their porches. A few dozen neighbors were massed in the street, watching intently as workers moved the excavator into position. People joined hands in a circle as a man offered a short prayer: "We thank you, God, for the women and men who take the lead in removing this blight, this structural refuse from our city. God, we take this time to pray peace into the world. For, Lord God, what is being done here is peace-giving work." Soon after, the operator raised the excavator arm and smashed it through the roof of a two-story house. Onlookers applauded as shingles, studs, siding, floors, tiles, and other materials splintered before collapsing into the basement.

I watched this scene with Edith, a Black, lifelong Detroiter in her eighties who lived on the block.[1] Edith set up lawn chairs in her yard, and throughout the day neighbors came by to sit, chat, and observe. Most were elders and longtime neighborhood residents. Their conversations recalled recent occupants of buildings being leveled, as well as the circumstances of their departures. There was talk of landlords asking for rent increases on houses where water leaked through the roof when it rained. Discussion of tax bills that went up every year while libraries were cut, schools were closed, and parks went unmaintained. Of factories that had been dormant for decades. People also spoke about their shared excitement at having empty buildings replaced with grass. These were not the first buildings razed on this block. Of the forty-eight buildings originally constructed there, just over half remained. Edith and her neighbors imagined that six more grassy lots might make

MAP 0.1. 35,364 demolitions in Detroit between 2010 and 2023.

Image by author. *Source:* City of Detroit, Detroit Land Bank Authority, State of Michigan.

FIGURE 0.1. An active demolition site.

Photo by the author.

enough space for improvised off-street parking or an extensive community garden. Without exception, Edith and others on her block preferred grass-covered lots to decomposing buildings. Nevertheless, at one point in the afternoon, Edith shuffled up her front porch steps and returned with a creased flyer someone had left on her stoop months before. Distributed by a nonprofit, the blue sheet cautioned readers against growing food directly in the city's empty lots due to the elevated presence of lead linked to demolitions that transformed lead-painted walls into dust that settled into the soil.

The crumpled piece of blue paper warning of possible lead contamination from demolishing buildings illustrates the central tension at stake in this book. Destructive processes that made structures seemingly disappear did not disrupt the systemic power relations that emptied Detroit's buildings. Detroiters queued up in municipal offices, at public meetings, and in front of news cameras to request that city officials dispatch demolition crews to tear down long-empty buildings next door or down the street.[2] People applauded when excavators rolled onto their blocks. For more than a century, Detroit and its surrounding region have remained among the most racially segregated and economically polarized parts of the United States.[3] Clearing away empty dwellings, factories, and other buildings that were the cumulative effects of discrimination made it possible to imagine places to live without the weight of racist disinvestment and loss. But knocking down buildings also created the conditions of possibility for surveilling Detroiters' homes. It reinforced profit-driven housing and work relations that left city residents precarious. Demolitions produced atmospheric and sedimented toxicities. When profits emerged from destructive processes, they tended to flow toward firm owners who were usually wealthy and white. Meanwhile, the predominantly Black and Latine Detroiters who related to demolitions as neighbors and laborers contended with them as sites of economic insecurity and emergent hazards. Building removals maintained racial whiteness as a location of wealth and well-being, while simultaneously compounding antiblack distributions of precarity and harm.

To be clear, racially unequal distributions of precarious work, profit, contamination, and other outcomes of building removal were not precipitated by biased contractors, regulators, or policymakers. There was no devious plot for tens of thousands of demolitions conducted in Detroit in recent years to engrain structural conditions of racial capitalism through white supremacy and antiblackness. It is important to stress this. It is also true that, in Detroit and elsewhere, administrative offices have wielded excavators and heavy equipment as tools of dispossession, leveling the places where racially and economically oppressed people live so that racially and economically privileged people can live there instead.[4] But that is not the case in the projects of intentional destruction examined in this book. For their part, demolition program staff worked to identify empty buildings in line with the perspectives of Detroiters in their neighborhoods. Drawing on research in urban planning, public health, and other fields, they imagined that tearing down these structures would remove barriers to Detroiters accessing formal sector employment and home financing.[5] Regulatory staff corralled demolition contractors to comply with environmental health and safety protocols. Rather than displacing people from their homes, demolitions were an effort to create a more livable city for Detroiters who already lived there. This book explicates how demolitions reinforced the very dynamics of racial privilege and oppression they appeared to be poised to eliminate. This happened even when people who designed programs, set policies, operated excavators, and enforced regulations were attempting to mitigate those very disparities.

For almost a century, what passes for urban policy in the United States has been organized around the idea that "demolition means progress"[6] and heralds the arrival of more just and inclusive cities. Across the twentieth century, cities leveled tenements and public housing projects in attempts to mitigate racist segregation and concentrated poverty.[7] In recent years, federal agencies have continued to allocate funds to demolish empty buildings, including $265 million directed to supplement local and state demolition funding in Detroit between 2014 and 2020. Following the late 2000s economic downturn that saw more than ten million people evicted from their homes across the United States, federal agencies held up Detroit's well-trod demolition routines as models for other cities to follow to dispatch with growing numbers of empty buildings. Recommendations that excavators tear down buildings came in places like Cleveland, Birmingham, Philadelphia, Jackson, and Memphis. As in Detroit, people living in these and other cities contended with empty buildings that materialized the entwined conditions of deindustrialization and racist disinvestment. As in Detroit, empty buildings were concentrated in racially and economically marginalized neighborhoods, with many hoping that clearing away empty structures would improve economic stability and environmental conditions for remaining residents. Rather than demolition as a process of clearing away the wreckage of disinvestment to make it possible to build a more equitable future, tearing things down itself seemed to offer a means of evening out entrenched inequities.

Examining the causes, processes, and consequences of demolitions in Detroit troubles the notion that the grass-covered lots created after demolition crews hauled away empty buildings contain a fresh start in the wake of racism and intersecting inequities. Instead, demolitions tended to reproduce the very conditions of inequity manifest in empty buildings, even if they were not intended to do so. Racist outcomes without racist intent are the calling cards of structural racism. In the United States and elsewhere, racial disparities in experiences and life chances continue to be relatively unchanged long after racist ideologies and policies have been seemingly rethought. Attending to demolitions in Detroit alongside people who experienced them as neighbors, laborers, and administrators provides a different vantage on this problem. It accounts for how racially unequal outcomes were produced through things like mortgage lending calculations, heavy equipment operations, regulatory paradigms, and the fallout radius of lead particles. This happened even when people who requested demolitions, designed programs to make them happen, operated excavators, and made regulatory decisions intended otherwise. More than a cautionary tale of unintended consequences, I argue demolitions make clear how racism is not simply an idea or institutional logic to be questioned. Racism shapes all our lives through unevenly constructed neighborhoods, buildings, worksites, and other places. Addressing racism and intersecting inequities will take more than dismantling systems with the promise of a clean slate. It demands accounting for structural damages and building up strategies of material repair.

DEFINING STRUCTURAL RACISM

In Detroit, boarded-over windows, tumbled-down chimneys, loose gutters, slumped roofs, and other features of empty buildings are the stuff of structural racism. Buildings make structural processes legible in the landscape. No matter what kind of building it is—a factory, a house, a warehouse, a skyscraper—the literal hundreds of thousands of structures that have been counted as empty in Detroit did not get to be that way by accident. When empty buildings first emerged in Detroit during the middle decades of the twentieth century, they marked how explicit policies and informal practices encouraged nearly a million white Detroiters to escape from an increasingly multiracial city for suburban municipalities that remained exclusively white. As this happened, many of Detroit's industrial titans were shifting production lines from slowly integrating city neighborhoods to all-white suburbs.[8] Explicitly racist policies nominally ended after midcentury uprisings and struggles for civil rights propelled the passage of antidiscrimination laws. But discriminatory practices continued apace, including financial institutions targeting majority-Black locations for foreclosure-prone adjustable loans. Alongside tens of thousands of mortgage foreclosures in recent decades, Detroiters have been emptied out of their homes by unaffordable municipal taxes. Attempting to shore up a diminishing tax base, Detroit's elected leaders boosted local property tax rates to some of the highest in the country.[9] Structural racism incorporates processes of white flight, capital disinvestment, and antiblack foreclosures that are differentially implicated in the making of empty buildings.

To name something as structural racism is to name it as a formation of racial capitalism. Building from a term first used by activists to describe the economic infrastructure of South African apartheid, the political theorist of the Black radical tradition Cedric Robinson broadened this concept to argue that capitalism has been predicated on racism since its beginning. On the origins of capitalist political economic relations in Europe, Robinson writes, "The tendency of European civilization through capitalism was not to homogenize but to differentiate—to exaggerate regional, subcultural, and dialectical differences into 'racial' ones."[10] With racial capitalism, Robinson and others locate interwoven structures of inequity, including racism, capitalism, coloniality, and heteropatriarchy, that render socially constructed categories into hierarchies of value.[11] These hierarchies are evident in the dispossession of Indigenous lands to create and subsequently maintain what is called the United States.[12] They are evident in economic relations that got their start through the theft and enslavement of African peoples to generate fortunes for European settler enslavers and their descendants.[13] They are evident in development paradigms that differentially allocate resources, contamination, displacement, and more depending on the degree to which a person or place conforms to normative, white, middle-class ways of being—all in the name of progress.[14] This book builds on these insights to grasp racial capitalism's "changing same."[15] This is to say it takes hold of inequities that might shift in appearance between past and present are structurally organized such that racism is always the cornerstone of profit.

Getting a handle on racial capitalism in the United States requires getting a handle on whiteness—and with it, white privilege and supremacy—as a structural condition. An idealized white, masculine, suburban homeowner is (and has long been) the gravitational center of moral and political economic life in the United States.[16] In a moment when people inhabit whiteness and other identities as flexible cultural constructs, it can be easy to lose sight of their persistence as structural conditions.[17] Nevertheless, philosopher and critic of racial liberalism Charles Mills helps to do so by identifying the stability of what he calls a "racial contract" as the basis of systems of power that have made and maintained private property in European metropoles and their colonial descendants.[18] The United States is emblematic but far from unique in its enactment of this contract, characterized by "the differential privileging of the whites as a group with respect to the nonwhites as a group, the exploitation of their bodies, land, and resources, and the denial of equal socioeconomic opportunities to them."[19] Importantly for my purposes here, Mills notes, "All whites are *beneficiaries* of the Contract, though some whites are not *signatories* to it." [20] Put simply, those of us who benefit from whiteness are entangled with it as a structural condition. We cannot wipe away the racial contract of white supremacy simply by saying we do not individually identify with it.

People benefit from the racial contract of white supremacy without signing onto it because racism structures disparities in life chances and experiences. Critical geographer of racial capitalism Ruth Wilson Gilmore provides a widely shared definition of racism when she writes, "Racism, specifically, is the state-sanctioned or extralegal production and exploitation of group-differentiated vulnerability to premature death."[21] Gilmore's definition underscores how racism is a system of violence that produces racial disparities in life expectancy.[22] By way of example, consider how the average Detroiter is expected to live 69 years, whereas the average resident of the city's suburbs is expected to live 76 years.[23] White Detroiters are expected to live eight years longer on average than Black Detroiters. Actuarial statistics of this sort reflect how Detroit has been a majority-Black city at the center of a majority-white metropolitan region since the middle of the twentieth century. At certain moments, laws ensured that the typical white resident of this region was paid a higher salary, had more reliable access to secure housing, and lived further from environmental hazards than the typical Black resident. Despite explicit policies of white supremacy ending in the late twentieth century following protracted civil rights uprisings, Detroit remains a majority-Black city at the center of a majority-white metropolitan region. The typical white resident of this region is paid a higher salary, has more reliable access to secure housing, and lives farther from environmental hazards than the typical Black resident. The racial contract persists even if its legal codifications disappear.

Detroit offers a diagnostic case of how the hinges between white supremacy and capital accumulation run deep. It is even in the name—Detroit. Inherited from the word French settlers used to name a trading center on a watery strait, this name claims the riverbend meeting place that Odawa, Bodwewademi, and Ojibwe peoples and their Anishnaabemowin-speaking relations would call Waawiiyaataanong. To build an eighteenth-century colonial outpost into a nineteenth-century city, French and subsequently British and American settlers incrementally dispossessed Indigenous lands and waters into settler property. In so doing, they extracted the timber, mineral deposits, real estate, and other resources that made their city into a global icon of twentieth-century industrial capitalism. Josiah Rector's environmental justice history of Detroit identifies how this transformation was facilitated by household and municipal debt instruments that sorted white and wealthy people into suburban neighborhoods and workplaces that would be most protected from the flow of industrial hazards.[24] Making such protections possible entailed shuffling Black, Brown, and impoverished Detroiters into central city neighborhoods and workplaces where they contended with toxic air, unaffordable housing, unclean water, and related harms.[25] Put simply, structural racism at the intersections of white supremacy, antiblackness, and coloniality is built into Detroit's foundations. Present-day conditions of inequity may manifest in emergent ways, but they are also entailed within systems of racial capitalism that have organized—and continue to organize—people through place.

This book turns to the process of tearing down empty buildings produced by racist disinvestment from Detroit to understand how the realities of structural racism remain. Tracing out unevenly distributed profits, contamination, and precarities produced by knocking down empty buildings surfaces how the structural conditions of white supremacy and its associated inequities can endure even as the environments in which they are embedded appear to be entirely transformed. Racist outcomes—and with them, capital—continue to accumulate through the aggregation of things like regional landscapes, asbestos fibers, algorithms, heavy machineries, and patches of earth. Ultimately, demolitions create vulnerability, abandonment, and deprivation for Detroiters, especially but not exclusively Black and Brown Detroiters. Those same systems also create stability, security, and wealth elsewhere—particularly but not always to the benefit of white people. By charting how racially unequal outcomes emerged from demolitions in Detroit, this book foregrounds how the material conditions of structural racism, especially the racial contract of white supremacy, endure despite interventions that are seemingly designed to even them out. It does not do so to suggest that formations of racial capitalism are so intractable that racist conditions of the past are destined to shape the present and future. On the contrary, I do so to demonstrate how paying close attention to the ways structural racism endures is an essential starting point to building up systems that address their cumulative harms.

STRUCTURAL RELATIONS

Empty buildings, demolition sites, and their aftermaths became places where Detroiters contended with the material conditions of structural racism. Bad actors certainly existed. They include demolition contractors who padded their profit margins by disregarding environmental protections. They also include demolition administrators who looked the other way as this happened. And yet, racially unequal distributions of benefits and harms also flowed in the absence of people and organizations who might be labeled as racists. Chapter 1 shows how empty buildings materialize structures of whiteness and private property connecting settler development paradigms with processes of antiblack disinvestment. Chapter 2 attends to systems that allowed Detroiters to shape administrative decisions about which buildings came down and which remained standing, but in so doing opened neighborhoods to increased scrutiny from municipal officials. Chapter 3 parses how removing empty buildings unlocked conventional home financing for Black Detroiters while also making it more difficult for them to secure affordable places to live. Chapter 4 examines how excavator operations created worksites in which white masculinity was a location of stable economic benefits that contrasted with antiblack precarities. Chapter 5 turns to asbestos abatement laborers, most of them Black Detroiters, who inhaled aerosolized toxins to complete work on time and within regulatory compliance. Chapter 6 works alongside Detroiters who confront a regulatory system that allows lead and other hazards to sediment from building components into soils. Together, these chapters show how racially unequal conditions endured through demolitions despite efforts to the contrary.

It would be helpful if I could point to a person, policy, organization, or state agency that designed demolitions to route precarities and vulnerabilities almost exclusively into the lives of Black, Brown, and poor people. Or to someone who designed demolitions such that any profits extracted or stability gained accrued to people who were almost always white and already wealthy. In the United States, gaining legal redress for racist harms is dependent on identifying concrete actors who make purposeful decisions.[26] Moreover, racism appears more tractable if we attribute it to a specific practice, group, idea, or person. Approaching white supremacy and related inequities as ideological problems makes it seem like those inequities would stop if only we could change the ways racist people think. Scholar of innovation and social inequity Ruha Benjamin cautions against this paradigm by demonstrating how the disparate benefits and harms that drive racial capitalism are encoded into "the machine" of technological systems and landscapes. In Benjamin's analysis, this machine "normalizes racial hierarchies—not as an ideological aberration from business-as-usual, but as an economic imperative that is built into the machine. . . . Likewise, changing individual sentiment from animus to tolerance, or even affection, will not transform the status quo so long as the underlying design of our socio-technical world is left in place."[27] Addressing racism takes more than identifying racist decisions or changing how people think. It demands changing the underlying systems that shape how our world works.

Benjamin and others working to elucidate the infrastructural dimensions of racial capitalism identify how disparities in opportunities and life chances are not simply a social problem. Empirically, racism is reproduced and reinscribed at the interface of social, technical, and material systems. These systems can range in size from roadways that cut through neighborhoods to algorithmic processes that allocate resources to devices that determine exactly how much contamination enters a person's breathing space.[28] For example, consider Johannesburg thirty years after a progressive constitution nominally ended the white supremacist apartheid project. Historian and anthropologist of technology Gabrielle Hecht describes how political commitments to environmental, economic, and racial justice did not dislodge the ways racism was baked into the very geographies of places like Johannesburg.[29] Apartheid institutions built shoddy housing for impoverished Black South Africans atop hazardous mine tailings, and in the wake of apartheid, impoverished Black South Africans still lived in shoddy housing constructed atop hazardous mine tailings. As Hecht puts it, "Long after the end of legalized racism, the proliferating residues of racial capitalism continue to sediment in financial tools, urban spaces, and health systems. Not to mention water, land, and air."[30] Racial capitalism becomes durable because it is physically constructed into the bodies and places through which people live. As this happens, inequities endure through even the most thorough efforts at social change and political transformation.

Building on these insights, this book identifies how the structural conditions of racial capitalism proliferate through systems that produce and maintain racist outcomes in the absence of racist people. In so doing, it contributes to demonstrating how the endurance of structural racism is not merely the side effect of so-called colorblind ideologies that allow those of us who benefit from the cumulative effects of racism to claim ignorance of our privileges.[31] Make no mistake, those ideologies exist. But as critical analyses of racial capitalism show us time and again, changing individual and collective understandings of race does not change how the violence of racism is a sociomaterial process enacted through landscapes in which some of us experience secure housing, healthy environments, and economic dignity while others do not.[32] Empty buildings clustered in Detroit's neighborhoods, employment practices in which suburban residents have a leg up, hazardous dusts that settle on the perimeters of demolition sites even when all regulations are followed—these and other conditions explored in the following chapters are all examples of how racism entails ongoing structural violence, or the kinds of violence that cannot be traced back to discrete people or motives but come from systems rolling forward.[33] Working from this vantage brings into view how racism—in this case, formations of white supremacist racial capitalism—becomes enshrined in and perpetuated by unevenly constructed buildings, neighborhoods, and environments.

Racist systems knit people into relations of privilege and oppression. Take the construction of dwellings as commodities to be bought and sold for a profit that sits at the core of the housing system in the United States. Until late in the twentieth century, real estate practices and financial institutions in this country were deliberately organized to produce wealth for people racialized as white by excluding everyone else, especially Black people.[34] This posed one of many structural barriers to Black families amassing intergenerational wealth.[35] When explicitly racist practices went away, housing transactions were open to anyone with the ability to pay, a form of inclusion that did nothing to address the centuries of exclusion that preceded it.[36] As a result, in the decades following the formal end of discriminatory housing policies, even as the wealth of Black, Latine, and Indigenous people in the United States has grown, so too have racialized wealth gaps between white Americans and everyone else, driven primarily by compound interest on past real estate profits.[37] In such circumstances, benefiting from white supremacy is less a question of what is in your head and more a matter of what is (or is not) in your bank account. In the absence of deliberate efforts to challenge those benefits, racial disparities are systematically primed to endure. They are maintained by a political economic system in which wealth accrues fastest to those who already have it.

Through an engagement with the ways racially unequal outcomes become structured in and perpetuated through things like municipal boundaries, excavator operations, and workplace atmospheres, this book traces how inequities are maintained without discrete actors at the wheel. In contending with such inequities as a problem of racist systems rather than deliberately racist people, policies, or institutions, I am not suggesting that it is impossible to discern who benefits from the violence of structural racism. On the contrary, following out how systems work makes it possible to understand how complicities unevenly build up and compound. Demolitions maintained the prevailing conditions of white supremacy and antiblackness in Detroit through neighborhood mapping, heavy machineries, environmental regulations, and other concerns. Attending to how that happened makes it apparent how the stable homes, healthy environments, and associated material foundations of racial privilege that some of us might take for granted exist only due to the concentration of insecurities, hazards, and precarities through which people experience oppression elsewhere. Like the intersections of racism with other systems of power, systems are multidimensional. This book takes racist systems as its point of departure to demonstrate how the analytic leverage of shifting racism from a violence of discrete actions into one of systemic conditions does not mean obscuring people. Indeed, racist systems make it clear just how some people and places amass benefits from persistent structural inequities while others bear the costs.

WHY DETROIT

Detroit and Detroiters are good to think alongside if you want to understand how structural racism endures, the ways people encounter those structures, and what it might take for things to work differently. The relatively brief interactions with Edith and her neighbors that I write about at the beginning of this introduction are emblematic of the ways I encountered city residents who were careful observers of the forces shaping their city. They took note of the ways Detroit yokes historical and contemporary processes that ripple out across the continent and around the planet. In conversation around an empty building or patch of grass, people narrate how techniques of colonial expropriation channeled subsequent waves of migration, mass production, suburbanization, deindustrialization, and gentrification.[38] At the same time, city residents have built long-standing practices of mobilizing front porches, worksites, public meetings, and neighborhood gatherings as sites for reckoning with an unjust status quo.[39] In Detroit, environmental and economic justice have long been interwoven struggles against white supremacy through which city residents worked toward more livable prospects in local, regional, and planetary dimensions.[40] This is to say that this book is grounded in Detroit. It builds in dialogue with Detroiters to gain vantage on structures, processes, and strategies whose ramifications extend far beyond their city.

I am not from Detroit. I grew up in the region of "Metropolitan Detroit," of which the city is the nominal center, and I have spent more years living in suburbs that sprawl out from the city than anywhere else. Detroit has long been part of my world, but not in the ways it would be if I could credibly call myself a Detroiter. This background is important, I think, because as political philosopher Antonio Gramsci helpfully suggests, "The starting point of critical elaboration is the consciousness of what one really is, and is 'knowing thyself' as a product of the historical process to date which has deposited in you an infinity of traces without leaving an inventory."[41] Plainly speaking, then, I am a white man who has spent a large part of my life living in a place that has been the proving grounds for iterative projects of white supremacy on this continent and in this world.[42] My inventory of these conditions, especially the ways structural realities of white supremacy, antiblackness, and racial capital have shaped my lived experience did not come until I was an adult. Assembling it only came with the benefit of time and support. But like any of us, I am the product of those processes. Passing childhood discussions of school district boundaries or reminders to lock the car doors when crossing the city limits may have seemed innocuous at the moment. But with this inventory at hand, they are foghorns in retrospect.

Something I know from experience is how people are products of systems. Many adults I knew growing up worked jobs that were in some way connected to making cars and their component parts. Some were engineers and managers. Some worked the lines. This work kept rents and mortgages paid, put food on the table, and sent children to college. Yet I did not live in a factory town. Our air, water, and soil remained relatively clean while contaminants settled dozens, hundreds, and thousands of miles away. Through the militancy of suburban property values, the public schools I attended were among the best funded in the state. It was in those public schools that I learned how race, no matter how you cut it, is a genetically meaningless concept and a politically powerful one. Stolen Ojibwe, Odawa, Bodwewademi, Shawnee, and Wendat lands combined with automotive capitalism kept the public university I attended relatively affordable. It was at that public university where I learned to notice the cumulative violence of colonialism and racism that forms the foundation of private property and capital. Connecting the social construction of race to its origins in the violence of racism is an important lesson. Learning it does not necessarily disrupt systems that are built into the world, including the very classrooms, institutions, and regions in which we learn. But simply because systems can prove difficult to change does not mean we stop trying.

Detroit and its region make racist systems blatantly obvious. They are also locations where people have continually worked to make systems otherwise. Geographer Sara Safransky talks about how hundreds of thousands of grass-covered lots created by demolitions make Detroit the iconic "city after property."[43] "After property" because, in some conjunctures, development agendas hold those lots within private property systems that are the mutual cornerstone of settler colonialism, racial capitalism, and white supremacy. But also, "after property" because Detroiters make moves to till subsistence gardens and imagine possibilities beyond private property in places seemingly shaken free of buildings and infrastructure. For Safransky, such possibilities enacted "a city built from collective daily practices of care, a city where Black life flourished—a city after property."[44] One example Safransky documents is the 2010 proposal from an urban agriculture startup to purchase 1,500 grassy parcels from the municipal government. Protests from Detroiters delayed the proposal for several years. Opponents did not object to interspersing crops and orchards in their neighborhood, or even to the wealthy, white city resident who was the project's financial backer. In public meetings and community forums, they took to microphones to demand the land be preserved in trust for all city residents rather than a private claim benefiting only one. Though elected officials eventually approved the sale at a price of $350 per lot, Detroiters living in the vicinity of transferred lots continued to make use of them as spaces to gather and grow food for their own purposes.

As Safransky demonstrates, the oppositional tactics Detroiters deploy in their struggles for a more livable and just city are often helpful guides to practical moves for a more livable and just world.[45] For that reason, when I first moved to Detroit in 2010, I was surprised to find that many people agreed about the urgency of demolitions, including municipal state actors and the activists who typically opposed their plans. People may have disagreed fundamentally on what should happen after buildings came down—with activists' plans for a sprawling urban commons organized by neighborhood stewards in which everyone's basic needs were met, contrasting sharply with state officials' visions of increasing tax revenue through profit-driven industrial agriculture, utility-scale solar fields, and new factories.[46] There were also diverging views on whether neighborhood residents or a central office of municipal employees should make decisions about which empty buildings should be torn down, and which ones might be salvaged for later use. But typically combative constituencies were nonetheless aligned on the need for building removals. They agreed that the tens of thousands of empty buildings in Detroit were products of ongoing racist disinvestment, that many structures could not be salvaged, and that demolishing them in significant numbers would better meet the needs of city residents. Indeed, when Detroiters confronted municipal officials about demolitions, it was almost always to insist that empty buildings were not being removed fast enough.

In this way, Detroit provides a helpful juxtaposition with the typical ways demolitions reshape places. It is well documented how proposals to tear down buildings are constitutive of an urban frontier that relies on displacing existing people and activities to create homes for more lucrative newcomers.[47] Urban ethnographer Catherine Fennell's account of public housing demolitions in Chicago's west side provides an illustrative example, since the elimination of social housing infrastructures to shelter the city's most impoverished residents made way for privately managed, mixed-income developments.[48] Across contexts, people facing eviction through urban development processes often resist demolitions—sometimes physically—to hold back the rising tide of dispossession through neoliberal privatization and its intersecting inequities.[49] In contrast, excavators have torn through hundreds of thousands of buildings in Detroit after they had been without residents for years, sometimes decades, before demolitions even became a possibility. City residents, especially longtime Black, Brown, and working-class Detroiters, cheering on excavator operators as they ripped through beams and foundations raised the question of whether demolitions might enact a different kind of politics. That is, in a world seemingly purpose-built to prop up the already privileged by undermining the already oppressed, could processes of tearing things down transform those systems to work otherwise? Not just metaphorically, but in a fundamentally material way. This question surfaced during my early conversations with Detroiters, and I returned to it over the next decade.

METHODOLOGICAL FOUNDATIONS

With more than six hundred thousand residents living across almost 139 square miles, Detroit is a relatively large place. It is large enough that this book is not an attempt to tell you how Detroiters act or think, or even how people in one neighborhood might. Instead, my goal has been to read city's landscape as the product of structures and systems, especially those related to white supremacy and racial capital. Racism happens through landscapes entailing not only people but also things like machines, concepts, buildings, standards, and the ground itself. To make those landscapes legible, my research bridged the political economic focus of what sociologist Michael Burawoy terms "the extended case method"[50] with the sociotechnical emphasis of what science and technology studies scholars Joe Dumit and Donna Haraway describe as an "implosion project."[51] This is to say that I tried to approach demolitions from as many vantages as possible—social, technological, material, institutional, economic, and so on—to detail procedures, key actors, and effects. As such, this book does not aim to provide a comprehensive vision of how my interlocutors experienced a particular moment in time. Instead, it works in conversation with specific people as they read the landscape of their city to analyze the ways racism and intersecting inequities become structured into place. In so doing, it surfaces instances in which people make moves to shift the racist status quo of specific places to work somewhat differently.

Empirically, this book is based on ethnographic and archival research conducted between 2010 and 2020. During that decade I lived in Detroit, conducting research for almost four years. This included periods of exploratory research during the summers of 2010, 2014, and 2015, as well as a period of long-term research between 2016 and 2019. Across this time, demolitions were never difficult to find. Sometimes I could spot the telltale swinging arms of an excavator from my fourth-floor apartment not far from Woodward Avenue on the central west side. In a flat city with relatively few buildings over two stories in height, that view stretched for miles. Early on, I would follow trucks bearing demolition company logos as they pulled excavators through neighborhood streets. Once at work locations, I introduced myself to demolition workers and others who came out to watch them. After these initial meetings, I spoke at length with several dozen demolition laborers, excavator operators, truck drivers, and contractors about their work and many let me know where they would be knocking down buildings in the future.[52]

I observed 433 demolitions in their entirety, as well as bits and pieces of almost a thousand others. I briefly spoke with hundreds of Detroiters who came out to watch demolitions near their homes. Thirty-four of these conversations developed into deeper relationships where I spoke regularly with people over the years.

Understanding the contexts and consequences of building removals required leaving the immediate locations where they happened. It meant spending days sitting with truck drivers as they carted building components to disposal facilities, completing a training program designed to funnel unemployed and underemployed Detroiters into positions as demolition and asbestos-abatement laborers, as well as traveling to national and regional conferences where state actors, regulators, and organizers from across the country gathered to discuss shared matters of concern. Attending to building removals from these various locations provided opportunities to understand where the physical components of demolished buildings ended up. They also provided opportunities to learn from people who related to demolitions as administrators, asbestos-abatement workers, compliance inspectors, and other roles. I complemented participant-observation in demolition-related activities and interviews with key actors with examination of the documentary record produced by demolitions in Detroit since the middle of the twentieth century. This included formal archives from municipal departments and public authorities, as well as city land records, demolition administration guidance, and regulatory documents I reviewed through freedom-of-information requests. In bringing together these different sources of information, I am not attempting to provide an episodic history of demolition across distinct moments. Instead, this book demonstrates how recent actions taken to level empty buildings were part of ongoing historical processes that were always constructed through place.

Ethnographic research prizes long-term relationships with people and locations as an antidote to superficial arguments. And yet, as anthropologists Gökçe Günel and Chika Watanabe detail, such research is not a refined product that emerges whole cloth, but a "patchwork" in which researchers' understandings and arguments emerge by piecing together interactions over varied formats.[53] Between 2013 and early 2020, I lived either in Detroit or some fifty miles away in Ann Arbor. This meant that even when I left the city proper, I could return for an evening neighborhood meeting, a weekend block party, or a day of work in a community garden. Initially, I did not see these routines as part of my research but as relationship-building contributions that could make research possible. But as meetings, backyard gatherings, and gardens became places where people gave their analyses of empty buildings, demolitions, and their consequences, I asked people for permission to share what I learned. For example, it was in a neighborhood gardening workshop that I first learned about the ways removing empty buildings could deposit hazardous materials into the surrounding soils, something that is the focus of chapter 6. Since leaving Ann Arbor at the start of the COVID-19 pandemic, I have maintained relationships with some interlocutors via phone and videochats, as well as virtual neighborhood meetings among Detroiters and various aspects of demolition administration. Across this book, I work to acknowledge the seams present in this research process rather than attempting to smooth them over.

My research raised questions around identity and power in research on racial capitalism. As a white man raised in Detroit's suburbs who was a student at the University of Michigan, I was a type of person whom many of my interlocutors could identify. Most people I engaged with through my research were Black and Latine Detroiters who could place me as someone simultaneously critical of the conditions of racial capitalism and immensely privileged within them. Often, they enrolled me and the privileges I carried—whiteness, masculinity, formal educational credentials, managerial class wardrobe, and a paycheck that did not depend on punching a timecard—to submit complaints about empty buildings to demolition agencies or to file paperwork with various administrative offices. At the same time, I gained relatively easy access to the diverse yet highly educated venues of demolition administration and the majority-white worlds of demolition contractors and property developers. One contractor attributed their interest in supporting my research to my legibility as a white man raised in Detroit's suburbs who was a student at the University of Michigan. Relational engagement, through research and otherwise, has sometimes been a means for privileged people to falsely claim lived knowledge of oppression.[54] My work does not seek to inhabit phenomenological experiences that are not my own, especially around Blackness, extreme poverty, and femininity. Instead, I approach my interlocutors as experts in their own experiences. Whenever possible, I foreground their words, ideas, and conclusions, including by respecting their moments of refusal.

The core observations of this book, especially around the ways building removals produced unequal distributions of benefits and harms, emerged in dialogue with people who talked through them with me on their front porches, in backyards, and at the sidelines of demolition sites. For this reason, I want to be clear that the people who appear on the pages to come are actual people, albeit anonymized in ways we agreed on. The chapters of this book move between individuals who were familiar with particular components of the demolition process: empty buildings, blight designations, siting decisions, heavy machinery, asbestos, and soil contamination. The Detroiters who spoke with me at great length about these topics were not movement leaders, policymakers, or elected officials. Most of the folks who taught me essential lessons about empty buildings, demolitions, and their consequences are the kinds of people who movement activists and theorists C. L. R. James and Grace Lee Boggs might have called "ordinary people" or "ordinary working people."[55] From their grounded vantages as laborers, neighbors, data analysts, machine operators, gardeners, and so on, ordinary people do not simply offer up how they experience complex structures, such as buildings, landscapes, racial capitalism, and white supremacy. Fundamentally, what they offer are analyses of why those structures remain as they are and what it could take to bring something different into being.

WHAT'S AT STAKE

If this book leaves you with one thing, I hope it is an appreciation for how destruction alone will not be enough to eliminate unjust systems. Across the United States and, indeed, the world, the mutually reinforcing violence of white supremacy and racial capitalism are evident. Given the world as it is, actions to topple statues, bulldoze walls, and raze buildings to the ground certainly appear to hold the promise of confronting structural racism head-on. But efforts to demolish the traces of racist disinvestment in Detroit show how destruction is not necessarily as liberatory as might be imagined. Detroiters gathered around and cheered as excavators ripped into empty buildings because their actions certainly appeared to remove the very infrastructures of inequity. For city residents and policymakers alike, demolitions appeared like a chance to change everything—to reset the balance of power so that residents of a majority-Black city no longer contended with the intersections of poverty, crumbling housing, and environmental contamination (figure 0.2). And yet, despite so many demolitions in recent decades, Detroit continues to be a city and region riven by antiblack distributions of poverty, crumbling housing, and environmental contamination. Actions to remove Detroit's empty buildings left the structural conditions that produced them relatively intact. In so doing, they show how tearing things down can change the world but not necessarily in ways that are guaranteed to create an equal playing field—to say nothing of a more equitable one.

Routinized demolition practices in Detroit reinforce how destruction can reproduce the interwoven systems of racism and capitalism that it might seem to eliminate. I am not alone in this argument. Karl Marx diagnosed capitalism as a system dependent on "bitter contradictions, crises, spasms. The violent destruction of capital not by relations external to it, but rather as a condition of its self-preservation."[56] The ongoing construction of new buildings on the periurban fringe of Detroit's metropolitan region alongside the prolonged emptying out of buildings within the city limits is itself indicative of the ways that capitalism's

FIGURE 0.2. **Demolition of building on Michigan Avenue and Shelby, 2006.**

Source: Image by Bob Oren. Courtesy of the Burton Historical Collection, Detroit Public Library.

promise of endless growth conceals a hollowed-out core.[57] As a matter of course, the destructive logics of capital are always predicated on racism.[58] By way of example, consider the wave of factory closures that crashed through Detroit in the 1950s. In a few short years, corporate decisions swept hundreds of production facilities out of an increasingly integrated city and into suburbs that were at the time almost exclusively white, some of which remain that way today.[59] Many Black workers who had made inroads on Detroit's production lines, including as members of radical union factions, found themselves out of work due to automation, whereas workers who remained employed were overwhelmingly white men.[60] My point here is that, literally and figuratively, moves that appear to dismantle landscapes of racial capital can be processes where things remain mostly unchanged.

In a moment when commitments to dismantling racism and demolishing white supremacy suffuse the vocabularies of justice-centered practices, there are important lessons to learn from paying close attention to the ways demolitions shook out in Detroit. For decades, so many people—among them, city residents, municipal employees, and neighborhood organizers—have hoped building removals would be catalysts of economic and environmental benefits for city residents. Despite this, demolitions have routinely transformed the debris of racist disinvestment into the stuff of contemporary antiblackness and white supremacy. For this reason, this book does not celebrate destruction as a stepping stone to structural change. Instead, it builds intellectually and politically from the more constructive aspirations of abolitionist organizing. Ruth Wilson Gilmore's summary of abolition is instructive:

> Abolition is not *absence*, it is *presence*. What the world will become already exists in fragments and pieces, experiments and possibilities. So those who feel in their gut deep anxiety that abolition means knock it all down, scorch the earth and start something new, let that go. Abolition is building the future from the present, in all of the ways we can.[61]

Detroit is a long-standing center of abolitionist struggle, including mutually informed waves of organizing against racist projects of enslavement, settler coloniality, and the carceral state.[62] This book does not chronicle the stories of abolitionist organizers and networks. Fundamentally, however, it brings their work on board when it insists that destruction alone will never be enough to construct a different possible world.

Rather than knocking everything down in hopes of unearthing a clean slate, ending racism and intersecting systems of injustice will take repair. Like Detroiters, any of us living on this continent live amidst what Black studies scholar Christina Sharpe calls "the wake produced and determined, though not absolutely, by the afterlives of slavery."[63] This is a world in which racism structures where we live, the scope of opportunities available to us, the air we breathe, who profits, who pays, and so much more. In his consideration of the philosophical ramifications of repair for enslavement and colonization, Olúfẹ́mi Táíwò discusses how movements to address enslavement, colonization, and their afterlives have been stymied by the fact that the people and institutions that set those systems in motion no longer exist.[64] Sometimes they have been gone for centuries. As such, those who inherit the spoils of racist systems can sidestep demands for change by pointing out that we have not personally dispossessed land, demanded racial wealth gaps, poisoned aquifers, and so on.[65] And yet, as Táíwò contends, the stakes of repair "aren't backward looking investigations into who did the wrong thing in the past; they are design choices about our present and future. Rather than trying to punish a wrongdoer, we may instead find ourselves trying to build a world that distributes risk in the right way."[66] In a thoroughly unjust world, repair means digging into conditions of structural injustice to construct systems that work differently.

To be clear, by invoking repair, I am not calling for apologies and sympathetic reconciliation. Writing around truth commissions and processes allegedly initiated to repair settler colonial violence, political anthropologist of settler coloniality Audra Simpson notes how calls to repair often suggest that "the cost of justice [is] pain and its value set within a market of sympathy. . . . This is the gestural architecture of settler states, the idea that repair will allow a joining, a concurrence, an equality, an assimilation."[67] Repair of this sort provides rhetorical gestures without material change. Building with Simpson, literary scholar Patricia Stuelke identifies how such antipolitical tendencies are embedded in contemporary intellectual calls for scholarly witnessing to the violence of racial capitalism without critiquing its beneficiaries. Such works are "exercises in absolution, they show, police and maintain the racialized boundaries of the human that secure the dominance of white settler subjects over economic resources and life itself, while allowing those settler subjects to feel not so bad about it."[68] By way of empty buildings and demolitions, the chapters to come connect risks and precarities borne by Detroiters who are typically Black, Brown, and impoverished to the profitable, quiet enjoyment that mostly white, almost always wealthier people experience elsewhere. I do not do this in search of apologies or to offer absolution. Quite the opposite. I do so to demonstrate how those of us who benefit from the histories and present of structural racism cannot deny our individual and collective complicities.

Ultimately, this book is about the ways demolitions that so many hoped would create clean breaks from racist systems mostly had the effect of reproducing those systems instead. My point in writing this book has been to think with people in Detroit around processes that produce empty buildings and turn them into grass-covered lots. In particular, I think with them in relation to the provocation spelled out on fencing used by one building removal contractor—*Let's create true and lasting change. Let's build a better world.* In places structured by the ongoing destruction of racial capitalism, how can people create true and lasting change? What does it take to build a better world? The chapters to follow do not offer a roadmap to a better world. However, alongside empty buildings, excavators, and people in Detroit, they open a vantage on what moving from destruction toward repair can and might entail. Because even as leveling buildings tended to compound racism and intersecting inequities, it also created a few locations where people moved machines, components, and materials to work against this status quo. Paying close attention to demolitions in Detroit makes clear how racism is never simply a social concept or a political process; it is always materially structured through the places people make their lives. Structures are not easily rethought or even knocked down. But they can be shifted, in fragments and pieces, to sometimes work a little bit differently.

PLAN

The chapters to follow examine how empty buildings come to be in Detroit, what it takes to demolish them, and the unevenly distributed fallout of destruction. They are arranged in three parts, and it may make the most sense if you read things in the order they are arranged. In the event you prefer to jump around, feel free. No matter your method, here are some signposts.

Part 1: Foundations provides an orientation to Detroit's empty buildings as problem spaces structured by enduring racism. Chapter 1 draws on the recollections of neighbors, former residents, and municipal records to provide a storied reading of a single empty building. From this building, it connects how antiblack processes of disinvestment and foreclosure that have separated people from buildings in the twenty-first century extend long-standing settler capitalist frameworks of whiteness and private property. At stake in this chapter are the ways white supremacy endures because it is iteratively structured into the everyday landscapes of neighborhoods and cities. Chapter 2 turns to the legal concept of blight. This concept emerged in the early twentieth century as a means of displacing Black, Brown, and poor people from their homes, but a century later is key to removing empty buildings from majority-Black, Brown, and poor neighborhoods. While Detroiters took up this designation to expedite demolitions, doing so required opening up their neighborhoods to municipal state surveillance. Detroiters illustrate how political concepts designed to enact antiblack outcomes continue to do so, even as the individual and institutional perspectives of the people deploying them change.

Part 2: Machineries examines how racist political economic landscapes endured through the routine operations of technical systems that were key to demolishing empty buildings. Chapter 3 considers how tearing down empty buildings stabilized property markets by shifting the computational calculus of financial institutions to expand eligibility for home mortgages and repair loans in Detroit neighborhoods. Given how exclusion from these markets has been a key enactment of structural racism, demolition administrators and officials highlighted these changes to secure hundreds of millions in public funding for building removals. Yet as Black Detroiters navigated increasing barriers to affordable housing in the wake of demolitions, they brought into focus how algorithmic indicators of market inclusion can obscure enduring inequities and undermine efforts for safe, stable homes in the actual world. Chapter 4 centers the heavy machinery that made large-scale demolitions possible. When Black Detroiters found work on demolition sites, it was almost always on more precarious terms than those of unionized excavator operators who were typically white, suburban-dwelling men. While heavy machinery operators attempted to recruit Black Detroiters into their ranks, they were stymied by the location of training facilities on the fringe of the metropolitan region that placed gateways to secure employment far from city residents and in the backyards of white suburbanites, especially the descendants of longtime union members. To this end, excavators provide a handle for tracing how racist disparities that underpinned Fordist industrial capitalism endure because they are embedded in regional landscapes.

Part 3: Aftermaths grapples with how demolitions produced unevenly distributed hazards that both reinscribed racist environments and created circumstances in which Detroiters challenged enduring material conditions of injustice. Chapter 5 unpacks how unemployed Detroiters routed into work as asbestos-abatement laborers made it possible for demolitions to comply with environmental safety regulations designed to protect surrounding residents. At the same time, those regulations also created spaces where abatement workers could inhale carcinogens themselves. As asbestos-abatement laborers construct airtight plastic enclosures and remove asbestos-containing components by hand, they raise key points about how good-faith promises of race-neutral regulatory protection can create antiblack occupational atmospheres. Chapter 6 turns to the ways soil-quality tests revealed that demolitions routed lead and other industrial contaminants into the surrounding earth. Unevenly contaminated soils made apparent how demolitions transformed the appearance of racism without addressing its constitutive logics. But soil testing also became the condition of possibility for some Detroiters who speculated about dredging up hazards from their neighborhoods in Detroit to deposit them in wealthy, typically white suburbs. In contrast with building removals, these imaginative and actual actions present a framework for structural change that moves beyond simply tearing things down to build up different possibilities for redistribution.

The book's conclusion builds from the chapters to reflect on the work ahead. Assessing the causes, processes, and consequences of empty building demolitions in Detroit makes evident how destruction alone is not enough to end racism and interlocking inequities. But demolitions did create moments in which Detroiters modeled what it can look like to move the material and social conditions of racist systems toward more reparative outcomes.

PART ONE

FOUNDATIONS

ONE

EMPTY

Detroit is known for empty buildings. It is possible you have encountered one of the literal thousands of gallery installations, news reports, or coffee-table books that center empty buildings in their representation of the city. Detroiters often express frustration with representations that ignore how more than six hundred thousand people make their lives in the city. Most buildings are actively in use rather than on the verge of collapse, and the long-standing association between Detroit and unused buildings quite literally crops Detroiters and the buildings they live in from view. At the same time, despite hundreds of thousands of empty-building demolitions in recent decades, empty buildings make themselves known across the city. An estimated thirty-eight thousand empty buildings stood in Detroit in 2023—more than in any other city in the United States. Some are the kinds of sprawling factory complexes and office buildings where soaring ceilings and missing equipment attract attention from visiting photographers. Most are small buildings, especially one- and two-unit dwellings that make up most of Detroit's building stock. In quotidian ways, these latter structures index how two million people once lived in Detroit. People do sometimes give empty buildings new uses. But, for the most part, after buildings sit empty for years and decades, state-funded crews eventually level them. In a straightforward way, empty buildings make targeted campaigns to demolish empty buildings possible—the sorts of campaigns that have occurred in Detroit for decades.

To be certain, empty buildings are never disconnected from people. Buildings signal disappeared people in belongings, marks, and administrative records. Grooves and depressions signal where people once routinely moved across a stretch of floor or where appliances and machinery once stood. Anthropologist of late industrial life Chloe Ahmann situates how places labeled "empty" create vantages on the conjunctures of empire and capitalism because "claims of emptiness encode whole value systems and have material effects. [Ultimately], vacant space, like ruined space, *is made*."[1] Empty buildings in Detroit provide particularly useful places to grapple with how, across shifting enactments of racial capitalism, value systems in which racial whiteness is a stable location of profit are durably structured into and through the landscape of the city.[2] Attending to the ways Detroiters identify buildings as empty to narrate their city on their own terms foregrounds how city residents excavated the connections between emptiness and profit extraction for themselves. When people encountered open doors, missing windows, sagging eaves, and other evidence of nominally empty buildings, they tended to spark stories about former neighbors and historical transformations. This is to say people drew on the tangible decomposition of Detroit's buildings as evidence of changing structural conditions. Sitting with their stories provides an orientation to the layered operations of racist and racializing systems that separate people from place in Detroit while simultaneously creating capital elsewhere.

A moment that helped make this clear to me occurred around LaShawn's front porch on Detroit's east side. LaShawn, a Black Detroiter in her forties, had grown up in the blue, two-story bungalow and currently lived there with her mother and several other relations. Autumn leaves dropped from the trees as LaShawn and I talked with Kenyetta and Walt, a Black couple in their sixties who had lived together a few blocks over since the 1980s. As we spoke, an excavator operator smashed through the house across the street—a two-story bungalow identical to LaShawn's home. The building had been built in 1920 and had stood at 2615 Bezner Avenue[3] for almost a century (figure 1.1). Wrapped in beige siding with green-painted trim, the house contained a kitchen, living room, dining room, bedroom, and bathroom on the ground floor; two bedrooms upstairs; and a basement below ground. By the end of the day, the house would be gone, with only an earthen

FIGURE 1.1. A boarded-up bungalow.

Photo by the author.

cavity in place of the basement. As the excavator picked apart the house, LaShawn, Kenyetta, Walt, and others who stopped by talked about the series of people who came and went from the house over the years. Conversations touched on factory closures, racialized geographies of the central city and its suburbs, absentee investors, and other systems that figure in the making of Detroit as a place.

When the demolition started, I asked Walt, LaShawn, and Kenyetta the question I posed almost every time I watched a demolition with someone: "Why do you think they are demolishing that building?"

Kenyetta: It's the same story across Detroit. People moved out and didn't take their buildings. White folks went out to the suburbs. Left Detroit with too many buildings and not enough people to fill them.

LaShawn: Well, there were people here, even after the white folks left. I remember when the Washingtons painted that green trim. It's been lately with all those LLCs, the tax foreclosures, and the investors. That's when people left.

Walt: And you can't forget that with the plants leaving, it's not like folks have reasons to come up here anymore. Why live with the Michigan weather if it's not like you're going to have a good paying job, you know?

These three brief reflections are indicative of observations made by people living around empty buildings across Detroit. Together, they reinforce why Detroit's long twentieth century is frequently enrolled as a case study of uneven development driven by the coupling of white flight and capital extraction.[4] At the same time, narratives like LaShawn, Kenyetta, and Walt's also complicate the idea that the emergence of empty buildings can be linked to a single epochal shift. Empty buildings index a cumulation of processes steeped in racial capitalist logics, including suburban expansion, tax foreclosure, and industrial contraction. LaShawn, Kenyetta, Walt, and their neighbors provide a granular focus on the conditions that emptied the beige bungalow. Though it is only a single location, it is emblematic of how empty buildings across Detroit are produced by political economic relations structured by racist inequities.

Like many Detroiters, Kenyetta, Walt, and LaShawn sought out state records to trace the ownership lineages of empty buildings in their neighborhood. In so doing, they constructed 2615 Bezner Avenue as a vantage on a century in which profits extracted from Black Detroiters have almost always flowed toward white-identified people and places. The beige bungalow is a particularly helpful location to work from because, as a place of dwelling, it offers a dense site of encounter with the ways racial capitalism articulates intimate and structural concerns.[5] Indeed, the family of European immigrants who built the beige bungalow in 1920 and held nominal ownership of it through the mid-1960s exemplifies how the shifting terrains of whiteness are built out of stable foundations of antiblackness. The Washington family who LaShawn remembered took up residence in a moment that corresponded with Detroit's emergence as the most populous majority-Black city in the United States. Generations of Washingtons lived in the home until 1998. After that point, ownership pinged between five investment trusts. None of these firms did much to maintain the building, nor did they pay municipal property taxes, and the bungalow cycled through tax foreclosure auctions. The last tenant moved out in 2014, and a group of neighbors boarded over the building's lower-level openings in 2016. Three years later, a private demolition firm received a publicly funded contract to demolish the beige bungalow.

Buildings are land relations.[6] In his history of Detroit, Kyle T. Mays describes it as a "city of dispossessions" in which the ongoing appropriation of Indigenous lands by settler capitalists created the conditions of possibility for antiblack displacement in the nineteenth and twentieth centuries.[7] The beige bungalow clarifies how these conditions extend into the twenty-first. When neighbors sought to understand the histories of 2615 Bezner Avenue told by state documents, they encountered a copy of the land contract issued for the building lot where the beige bungalow was constructed. The seller was A. M. Campau Real Estate, an investment firm organized by descendants of a family of French settlers. In the eighteenth century, members of the Campau family staked claim to large, forested stretches along what is now the Detroit River, with those thefts formalized into private property by French, British, American, and Canadian settler states. For almost two hundred years, Campau heirs amassed profits from the land through timber sales, agricultural operations, and leases. With Detroit's population booming in the early twentieth century, sectioning the land into rectangular lots provided yet another opportunity to transform it into a capital fund. One of those lots, measuring thirty feet in one direction and one hundred in another, became home to the beige bungalow. In other words, this building sits at an intersection of how contemporary processes that create empty buildings build upon Detroit's origins as a settler colonial claim.

A storied reading of empty buildings like the beige bungalow brings whiteness into focus as the common denominator in Detroit's development as a settler colonial entrepot and icon of late industrial abandonment. Explanations for the concentration of empty buildings in Detroit sometimes hinge on population metrics—1.8 million city residents counted in 1950, 1 million in 1990, and 639,000 in 2020. With assistance from neighbors, former occupants, and municipal records, the beige bungalow tracks a more complicated path of racist disinvestment. This sweep includes the flight of white Detroiters to garrison suburbs as a means of avoiding integrated city neighborhoods and antiblack skews of foreclosure in recent years. At the same time, however, attending to conditions that built, maintained, and emptied the beige bungalow connects how racist circumstances of suburbanization and eviction elaborate upon colonial systems that fueled Detroit's expansion in earlier years. I do not tell this story chronologically—that is, beginning with settler enclosures of Indigenous lands, trafficking through the binary construction of a mostly Black central city ringed by mostly white suburbs, and arriving at contemporary circuits of tax foreclosure and disinvestment. Rather, I approach the coupling of antiblackness with coloniality alongside Kenyetta, Walt, and others as they peel back the layers of buildings for themselves. Doing so sits with the ways people encounter empty buildings as sites for the coproduction of antiblack housing policies, predatory foreclosure practices, and settler property development paradigms.

At stake in 2615 Bezner Avenue are the ways that relations of what legal scholar of racism and inequity Cheryl Harris describes as "whiteness as property" become durably embedded in everyday landscapes like buildings and neighborhoods. The point, as Harris and others identify, is how white supremacy is more than a question of how individual people or groups think. It is a matter of property systems in which being slotted into racial whiteness is a stepping stone to accumulating wealth. In Harris's summation, "Whiteness is an aspect of racial identity surely, but it is much more; it remains a concept based on relations of power."[8] Detroit's empty buildings are products of those power relations. They materialize how profits extracted from something as quotidian as a beige bungalow sitting on a thirty-foot-wide lot cannot be disentangled from recursive conditions of antiblack disinvestment situated within ongoing settler colonial dispossession. Buildings may be constructed and emptied out as ownership changes hands from investment firms to people and back again, but the system underlying those transactions remains relatively unchanged. Across them, the people and places who profited from the collateralization of land into property, the construction of buildings, and the removal of people from those structures have almost always been white. In this regard, the making and emptying of Detroit's buildings provide a vantage on how the places where we live are structural locations in which uneven relations to whiteness as the foundation of capital accumulation are made and inherited.

SEEING DETROIT

In 2017, a real estate holding company covered empty storefront windows in prominent downtown locations with invitations for viewers to "See Detroit Like We Do." Along Woodward Avenue, the words floated above images of almost entirely pale-skinned crowds gathered in city streets. On social media, people were quick to observe how the images whitewashed a city in which more than 80 percent of the residents at the time identified as Black. In response to criticism, the holding company stripped the vinyl printings from windows and issued an apology. According to a message posted to the company chairman's feeds, "We screwed up badly. . . . Although not intended to create the kind of feelings it did, the slogan/statement we used on these graphics was tone deaf, in poor taste and does not reflect a single value or philosophy that we stand for."[9] The statement may have controlled damage to the company's reputation, but it did not change anything about the material conditions of uneven development in Detroit. Indeed, scrubbing the campaign from public view did not change crowds moving around downtown streets, nor did it address how public resources were increasingly channeled into the city's central districts, which were wealthier and whiter than other neighborhoods.[10] Far from a color-blind vision, the request to see Detroit's emptied buildings through the gaze of urban development confirmed long-standing suspicions that developers' visions for central neighborhoods were geared to the production of exclusive enclaves for affluent, typically white people.[11]

Almost immediately after apologizing for the ill-fated marketing, the executive who issued the apology also attempted to wriggle out of it, writing further:

> Who cares how "we see Detroit"!?! What is important is that Detroit comes together as a city that is open, diverse, inclusive and is being redeveloped in a way that offers opportunities for all of its people and the expected numerous new residents that will flock to our energized, growing, job-producing town where grit, hard work and brains meld together to raise the standard of living of all of its people.[12]

Contrary to this executive's insistence, how people see place is immensely important. Cultural historian of urban development Rebecca Kinney notes how early-twenty-first-century representations of Detroit focus on empty buildings in ways that portray the city as "barely populated and laid dormant, just waiting to be discovered and used to its full potential."[13] Whether deliberately or accidentally, claims about the vacancy of late-industrial places like Detroit overlook blatant evidence of ongoing use.[14] Within the context of Detroit's nearly 139-square-mile municipal footprint, to exclusively home in on empty buildings without turning to see ones in which people make lives is to efface the hundreds of thousands of people—especially hundreds of thousands of Black folks—who call the city home. Most Detroiters I met had desires reflective of the real estate executive's pitch for an "open, diverse, and inclusive" city. However, they also centered the historical conditions that produced empty buildings to begin with, especially their connections to ongoing disinvestment from the majority-Black city.

I talked through the "See Detroit Like We Do" campaign with Walt on a warm summer evening as we cast for fish from a rocky embankment along the Detroit River. A graying man in his late fifties, Walt had lived on Detroit's east side for most of his life. Friends and relations routinely stayed in the two-story brick house Walt and his wife, Kenyetta, had shared since the mid 1980s. When we met in the summer of 2014, he was working as a hospital maintenance technician at a hospital in a nearby suburb. Walt's two-decade-old truck was out of commission, and a mutual acquaintance introduced me as someone who could give him a lift. Walt patched the truck up in short order, but we saw each other every few weeks. Fiddling with his reel, Walt responded to the ill-fated marketing campaign to see Detroit as a place of white enjoyment. "Make no mistake, I think it's a good thing to have new people to living in the city," his deep voice echoed. "I just wish there was some appreciation for the longtime folk who've been holding the city down. We've seen the jobs dry up, the schools close, folks leaving, bankruptcy. But we care about the city. We're still here." Like most long-term city residents I spoke with, Walt took no issue with new people coming to live in Detroit. He was frustrated by redevelopment efforts that did not have space for people who had called the city home for decades.

Night set in as Walt and I loaded gear into his truck bed and made our way back to his house. Streetlights illuminated our way, including the handful of boarded-up buildings on each of the blocks we drove through. Plywood coverings over windows and doorways buffered against the removal of wiring, plumbing, and other essential components from inside buildings in hopes that people might make regular use of them in the future.[15] Sometimes empty buildings gained new occupants, as was the case with the house directly across the street from Walt and Kenyetta. Two years earlier, a pair of brothers had pried the plywood off the front doorway, climbed inside, and incrementally worked to make the structure usable—fixing windows and doors, adding a furnace, rebuilding the kitchen and bathroom, running new plumbing. In the evening, the glow of a television illuminated a front window. However, as has been the case for most empty buildings in Detroit since the late twentieth century, many of the boarded-up structures would eventually be subject to municipal demolition orders. Demolition crews had knocked down two of the thirty-six buildings that once stood on Kenyetta and

Walt's block. Neighbors had filled the gaps created by the absent structures with lawn furniture, children's toys, and a fire pit. In a way that was typical of many (but certainly not all) of Detroit's blocks, buildings in active use stood directly next to ones that had been empty for varying periods of time. Across the city, an empty building did not necessarily signal a future demolition, even though that was often the result.

Despite the darkness, Walt referred to his surroundings as if they were in plain view. As we turned down Bezner Avenue and passed the bungalow—its lower floor boarded tight and the top windows yawning open—Walt pivoted back to our earlier conversation on seeing Detroit. "Look at these vacants. People think they happened overnight when white folks left. That just ain't it. We built a solid Black city. But over the years with plants leaving and bankruptcy, that's when these vacants came up." Walt pointed to how during the second half of the twentieth century—a period when Detroit's population shrunk by 800,000 people—the number of white-identified city residents fell by 92 percent. For the most part, they relocated outside the city limits into the collar of suburban and exurban polities where elected leaders loudly pledged to maintain all-white neighborhoods.[16] Alongside explicit commitments to segregation, a key plank of these pledges was draining Detroit of economic life by enticing industrial firms large and small to move outside the city limits.[17] Suburbanization of production created empty factories and machine shops along Detroit's industrial corridors that prefigured broader deindustrialization when executives later shifted operations offshore. Racist foghorns have quieted to whistles in recent decades and certain suburban polities are more integrated than others. However, Detroit remains a majority-Black, resource-strapped city ringed by a majority-white, significantly wealthier suburban region.

Detroit thrived despite the deliberate parasitism of its suburbs. Even as white Detroiters abandoned the city during the second half of the twentieth century, the number of Black Detroiters more than doubled over this same period. Such growth represents the tail of the Great Migration of African Americans from the US South to northern and western cities.[18] Between 1980 and 2020, Detroit was the largest majority-Black-identified city in the United States.[19] Progressive Detroiters operating through participatory action in local government, organized labor, and education systems worked to foster a city that supported the material interests of Black residents.[20] Their movements, especially against police brutality and for guaranteed income, reverberated in and beyond Detroit.[21] But cuts to state and federal funding for city services, combined with declining local tax revenues brought on by industrial loss, continually undercut municipal efforts to support city residents.[22] When a state-imposed manager used municipal bankruptcy proceedings to gut public services beginning in 2013, his moves were merely the culmination of decades of maneuvers to diminish local democracy in Detroit. Despite pledges that austerity budgets would trickle down into increased population, the number of city residents continued to decline, driven particularly by Black middle-class Detroiters relocating to suburban municipalities with more reliable services.[23] As Walt observed, the inflection point of white flight from Detroit in the mid twentieth century was only one of many antiblack processes bound up in the creation of empty buildings.

Some people might question the binary of Blackness and whiteness through which Walt sees the sweep of Detroit's recent history. But he is far from alone in defining Detroit and its broader region this way. Census tables correspond imperfectly to race as a lived reality, flattening complexities that people navigate in their lives.[24] Yet even with their imperfections, statistical tabulations point to local geographies of racial meaning. Scholar of racism and uneven development Clyde Woods demonstrates that these "specifically regional forms" of sociospatial organizing are indicative of how white supremacy is structured in the Americas.[25] In Metro Detroit, those regional forms are such that the central city symbolizes intergenerational efforts to build African American working-class power in the face of resistance from typically white and significantly wealthier elites.[26] Billboards with the slogan "Majority Black Detroit Matters" dot the city, encouraging viewers to join movements to secure living wages, affordable housing, utility access, and other rights for city residents. Black identities and experiences are always multidimensional. People inhabit racial systems in tandem with gender, class, nationality, and other structures of power.[27] Analytically and politically, however, taking claims to Detroit as a Black place and a Black city seriously does not mean ignoring these complexities. On the contrary, it keeps in view how people inhabit the city's landscape as part of a racial construction that is freighted by struggles for and challenges to Black lives.

Holding the conceptual understanding and demographic reality of Detroit as a majority-Black city also makes apparent how ostensibly race-neutral visions obscure antiblackness. The development executive's social media posts apologizing for the abandoned "See Detroit Like We Do" campaign prompted chains of

TABLE 1.1. Racial demographics of the City of Detroit, 1900-2020.

Year	Detroit	Black	Native/ Indigenous	White	Asian	Multiracial	Hispanic/ Latine
1900	285,704	4,111	16	281,575	4	—	—
1910	465,766	5,741	41	459,926	58	—	—
1920	993,678	40,838	155	952,065	620	—	—
1930	1,568,662	120,066	350	1,446,656	1,590	—	—
1940	1,623,452	149,119	434	1,472,662	1,237	—	5,156
1950	1,849,568	300,506	730	1,545,847	1,734	—	—
1960	1,670,144	482,229	1,426	1,182,970	2,780	—	—
1970	1,511,482	660,428	2,914	838,877	4,478	—	27,038
1980	1,203,339	758,939	3,420	413,730	6,621	—	28,970
1990	1,027,974	777,916	3,655	222,316	8,461	—	28,473
2000	951,270	775,729	3,319	116,599	9,519	22,041	47,167
2010	713,777	590,226	2,636	75,758	7,559	15,900	48,679
2020	639,111	496,534	2,931	68,407	10,193	31,205	51,269

Source: United States Census.

hundreds of comments. Some challenged the firm to begin taking the concerns of longtime city residents seriously as a step toward taking the concerns of Black Detroiters seriously. Many expressed dismay that the campaign was canceled to begin with. One illustrative reply with hundreds of likes came from someone who identified herself as a white woman living in a central city neighborhood:

> For someone to take this campaign and see the words "See Detroit as we do" and turn it into a race issue. . . . It's you that's keeping racism alive. Everything can be turned different ways and misconstrued. I'm personally sad to see this campaign go because I do see the city the way they see it—and know that the banner had nothing to do with racism. #riseabove #coexist.

This comment is emblematic of how questioning the latent backdrop of white supremacy can elicit claims that people are misrepresenting that backdrop to "turn it into a race issue."[28] But seeing Detroit's contemporary landscapes for what they are demands taking how their conditions of production are, fundamentally, steeped in racism. Empty buildings in particular provide orientations to the imbrications of white supremacy and antiblackness that shaped the creation of a majority-Black Detroit at the center of a majority-white region.

BUILDING WHITENESS

More than 95 percent of the buildings standing in Detroit in 2023 were constructed before 1958. Between 1910 and 1958, nearly five thousand new structures were built in the city each year. Less than thirty thousand total were built in the subsequent six decades combined. The skew of construction years means most of Detroit's buildings, especially its dwellings, were built prior to the end of federally sanctioned racial segregation in the United States. Kenyetta helped reinforce this for me when we were discussing how her grandparents found each other in Detroit during the early decades of the twentieth century. A massive scrapbook sat on the kitchen table, the kind that creaked as Kenyetta turned through laminated photographs of weddings, birthdays, and family reunions. The images chronicled how relatives moved to the city from Alabama, Arkansas, Ohio, and Tennessee. Kenyetta came to a yellowed 1923 newspaper advertisement for the "last close-in property at subdivision prices"; the cross streets included those where we currently sat. Adding that she had found it in the attic soon after moving in, she observed,

"You know, this house wasn't built for us. Wasn't meant for us." She pointed to a part of the page that read: "Restrictions are drafted to exclude any unwanted element, thus ensuring you that you will have good neighbors from the same social level as yourself." Kenyetta paused while I scanned the page and then asked, "You know what that means, restrictions?" The words chugged with gusts of breath: "reee-stric-shuns." "Whites only."

Kenyetta's scrapbooked advertisement points to the tightly wound knot of whiteness and the construction of arbitrary boundaries around where people can and cannot live. For the past century, Detroit has remained among the most racially segregated municipalities and metropolitan regions in the United States.[29] During the first seven decades of the twentieth century, racist segregation was entirely legal, and Black people who took steps to integrate explicitly coded all-white neighborhoods were typically met with violence from white mobs.[30] For Black newcomers arriving in Detroit from the rural south, especially African American people like Kenyetta's grandparents, their moves confirmed how northern cities were not a reprieve from interpersonal and structural antiblackness.[31] An amalgam of racist, classed, and xenophobic restrictions channeled many European immigrants landing in Detroit into the same "unrestricted" neighborhoods where Black Detroiters lived. However, most European arrivals moved on from these areas, especially as they acquired homes in neighborhoods governed by antiblack deed restrictions and homeowners' associations. Dwellings like the one at 2615 Bezner were quite literally built for them. Despite this, initial occupants can skate over the enabling relations of whiteness bound up in the construction of those buildings.

I met Maddie, one of the original inhabitants of the beige bungalow, as I was leaving Kenyetta and Walt's house late on a summer day. She was idling partway down the block in a black luxury sedan and pulled forward as I walked toward my car. The window rolled down and a head of meticulously curled silver hair leaned out. It belonged to a short white woman in her mid-eighties. She introduced herself and explained that she had recently flown in from Florida and was on her way to a family gathering in Port Huron. The car was a rental. Maddie asked, "You look like one of those kids I read about in the news. The ones who are rebuilding Detroit. Your house is beautiful." I explained that, no, the house with the gleaming white trim, bright red brick, potted impatiens on the porch, and yellow roses under the windows belonged to Kenyetta and Walt, who had lived there for decades. Maddie moved on to describe how she was detouring through Detroit and several suburbs on the east side to visit the places she had lived before moving to Florida in the 1980s. She had gotten turned around trying to locate the house where she had spent the first fifteen years of her life. Though Maddie had the address memorized, she could not find the elementary school she used as a landmark. According to city records, it had been demolished about a decade before.

Maddie had overshot her old house by three blocks. After I pointed her in the right direction, she asked if I would mind accompanying her on the drive. As we introduced ourselves, Maddie quickly narrated a schematic family story. She was born in 1932, the youngest of six children. Her parents, Lidia and Albert, were born only a few dozen miles apart where Germany and Poland are now. They met in Detroit around 1914. Albert followed a brother who had secured work in a pharmaceutical factory. They lived in a near-east-side neighborhood that was home to mostly Jewish, Black, Polish, and German Detroiters. By 1915 Lidia and Albert were married, with Maddie's eldest sister born shortly after. Family lore said that the family changed its name to Peck from Pęk, Albert's given surname, after losing out on an attempt to buy a house when a real estate agent refused to sell to "foreigners." In 1919, Albert and Lidia took an eastbound Mack Avenue streetcar to purchase a small lot on a recently paved street. The couple subsequently ordered a kit for a three-bedroom, one-bathroom bungalow from a catalog in a local department store. Maddie had raised three children in Detroit's northeast suburbs and moved to Florida following the death of her husband. With her children all living near Chicago, she had not been back to Michigan in almost a decade.

Maddie covered this narrative in the time it took to drive three blocks because the speedometer barely cracked five miles per hour. We also paused to examine a church that Maddie recalled trudging to multiple times each week. In Maddie's time, the church was Catholic. It now housed a Baptist congregation. Our pace quickened as Maddie steered onto the block with the beige and green bungalow. We soon slammed to a stop in front of the structure. "Oh dear," Maddie stammered. We sat in silence for a few moments, with Maddie blinking tears back. She explained how, on her previous visit, the house had been in good repair. An older woman had waved from the front porch as Maddie drove past. Now, the windows were boarded over, and the house was partially obscured behind grasses so tall they rose above the front porch elevation. Speeding back around the block, Maddie reflected on what she had seen. In her words, "People like my dad and mom worked hard to build this neighborhood. They built this city. It's such a shame to see it like this." When I asked what she meant by people like her parents, Maddie replied, "Immigrants. Blacks and whites, we were all immigrants to this city." We pulled back in front of Walt and Kenyetta's house and I stepped out of the car. As I did, Maddie wished me, "Good luck rebuilding the city," and drove away.

I never saw Maddie again. We exchanged numbers and my calls went unanswered. But my brief car ride with her helps to illustrate a presentation of Detroit's history that is especially prominent among white former Detroiters and their kin. They relate to the city as a place created by racially symmetrical movements of people. To be sure, crediting Detroit's twentieth-century emergence as a global industrial center to people who labored to build households does important work in pushing against corporate biographies of the city that typically center capitalists whose names were often stamped on products rolling off factory lines. But equating the experiences of European immigrants with those of African American people is a false equivalence.[32] During the early decades of the twentieth century, the hundreds of thousands of European immigrants living in Detroit matched the number of Black Detroiters. Men from Southern and Eastern Europe, like men from the US South, were recruited specifically as labor for the city's growing industrial enterprises. Despite passing the xenophobic muster of migration quotas that barred entry to people from most of Asia, Africa, and Latin America, people like Maddie's parents received a hostile welcome.[33] Lidia and Albert's fears of losing out on the building lot are just a single example of how access to housing and employment often required immigrants obscuring connections to places of origin. In the end, however, the family moved into an exclusively white neighborhood without incident.

Family-name changes like the one Maddie's parents undertook trace how individual identities are always tethered to structural conditions. The move from Pęk to Peck is an instance of what keen observer of white supremacy James Baldwin terms "the price of the ticket" available to many, though not all, European-descended people arriving to the United States. Racist systems undergirded life in Europe, but they were not identical to logics of white supremacy in the Americas.[34] As a result, migration from Europe often presented an opportunity to move from marginal positions into ones of racial privilege. In Baldwin's telling, "*Giorgio* becomes *Joe*, *Pappavasiliu* becomes *Palmer*, *Evangelos* becomes *Evans*, *Goldsmith* becomes *Smith* or *Gold*, and *Avakian* becomes *King*. So, with a painless change of a name, and in the twinkling of an eye, one becomes a white American. Later, in the midnight hour, the missing identity aches."[35] Denying geographic and ethnic origins—the price of the ticket—takes a toll on people. But that cost provided a stepping stone to material benefits that the heightening of antiblack constraints amidst an incomplete emancipation kept out of reach of freed people and their descendants.[36] As people with no conception of whiteness as a racial characteristic were—willingly and not—interpellated as "white," they were folded into whiteness as a structure of power relations rather than a question of individual identity. For people like the Peck family, changing the spelling of their name was one aspect of a slide into whiteness that brought with it a house in a newly built neighborhood that was explicitly closed to Black Detroiters.

Whiteness is chimeric. During the early decades of the twentieth century, when Detroit's population was surging, newly built dwellings on newly established streets were not available to just anyone. Buildings like the beige and green bungalow are the material artifacts of procedures that deliberately conditioned access to neighborhoods based on a shifting structure of whiteness. In their exploration of the American Midwest as an "imagined heartland," anthropologists Britt Halvorson and Joshua Reno describe the region in which Detroit sits as a model of white supremacist spatial organization. They note, "Who counts as white is never merely a descriptive labeling of one person or group because it is part of much more pervasive political projects that seek to organize and control social and economic resources and privileges on the basis of race."[37] People who benefit from these political projects can find them easy enough to ignore or consign to an irrelevant past. Maddie's read of 2615 Bezner does just that. For her, the emptied dwelling demonstrated a lack of care for the labors of people like her parents, "Blacks and whites" who built up the neighborhood and Detroit more generally. Such a reading obscures the conditions of explicitly racist segregation tuned to disentangle whiteness from its others and, especially, to restrict Black people to a limited set of neighborhoods. Maddie may have forgotten or been unaware of those conditions, but Kenyetta retained evidence of the antiblack character that shaped the construction of her neighborhood.

SETTLER SPRAWL

Detroit is a notably low-rise, sprawling city. Vanishingly few buildings over six stories exist outside the municipality's central downtown districts. Even in 2024, 60 percent of the city's 139-square-mile land area is restricted to the construction of detached dwellings—that is, single-family homes. To travel across the city is to traffic through a gridded landscape in which strips of churches, salons, hardware stores, gas stations, restaurants, supermarkets, and the occasional apartment building ring blocks upon blocks of one- and two-story dwellings. Detached dwellings quickly materialize disappeared residents.[38] In addition, leaving a building unoccupied through a single Detroit winter can burst pipes and heave previously well-maintained floors. With each freeze-and-thaw cycle, leaking roofs and foundations make structures increasingly difficult to repair. Contemporary observers, including most of my interlocutors, tend to explain Detroit's low-rise landscape as evidence of how mass-produced automobiles are built into the fabric of the Motor City.[39] Indeed, Detroit's metropolitan region powered the trend of car-centric urban and suburban design that was replicated across the United States.[40] Despite this, low-rise blocks filled with individuated dwellings like the one where Lidia and Albert built their home existed before cars became a mass-market consumer item. Their repetitive landscape emerged from an already existing foundation of settler-colonial-capitalist development seated in demands to gobble up land and render it into a profitable fund.

LaShawn, Kenyetta, and Walt were members of a block club that did what it could to maintain the empty buildings in their neighborhood. Like groups across the city, much of their work involved using plywood sheeting and tools delivered by municipal employees to close access to unoccupied structures.[41] Boarding over open windows and doorways kept children from playing in buildings. It also helped keep some rain and snow from seeping into structures, preserving them for possible future occupants. Around Bezner Avenue, residents took a further step of mailing letters to the nominal owners of empty buildings. Those letters requested that the people who nominally owned buildings make them habitable or arrange for demolitions. Identifying those people required trekking to a squat commercial building near one of Detroit's downtown casinos where staff in the county register of deeds office worked. Sometimes the owner was one of the public offices that acquired empty buildings for the purpose of demolition. Often, as was the case for the beige bungalow, it was someone listed as the local agent of a property investment company. On one of these visits, Walt asked the county staffer assisting us how far back their records went. She replied, "We have every deed since the beginning on file here in the office." Given their interests, Walt, Kenyetta, and their neighbors focused on present-day records. But, curious about the so-called beginning of their neighborhood, they also paged through reproductions of the oldest ones, which dated to 1734.

Marking 1734 as Detroit's "beginning" is a settler construct. The City of Detroit took its name from Fort Pontchartrain du détroit du lac Érié, a French garrison established in 1701. The fort, positioned in the straits of the river running between two lakes, began the occupation of what Anishinaabeg named *wawaiiatanong*, "a round or circular place."[42] Prior to European arrival, *wawaiiatanong* was the meeting ground for representatives from multiple Indigenous sovereignties, including Anishnaabemowin- and Huron-speaking nations. French commanders established the fort in hopes of recruiting Indigenous collaborators to fend off British and Haudenosaunee competition in the fur trade. Eight months after the French established the fort, colonial officials counted some six thousand people living in its vicinity, including three Anishnaabemowin villages.[43] Occupation governors—sometimes with nominal consent from Indigenous leaders, but typically without it—granted settlers permission to establish farms, orchards, and dwellings on the lands around the fort. In 1734, Jacques Campau, a French colonizer who had previously relocated to the fort from Montreal, received such permission for the area where the beige bungalow once stood.[44] Campau and his heirs claimed that land as their property for almost two hundred years until they sold it to people like Albert and Lidia Peck. Situating the beige and green bungalow within these enabling conditions helps to specifically ground how Detroit's present-day geography—especially a sprawling landscape overwhelmingly composed of detached dwellings—originated in settler capitalist designs of turning land into property.

Detroit's eighteenth century entailed transfers between three occupying forces of settler colonization. In 1760, British regiments seized what they called Fort Detroit and its surrounding villages as part of a coordinated effort to eliminate French colonial outposts. By 1796, the settlement was one of the first added to a growing American empire. Handoffs between imperial sovereignties made for what historian Kyle T. Mays describes as "a place of cultural exchange and violence."[45] British officials marked their occupation by murdering Odawa, Bodwewademi, Ojibwe, and French people who opposed it. American officials forced Indigenous nations to sign treaties that dispossessed lands to the settler state and removed their peoples to reservations.[46] Colonial transformations created settlers' claims to land as their heritable property. Land grants issued to settlers by Indigenous authorities were typically time limited and conditioned on routine trade in crops, fish, and other goods.[47] By contrast, British and American land offices established in Detroit claimed legal dominion over the entirety of the Great Lakes region by formalizing settlers' farms and dwellings into evidence of permanent property rights.[48] Settlers' "private claims" stretch along the entirety of Detroit's present-day riverfront. For good measure, American officials extended these claims by allowing claimants to enclose grazing lands that Indigenous and French laws held as commons.[49] Through the private claims process, the Campau heirs became one of Detroit's largest landowners, amassing titles to almost a fifth of the city at the onset of American settler administration.

Like many of Detroit's settler capitalists, members of the Campau family claimed Indigenous and African people as their enslaved property. Black and Indigenous studies scholar Tiya Miles historicizes how competing Indigenous and settler sovereignties, as well as densely forested river landscapes, created possibilities for freedom that made it difficult to establish systems of chattel enslavement in Detroit.[50] Despite this, settlers attempted to do so for more than a century. Laws claiming Detroit as the territory of the United States nominally banned slavery in the region beginning in 1787, but they provided for the continued enslavement of people held in bondage during British administration. When US territorial laws eventually abolished slavery in Michigan, they did so while simultaneously conditioning citizenship in the settler state on white supremacy. Alongside treaties restricting movements of Indigenous people, Black people moving to the region were required to demonstrate proof of their freedom and $500 in seed capital.[51] Similar restrictions did not apply to white settlers. Black Detroiters born into nominal freedom encountered routine violence from white city residents seeking to cash in on bounties offered by slaveholders elsewhere on the continent.[52] African-descended, property-owning men received the right to vote in Detroit's municipal elections only in 1870, following the legal abolition of chattel slavery in the United States.

For much of the nineteenth century, the area that became Bezner Avenue remained part of an agricultural belt. It was midway between the center of Detroit's inland trading port and the lakefront retreats of the city's growing merchant elite. The Campau family collected significant rents from tenants farming and living on their inherited property. In a show of how dispossessing and renting land is the cornerstone of obscene wealth, the Campau family trust is credited with creating Michigan's first millionaires.[53] Describing how the family's late-nineteenth-century wealth grew out of colonial holdings, one journalist wrote, "You could not turn to the right or the left in the City of Detroit without running over Campau lots, seeing Campau houses, encountering Campau tenants."[54] Members of the family gained controlling interests over the network of canals and railroads running from Boston and New York through the Great Lakes.[55] Decisions about what to do with Campau land claims were routinely a site of bickering among relatives over who should control the greatest share of the profits, but family members were in agreement about constructing a railway spur from the riverbank through their holdings just west of what became Bezner Avenue.[56] In the middle of the nineteenth century, the spur shuttled metals, coal, and lumber extracted around the northern Great Lakes into workshops where they emerged refashioned into stoves, carriages, rail cars, and other commercial goods to be ferried back to the docks. Today, that same rail line links Detroit's three remaining automotive manufacturing facilities into global logistics networks.

With Detroit exploding into one of the most populous cities on the continent early in the twentieth century, the Campau heirs, like most all the city's capitalists, moved to cash in on property claims created through colonial occupation. When Albert and Lidia Peck paid off their land contract, it was the first time the recorded owner on file was not a direct descendent of colonizers who had originally expropriated the land during the early colonial period. Though a few of Detroit's landholders concentrated on building their holdings into factory corridors or clusters of brick and steel apartment highrises, most moved to segment existing farms into grids of detached dwellings hemmed in by low-rise commercial thoroughfares. Real estate companies like the Campau family firm tied purchasers' acquisitions of rectangular plots to restrictive covenants that spelled out the kinds of buildings people could construct there. They also barred selling or leasing to anyone who was not white. With tens of thousands of additional people arriving in Detroit each year, the sprawling, low-rise housing system left the city woefully short of dwellings necessary to house newcomers.[57] Advocates for white workers and Black Detroiters across classes pressured landowners to increase housing construction, especially of denser apartments. But landowners insisted on sprawling designs. In so doing, they kept up pressure to expand further inland from the river along radial avenues shooting out from the city's central business district.

When Kenyetta, Walt, and their neighbors filed out of the county register of deeds office, they carried pages scribbled with the lineage of people and corporate entities who had claimed ownership of the now-empty buildings in their corner of Detroit. As we drove across the east side, we passed over a couple of the expressways carved through the city in the middle of the twentieth century to create racetracks for white-collar commuters moving between Detroit's downtown skyscrapers and their suburban bedrooms. We also passed a road named Joseph Campau. Running north-south, the road sits at what was once the boundary of one the family's colonial farms. Campau is not an outlier, with many of Detroit's thoroughfares tracing routes carved by property claims made by Detroit's early colonizers and their descendants, such as Beaubien Street, Dequindre Avenue, Moross Road, Chene Street, Meldrum Street, and Mack Avenue. After selling their land holdings, most of Detroit's settler capitalist families took their wealth elsewhere. But street signs and property deeds index how settler profiteers like Campau remain materially present in the landscape. Twentieth-century Detroit mass-produced the conditions for white Americans to drive to the suburbs. Sifting through the layers of property claims associated with 2615 Bezner Avenue situates how sprawl took hold in Detroit long before cars rolled off the city's assembly lines. Antiblack and Indigenous dispossession have been ongoing motors for extracting wealth from Detroit since settler capitalists began making ever more expansive claims to what became the city.

SWEATING PROPERTY

Kenyetta, Walt, and their neighbors spread papers with the information they retrieved from the register of deeds office across the wooden surface of LaShawn's kitchen table. They had counted eighty-six empty buildings within the six-block vicinity: seventy-nine detached dwellings, one apartment building, five commercial storefronts, and one church. Just under half the structures were held in the portfolios of various government offices—a signal that they could already be in the demolition queue. Holding companies with names like Invest Detroit, Innovative Property Solutions, and ESV LLC held titles to the others, including the beige bungalow. Around the table, people pored over stacks of ownership records to identify addresses closest to their home. LaShawn scanned the deed transfers related to 2615 Bezner Avenue. She identified the owner listed in the register of deeds as Exit Strategy May 5 LLC, a holding company with a post office box in Detroit's western suburbs. With looping print, LaShawn wrote out a note, folded it into an envelope, and addressed it to the firm.

> *To Exit Strategy May 5 LLC:*
>
> *I live across the street from the house your company owns at 2615 Bezner Avenue in Detroit, Michigan. It has been empty for two years (since 2014) and is falling apart. My neighbors and I boarded over the windows and doors, but it is still not usable. Please make it possible for new people to come live in the house or demolish it.*
>
> *Sincerely,*
>
> *LaShawn Hitchins*

Others at the table penned similar notes. Most were addressed to post office boxes and office parks in nearby suburbs. Some of the people gathered in Kenyetta and Walt's house had experience with letter-writing campaigns as effective strategies for inducing landlords to address shoddy housing conditions. However, unlike those instances, the anonymized corporate people listed on ownership documents for empty buildings never responded.

In 2020, more than half of Detroit's buildings were nominally owned by corporate shell companies like Exit Strategy May 5 LLC. On average, each firm claimed ownership of dozens of structures.[58] Compare this with 2000, when three-quarters of the city's buildings were owned by their immediate occupants—that is, owner-occupied housing or business-occupied commercial and industrial buildings. Small-scale landlords held most of the rest. Geographer Joshua Akers and colleagues describe this shift as part of the move toward "liquid tenancy" across the United States in which property ownership is increasingly concentrated in the hands of large-scale firms that harness state-facilitated eviction proceedings to extract maximum profits.[59] The emergence of such tenancy relations in Detroit has been specifically enabled by state tax foreclosure statutes. Under these statutes, if municipal property taxes for a particular address are unpaid for three years, county administrators are required to auction off an ownership deed to the highest bidder. In Detroit, where a shrinking number of residents have shouldered the costs of sustaining local services, tax rates are among the highest in the country. So are the rates of tax foreclosure. Following concentrated cuts to manufacturing employment, many Detroiters struggled to pay inflated tax bills. Between 2007 and 2017, county administrators foreclosed on more than 160,000 structures in Detroit, almost half the buildings in the city—some more than once.[60] Annual auctions for tax foreclosed buildings became frenzies where investment companies placed 90 percent of the winning bids.

LaShawn paged through a sheaf of papers that documented ownership transfers at 2615 Bezner Avenue from the time Albert and Lidia Peck sold it in 1965. After renting the bungalow to tenants for eighteen years, the Pecks sold it to Gloria and Kelvin Washington in exchange for around $15,000. LaShawn's mother recalled the Washingtons as a quiet family with two children who kept to themselves. After both older Washingtons passed, their eldest child, a woman named Shonda, inherited the family home. When Shonda passed in 1998, her relations sold the dwelling for $22,500 to a property management firm based in suburban St. Clair Shores. The firm rented 2615 Bezner to tenants until the county treasurer foreclosed on around $10,000 in unpaid city property taxes. A limited liability corporation (LLC) registered in suburban Dearborn acquired title to the beige and green bungalow with a winning bid of around $7,500. Five years later, when county officials again foreclosed on the building for unpaid taxes, the winning bid of less than $2,500 came from an LLC registered out-of-state. Another round of tax foreclosure saw a deed issued to Exit Strategy May 5 in exchange for $500. In 2017, with its front stoop missing and rain trickling through a hole in the roof, the building entered the auction a final time. Without a single bid, the title transferred to the Detroit Land Bank Authority, which eventually contracted a demolition firm to level the building.

2615 Bezner's route through three cycles of tax foreclosure resembles the paths of buildings across the city. Between 2001 and 2014, classified ads offer 2615 Bezner Avenue for rent and land contract with advertised rates of $200 to $700 each month. Despite this, after 2001, none of the corporate entities that collected monthly payments from tenants paid a single dollar in property taxes. At a training for people looking to learn how they could leach "passive income" out of tax foreclosure proceedings, one speculator boasted of how he paid off a luxury car and student loans using land contract payments he collected from people living in houses he acquired through the annual auction. Summarizing his strategy, he said, "You've gotta get it, sweat it, forget it." Because winning auction bids typically came in at a few thousand dollars, "after a security deposit and first month's rent, it's basically pure profit." Current speculators reminded would-be practitioners that county officials would likely seize the property deed and auction it off once more after three years of unpaid taxes. However, as long as building owners did nothing more than place the winning bid, their profit streams remained secure. As a result, Detroit's housing-justice organizations were overwhelmed by tenants contending with landlords who refused to address unstable floors, leaky roofs, faulty electrical wiring, plumbing backups, and other conditions in buildings they acquired on the cheap through tax foreclosure.[61] Like the beige bungalow, thousands of buildings became increasingly unsound with each tax foreclosure cycle.

Rental and land contract payments made by Detroiters on buildings that experienced one or more cycles of tax foreclosure fed into capital networks that were simultaneously global in scope and concentrated in the ring of municipalities that surround the central city. Webs of shell companies and holding corporations make it difficult to link Detroit's buildings to discrete human owners. However, following the conclusion of annual foreclosure auctions, Detroit-based journalists routinely flagged how some of the entities that snapped up ownership claims to land and buildings were registered in the United Kingdom, Florida, California, and other places thousands of miles from the city.[62] At the same time, more than 80 percent of winning tax foreclosure bids come from entities based in the metropolitan region encircling Detroit. Since the 1960s, Detroit's housing-justice activists have observed how monthly payments extracted from Detroiters for dilapidated dwellings have increasingly transited past the city limits to landlords and financial institutions based in its suburbs.[63] During decades of legal segregation, it was easy to account for the racialized character of profits, since suburban wealth was almost always white wealth. Geographically triangulating the racial identities of suburban speculators is currently less straightforward.[64] In the early decades of the twentieth century, suburban Detroit's wealth has been mostly, but not exclusively, held by white-identified people. Despite the changing beneficiaries of suburban wealth, landlords who fail to keep Detroit's buildings in good repair have consistently done so while extracting monthly payments from the city's majority-Black populace.

Some of the same speculators who scooped up tax-foreclosed properties in Detroit also amassed holdings in its suburbs. And yet, the same entities that allowed structures in majority-Black Detroit to become increasingly unusable kept buildings in majority-non-Black suburbs in good repair.[65] Detroiters, housing-justice advocates, and municipal administrators were perplexed by such operations, which positioned residents of the majority-Black central city as less deserving of decent housing conditions than white suburbanites with similar incomes.[66] Landowners claimed their decisions were motivated by different rental rates rather than the identities of the people paying them. While this explanation helped building owners sidestep legal discrimination charges, it is a particularly illustrative case of what Black studies scholar Keeanga-Yamahtta Taylor describes as "predatory inclusion." As Taylor details at length, federal, local, and state policies enacted to outlaw explicit discrimination in housing, employment, and other domains have also "created the conditions for continued extraction" because they did not address the political economic imbalances perpetuated by centuries of legal discrimination.[67] So often, racism and intersecting inequities endure in acute and structural ways under the alibi of "market forces."[68] These forces materialized each time the nominal owners of Detroit's buildings deferred maintenance or refused to pay municipal taxes while simultaneously collecting rents from Detroiters who lived and labored in those structures.

When state officials introduced tax foreclosure proceedings in Michigan in 1998, they framed the threat of losing ownership deeds as an incentive for deedholders to be "responsible" and make good on contributions toward municipal services.[69] Legislators went so far as to ban deedholders who were behind on their taxes from participating in annual auctions. This largely blocked owner-occupants from regaining ownership of their dwellings, but it did not block investment firms that could slip off one corporate name and put on another.[70] Though tax foreclosure proceedings occurred across the state, the annual shuffle of tens of thousands of buildings into the hands of opaque limited liability corporations was concentrated in Detroit. With each passing year, investors' refusals to make tax payments undermined Detroit's municipal balance sheets just as their refusals to make repairs quite literally undermined the city's buildings. This churn ultimately slowed around 2019, following intensive organizing by city residents and organizations to transfer investor-owned, tax-delinquent buildings to existing tenants rather than auctioning them off to the highest bidder. Despite meaningful changes going forward, the damage of decades of routinized foreclosures was already running its course. The scale of deferred maintenance—busted pipes, cracked foundations, missing windows, nonfunctioning heat, holes in the roof, and more—placed many buildings structurally beyond repair. Nearly every single one of the nearly thirty thousand buildings demolished in Detroit between 2014 and 2020 was leveled directly following a cycle of tax foreclosure.

The extractive relations of racial capitalism are manifestly global, but they are always embedded within more proximal geographies. For instance, locations like 2615 Bezner Avenue have been sites for simultaneous accumulations of deferred maintenance, past-due tax bills, and rent receipts. Beyond this single building, LaShawn, Kenyetta, and Walt's neighborhood is demonstrative of the ways empty buildings typically move through contemporary processes of tax foreclosure as part of their final steps toward demolition. In 2016, neighborhood residents counted eighty-six empty buildings. All but two had been previously auctioned off through tax foreclosure. By 2022, just four of those buildings—three houses and a convenience store—had new users. City-funded crews had demolished fifty-seven other structures, with two dozen more structures in the queue to be razed. Like the beige bungalow, these buildings were missing integral heating and plumbing systems. With each freeze and thaw cycle, their floors heaved and buckled, leaving them precariously close to collapse. Frayed electrical connections sometimes set empty buildings alight. Such conditions were the active result of state-facilitated tax foreclosure processes that created the conditions for investors to scoop up buildings at low costs, sweat them for rents, refuse to make repairs, and offload the consequences to publicly funded demolitions. In so doing, they index the sorts of predatory relations that produced the recent scale of empty buildings in Detroit, especially as investment firms with links to Detroit's majority-white suburbs have marshalled buildings in the majority-Black central city into reliable sources of profit.

WHITENESS AS SPATIAL RELATION

Let's return to the day when a demolition crew knocked down the bungalow that stood at 2615 Bezner Avenue on Detroit's east side. Over the course of that day, neighbors came and went from LaShawn's front porch. Kenyetta, Walt, LaShawn, and a few others chatted as crews worked on buildings up and down the block. Together, we watched them topple four houses, including the beige bungalow across the street from us. Conversations came to a halt whenever a crash and a plume of dust signaled that an excavator operator had pulled loose whatever remaining structural element was holding a building upright. As I typically found when sitting with people watching crews raze buildings in their neighborhoods, the mood was equal parts reflective and anticipatory. Though she would have preferred new neighbors, like many Detroiters who had lived with a growing number of empty buildings on their block for years and decades, LaShawn was content with the demolitions. In her words, "I just hope we can put these buildings and all that in the rearview. That this means the future for our block and our city is bright." Others on the porch expressed similar sentiments. While people missed departed neighbors, they were frustrated by the empty buildings created by their absence. Resonating with residents' front porch conversations across the city, the trio narrated leveling the empty buildings around them as a key step toward a different future for their neighborhood and their city.

Seeing how a bungalow-style house was built, inhabited, emptied, and eventually demolished at 2615 Bezner Avenue provides an exemplary case of racist systems that have shaped Detroit as a place. It brings into relief conditions and systems in ways that amplify how Detroiters like LaShawn, Walt, and Kenyetta encounter and understand them. As Detroiters piece together memories, ownership claims, and ways of seeing empty buildings in their city, they grapple with just how narratives of industrial contraction and population loss due to white flight do not completely explain why hundreds of thousands of empty buildings came to be in Detroit. Those processes are at work. The targeted closure of Detroit's manufacturing facilities accompanied by the coordinated flood of white Detroiters to segregated suburbs figures prominently in the making of emptied buildings. However, twenty-first-century motors, including but not limited to tax foreclosure, also play significant roles in displacing Black people from a majority-Black city. Underlying all of it, literally as much as figuratively, are settler capitalist paradigms that prioritized sprawl as a means of rendering land into property to be hoarded and leveraged for maximum profits. Detroit's empty buildings track the intergenerational operations of racial capitalist accumulation. They point specifically to the ways that, despite its many permutations, removing people from Detroit has consistently been a racist process that generates wealth elsewhere.

Attending to buildings like the beige bungalow surfaces a question that sociologist of the Black radical tradition W. E. B. Du Bois asks to illustrate the co-constitution of racial whiteness and colonial capitalism: "But what on earth is whiteness that one should so desire it? "[71] For Du Bois, "I am given to understand whiteness is the ownership of the earth forever and ever, amen." Writing in the early decades of the twentieth century, Du Bois demonstrates how enactments of racism in the United States, especially its conditions of white supremacy, are embedded within "the current theory of colonial expansion." In his words, "Bluntly put, that theory is this: It is the duty of white Europe to divide up the darker world and administer it for Europe's good." Du Bois and those building with his insights make clear how whiteness is structural. It is a political economic system in which power, privilege, and oppression articulate through claims to property ownership.[72] At the origins of colonial occupations, access to the knotted relations of whiteness and property was constrained to a narrow band of settler capitalists who extracted immense wealth by claiming stolen land as their own. And yet, as those occupations wore on, their claims made it possible to concretize the profitable circuitry of whiteness through antiblack segregation and tax foreclosure. The granular scale of the beige bungalow magnifies how settler property claims form the foundation of expansive structures of inequity.

Moving across the stories that municipal records and neighbors tell about the 2615 Bezner Avenue, it becomes apparent how Jacques Campau and Detroit's original settler capitalists may be long dead but the systems they set in place continue to metastasize. Extractive property relations that codified white supremacy through Detroit's sprawling neighborhoods, as well as who gained priority access to suburbs beyond the city limits also reverberate in buildings that break down a bit further with each cycle of tax foreclosure. To be sure, whiteness and private property are unequal by design. 2615 Bezner Avenue generated only a small piece of the immense wealth that Detroit's settler capitalist families extracted by claiming stolen land as their property. And yet, the incremental gains afforded to people like Lydia Peck opened doors that were purposefully closed to her former Black neighbors. Detroiters like Kenyetta, Walt, and LaShawn contend with buildings that break down as investment firms profit with each round of tax foreclosure. Sitting with the construction and repeated emptying of a dwelling on Detroit's east side lays out how the privileges that accrue from the spatial relations of whiteness and property are not merely artifacts of past inequities. Conditions of coloniality and antiblackness cannot be scrubbed from view or simply forgotten—much as some may hope. They are structures through which racist distributions of benefits and harms are inherited and accrue force in the present.

TWO

BLIGHT

The tires of Andy's car crunched over freshly fallen snow on the afternoon we rolled slowly up and down the blocks of Detroit's west side. Andy, a white man in his thirties, drove along a route mapped out on the car's GPS, while I sat in the sedan's passenger seat. Claude, a Black man in his fifties, was sprawled out in the back. Shoulder against the window, he aimed a tablet computer to photograph each building and lot as we drove by. After taking an image, he would key in a few survey responses describing the location. It was halting work. Andy would pause for a few moments following each shot to allow Claude to tap out his responses and queue up the next entry.

"You OK?" Andy would ask.

"I'm good," Claude would respond."

Then the car would crunch forward a few meters and we would repeat the process. Magnetic placards slapped to the sides of Andy's car announced "MOTOR CITY MAPPING OFFICIAL BUSINESS" to anyone who read them. The flashing orange light fixed to the roof added a further air of officialdom. A few drivers laid on their horns as they sped by on main roads, and many people waved as we drove by, as they were shoveling out driveways and sidewalks. But for the most part it was an uneventful drive, filled only with the sounds of tires compacting snow, Claude's fingers thumping on the tablet screen, and a top-forty station barely audible on the radio.

Our quiet routine was broken by a rap on my window followed by "Did you just blight my house? Tell me you didn't just blight my house!" The interrogation came from a Black woman, who appeared around Claude's age. She was wheezing, with footprints indicating her pursuit of our car over much of the block. A waft of icy air pierced the cabin as I rolled down the window and asked for her address, adding that I did not think so. She gave a street number just a few houses back. The one with Christmas garlands twisting in the breeze and a piece of plywood fitted over a window. I could hear Claude's fingers thumping on the tablet behind me as he keyed in the address. In the few moments it took for him to load the entry, the still breathless woman described how her grandparents had been evicted from their home in the 1940s or '50s when it was "blighted" to build the spindle of expressway that links Detroit's central business district to its northeastern suburbs.[1] Likewise, she recalled another eviction in her youth when her family was "blighted" out of an apartment building on the near west side that became the site of a university expansion project. In both cases, people had come through and photographed the neighborhoods before they were flattened. After recalling these displacements for several minutes, the woman concluded we must be there to accomplish similar work.

Claude slid over in the backseat and motioned the woman inside. She introduced herself as Dorothy, and Claude walked her through his description of her home. The address and a photo were followed by selections from a standard survey:

STRUCTURE: **Yes** / No
OCCUPIED: **Occupied** / Unoccupied / Partial Occupied / Possibly Unoccupied
USE: **Residential** / Commercial / Mixed / Industrial / Institutional / Parking Lot / Park / Garden / Unknown
UNITS: Garage or shed / **Single-Family** / Multifamily / Apartments
CONDITION: Good / **Fair** / Poor / Suggest Demolition
FIRE DAMAGE: Yes / **No**
DUMPING: Yes / **No**

In a textbox Claude added a note about meeting Dorothy. Upon reading it, Dorothy noted how there was not a category for "blight." With an incredulous tone, she asked, "So you didn't blight it?" Claude gave an emphatic "No, ma'am," before explaining how his grandparents too had been "blighted" from a home in Cincinnati in the 1940s. That's what had brought them to Detroit. Dorothy smiled at this and opened the door to exit the vehicle. But she shut it quickly to list several buildings nearby: a burned-out brick house around the corner, the boarded-up dollar store on a major intersection, and an unused elementary school. "Could you please make sure those get blighted so the city can come tear them down?" With that, Dorothy stepped out into the chill.

Dorothy's fear of being once more "blighted" from her home gestures to the ways this label is integral to the process of building removal. Indeed, large-scale destruction of Detroit's built environment emerged in response to large-scale blight. In recent decades, municipal offices and other agencies operating in Detroit have drawn on procedures embedded in state laws on "blighted area rehabilitation" to level hundreds of thousands of structures.[2] These statutes, first enacted in the early twentieth century, allow staff from municipal offices to seize and demolish buildings they identify as likely to "endanger the health, safety, morals, or general welfare of the municipality."[3] Similar statutes exist across English language contexts.[4] Legal frameworks reflect how *blight* transformed from a class of plant diseases into an authorizing concern of urban planning and public health surveillance.[5] For more than a century, Detroit's residents, activists, researchers, investors, and policy specialists have been attuned to the existence and effects of blight in their city. But, despite broad agreement that blight poses an existential threat to cities and their inhabitants—Detroit and otherwise—no fixed definition exists.[6] In the early twentieth century, *blight* described crowded housing conditions, buildings without utilities, and places local elites found unseemly. Since the closing decades of the twentieth century, however, *blight* has increasingly referred to any building that appears open and without regular occupants. Across this shift, addressing the menace of blight remains a stable conceptual and legal footing for large-scale demolition projects.

Only structures formally labeled as blighted can be routed to publicly funded demolitions. In recent years, blight designations have drifted between staff in various municipal offices and public authorities that deploy building inspectors in response to reports from city residents. These offices, endowed by state statute with powers to legally seize and demolish buildings for the purposes of "blight elimination," operate as what Michel Callon and other science and technology studies scholars might describe as "obligatory passage points" for the transformation of Detroit's built environment.[7] Chronically understaffed since their formation in the first decades of the twentieth century, these offices have never had sufficient personnel to observe Detroit's almost 139 square miles on their own. Instead, they have relied on reports and images submitted by city residents, companies, journalists, and researchers who document neighborhood conditions. Empirically, the Motor City Mapping project provides a central vantage on more than a century of efforts to bring the extent of Detroit's alleged blighted buildings into focus. This includes photographic surveys funded by private wealth, discussions among neighbors, building inspection routines, and street-by-street image collection modeled on Google's Street View platform.[8] Across them, searching for blight constitutes relationships in which "seeing like a city" is not a myopic view from city hall.[9] It is state actors responding to detailed visions created from the ground.

Across the United States, administrative projects to remove allegedly blighted buildings have been routinely designed to remove racially minoritized people, especially but not limited to Black communities, from place. Dorothy's and Claude's recollections mark how these actions were typically enabled by photographic surveys that made buildings and their residents legible to administrative offices tasked with "improving" the landscape. Consider a 1938 survey organized by a local university that produced a building-by-building account of the city. The results showed the most severe concentrations of overcrowded dwellings with dysfunctional utilities and other conditions of what was then identified as "blight" in the city's most impoverished majority-white neighborhoods. Despite this, corporate leaders and municipal officials ensured that majority-Black districts in which some, but not all structures were dilapidated were the first to be leveled in pursuit of "blight elimination."[10] Surveillance and Black studies scholar Simone Browne describes such outcomes as products of "racializing surveillance [which] signals those moments when enactments of surveillance reify boundaries, borders, and bodies along racial lines, and where the outcome is often discriminatory treatment of those who are negatively racialized by such surveillance."[11] Like Dorothy, many Detroiters were apprehensive about Motor City Mapping and other contemporary efforts to scour their city for instances of alleged blight due to lived experiences of being displaced following such projects. And yet, like Dorothy, Detroiters also took up the category of blight to identify empty buildings they hoped municipal offices might remove from their neighborhoods.

At stake in this chapter is whether the conceptual and legal toolkit of blight—a toolkit that originated in efforts to encode racial capitalist accumulation through white supremacy as an artifact of spatial management—could be wrenched from its antiblack foundations and repurposed to support some of the very people it once harmed. The prospects of such a transformation were on display in the exchange between Claude and Dorothy in which she sought to ensure her house had not been "blighted" while also attuning us to buildings she thought should be. Despite fears that the Motor City Mapping project and subsequent rounds of blight identification would unleash a wave of evictions and displacements of Black, Brown, and poor Detroiters from their homes, no such wave materialized. For many observers, efforts to figure what and where blight is through the literal and figurative hands of Black Detroiters—people like Dorothy, Claude, and their neighbors—made it possible for municipal offices to survey the city and remove buildings without replaying antiblack outcomes. But as camera-mounted rigs fanned out along roadways, they carried forward projects of focusing heightened scrutiny on the places where Black Detroiters lived as a condition of tending to the well-being of Detroit as a city. Tracing how blight surveys routinize surveillance despite intentions to the contrary ultimately show how technologies of spatial governance can construct racist outcomes even when the people wielding them seek to do otherwise.

BLIGHT IS A POLITICAL DIAGNOSIS

Just about everyone I met in Detroit used blight as a commonsense category. When I would introduce myself as someone following the process of producing and demolishing empty buildings, most people—city residents, administrative staff, researchers, journalists, and demolition workers—would narrate my interests back to me in terms of "blight." Sometimes, people used "blight" interchangeably with "empty structures" and "vacant buildings." In other moments, it became apparent that blighted buildings were always empty, but empty buildings were not always considered blight. Neighbors sometimes disagreed about whether the empty building across the street or down the block was a structure awaiting new occupants or a blight to be reported to demolition coordinating agencies. Likewise, scholarly research frequently attempts to parse the distinction between unused buildings that can be made habitable and blighted ones that should be torn down.[12] Urban planners, engineers, and building scientists draw upon analyses of foundations, windows, roofing, and neighborhood sociality to suggest there are "tipping points" for when the absence of maintenance transforms into blight.[13] Yet, it is helpful to be mindful of how blight is fundamentally a political diagnosis rather than a straightforward technical question. For neighbors and administrators alike, labeling a building as blight constructs it within a terrain of action in which demolition becomes possible. Such actions are contingent on the sociolegal construction of blight, which tracks how the visible material consequences of racism shifted from buildings overflowing with people to ones without occupants altogether.

Consider the following disagreement between Dorothy and her friend Mavis, a Detroiter in her seventies who had previously worked alongside Dorothy in a now-shuttered metal stamping plant. A few years after Dorothy pursued Claude and Andy's Motor City Mapping car, we were reclined in creaky folding chairs in Mavis's fenced-in yard as the pair recounted stories from their years of friendship. Over the top of the fence, dozens of plywood-covered windows were visible in the empty houses that surrounded Mavis's home. Basking in the glow of late afternoon sun, Mavis pivoted the conversation: "I'm looking forward to the day the city comes and takes care of all this blight." She was particularly animated about the two-story white house immediately next door, which slanted toward her own on account of a compromised foundation. While that structure had slouched sideways for years, others we could see had been vacant for only a short while. They included the small brick house where tenants had recently departed after their landlord refused to repair a faulty hot water heater. Members of Dorothy's church congregation had worked to nail plywood over the windows and doors in hopes that new occupants might move in some day. But given that the number of empty buildings in her corner of the city only seemed to grow, Mavis imagined the need for demolition crews to roll through.

Mavis's backyard appeal for "the city" to address blight was an appeal to administrative offices tasked with issuing demolition orders. Decisions made in those offices were guided by municipal ordinances that allowed Detroit's building inspectors to levy "blight violations" on buildings that were empty and in danger of collapsing onto an adjacent structure or were documented as having been left open to the elements for at least 180 days. In cases where administrative staff could prove such conditions were met, state statutes empowered them to seize and level buildings for the purpose of addressing "blighted areas," which it defines as follows:

> Blighted area means a portion of a municipality developed or undeveloped, improved or unimproved, marked by a demonstrated pattern of deterioration in physical, economic, or social conditions [or] any other similar characteristics which endanger the health, safety, morals, or general welfare of the municipality. . . . It is expressly recognized that blight is observable at different stages of severity, and that moderate blight unremedied creates a strong probability that severe blight will follow. Therefore, the conditions that constitute blight are to be broadly construed to permit a municipality to make an early identification of problems and to take early remedial action to correct a demonstrated pattern of deterioration and to prevent worsening of blight conditions.[14]

Within the architecture of a state law enacted in 1945, the definition of blight is purposefully nonspecific. Blight can be anywhere, with conditions that "are to be broadly construed" to encompass anything that might labeled as threatening the well-being of the municipal body politic.

Blight arrived in Detroit decades before laws defined it, much as it did in cities across the anglophone world. It was in this early-twentieth-century moment that practitioners in nascent fields of urban planning and health advocacy adapted blight from a category of crop and plant diseases into a classification for allegedly troublesome built environments.[15] In an essay that traces the emergence of blight as a category that demands coordinated public attention, architectural historian Andrew Herscher suggests that the ways this transformation has taken place in Detroit are emblematic of how it has played out across the United States. For Herscher, the hinge between popular and statutory understanding of blight formalized during the early twentieth century "translates the inadequate housing of communities disenfranchised by racism and class prejudice into a menace to the health, security, prosperity, and property value of the entitled."[16] By way of example, take a 1910 pamphlet, "Civic Welfare and the Dwelling," issued by Detroit's health commissioner to describe the alleged blight of "unsanitary and overcrowded homes" across their city. The pamphlet warns, "Nothing can so effectually destroy a city's future as the disproportionate increase of homes that are unsanitary, damp, dark, unclean, unattractive, unventilated, overcrowded, and immoral. [It] disheartens the poor, preys upon the immigrant, . . . packs it with hungry humanity and then raises the rent upon it."[17] The pamphlet concludes with encouragement to readers to advocate for legislative changes to enable municipal offices to intervene to address the moralized material landscapes of blight.

As Detroit's population exploded between the mid-1910s and the 1940s, teams of university students, municipal employees, and residents repeatedly fanned out across the city in attempts to identify blight. At least once each decade, with cameras in hand, people walked up and down every block, photographing buildings and talking to people who answered knocks on their doors. Their surveys documented the lived reality of discriminatory housing systems, with areas restricted to white Detroiters setting the standard for "good wholesome neighborhoods" with newly built dwellings sitting on large lots and wide streets.[18] Meanwhile, the city's "blighted areas" were those in which the city's Black, Jewish, Latine, Asian, and recently arrived immigrant residents were permitted to live.[19] Well-maintained dwellings, especially those owned by Detroit's Black elite and middle classes, were photographed on the same blocks as crumbling rooming houses in which the city's multiracial working poor waged conflicts with landlords who demanded rent increases on structurally unstable buildings for which they refused to provide operational utilities.[20] For many white Detroiters, surveys on racialized and classed housing conditions confirmed racist sentiments that whiteness and wealth were a bulwark against dilapidation caused by nonwhite and impoverished white people.[21] Nevertheless, people who lived with shoddy foundations, jury-rigged electrical wiring, and crowded apartments were typically clear-eyed about how such conditions reflected systemic actions rather than the alleged immorality of their inhabitants.[22] Neighborhoods deemed blighted and racial disparities in who lived there existed because a constrained housing supply for nonwhite Detroiters was exceedingly profitable.

The meaning of *blight* in Detroit and elsewhere changed markedly in the 1960s. This occurred as industrial firms and white residents relocated from increasingly integrated cities into reliably segregated suburban municipalities. In 1962, Detroit's city planning office warned, "blight is eating away at Detroit faster than efforts to control it."[23] The central issue of blight at stake for Detroiters who called municipal offices and for the staff who picked up the line began to shift from occupied buildings in states of alleged disrepair to focus on the growing presence of buildings identified as "vacant and abandoned."[24] This local trajectory mirrored trends playing out across the United States as popular and professional definitions of *blight* moved from buildings that were falling apart in ways that posed safety risks to their immediate occupants to buildings that were falling apart due to the absence of human occupants altogether.[25] Beginning in the 1970s and continuing through the 2020s, municipal officials made annual promises to eliminate blight through tens of thousands of demolitions in the years to follow. Commenting near the start of this routine, two Detroit-based journalists observed, "Detroit's thousands of abandoned structures are much more than an eyesore and an immediate danger to those who live near them; they are one especially visible and undeniable consequence of decades of racism, corporate greed, and inhuman callousness."[26] Despite a seeming inversion in what counted as blight, from places with too many occupants to those with too few, the reasons such places existed remained the same.

Unpacking blight as a political concept is an exercise in pinning down a floating signifier. Cultural studies theorist Stuart Hall uses this term, *floating signifier*, to name how the meaning of racial categories "can never be finally fixed, but is subject to the constant process of redefinition and appropriation."[27] Race is a fundamentally political concept whose ramifications and very definition shift around depending on sociohistorical context. Like the floating signifiers of race with which it is enmeshed, blight has no inherent referent. But following the conditions around which blight is enacted—whether packed buildings in the early twentieth century or vacated ones in the decades to follow—offers a useful vantage on how inequities of racial capitalism take place. As a concept of law and urban administration, blight has been repeatedly critiqued for obscuring how unsound built environments are the products of racist political economies, rather than due to the inability of individual occupants to conform with an "image of care."[28] Such critiques are well-placed, since as a sociolegal category, blight was constructed as a moralizing label that made it possible for state actors to scrutinize the lifeworlds of oppressed people. But people like Dorothy, Mavis, and other Detroiters do not simply reproduce images and imaginations of blight formed a century ago. Their identifications of blight as a feature of their neighborhoods are appeals for assistance from municipal institutions empowered to remove empty buildings.

KNOWING THE CITY

It may seem obvious, but before administrative staff tasked with managing publicly funded demolition programs could allocate funding and dispatch a team to level an empty building at a particular address, they needed to know there was an empty building there to begin with. This was easier said than done. Staff in Detroit's municipal offices have proposed annual surveys of the city's buildings since the time blight first came on the scene.[29] By tasking municipal employees to walk the city's streets in search of overcrowded buildings and, later, empty ones, they imagined it would be possible to address issues before residents complained. These visions never became reality. Except for occasional projects like Motor City Mapping in which city residents were marshalled to go up and down blocks to find empty buildings, the costs of maintaining a systematic picture of Detroit's built environment always exceeded the limited funds available in the municipal budget. Instead, employees in what is currently Detroit's municipal Buildings, Safety Engineering, and Environment Department (BSEED) have spent decades requesting that city residents report "dangerous buildings" in their neighborhoods. Upon receiving a report, BSEED inspectors visit the building to assess if it is structurally unsound enough to be demolished. With only a handful of inspectors tasked with assessing whether thousands of reported buildings meet municipal definitions of blight, this process can take years. Extended timelines became a source of friction between overstretched building inspectors and the frustrated residents they relied on to have a picture of the city's changing landscape.

Mitch, a Black Detroiter in his fifties, had worked for some time as a BSEED inspector, a role that involved driving around the city, visiting addresses on a seemingly endless spreadsheet. In a given day, Mitch would make a few dozen stops. At each, he climbed out of his truck, photographed the building, and wrote a quick assessment of whether it met municipal standards of blight. Had it been open to the elements for 180 days or more? Could it collapse if someone walked inside? For structures slumping over or those with holes in their roof, or ones showing signs of fire damage, Mitch's answer was typically yes. Empty buildings that appeared otherwise sound with plywood boards hammered over their windows and doors got a note to return in a year. On rare occasions, Mitch rolled up to find people living or working in buildings he anticipated would be empty. He crossed those addresses off the spreadsheet entirely. Mitch and his coworkers filed their reports into a database containing information on each of the almost 400,000 addresses on file in the municipality. If an inspector labeled a building as blight, office staff mailed a notice to the registered owner warning of a potential demolition order. Sometimes, owners staved off such orders by arriving to municipal offices with photographs showing they had boarded over openings or shored up shaky foundations. More often, the structures inspectors classified as blight entered the demolition queue.

Entries on the spreadsheet that guided daily workflows for Mitch and other inspectors came from calls and online reports of empty, dangerous, or blighted buildings. Some of those reports came from municipal fire fighters, health department workers, and public works employees who crisscrossed Detroit's neighborhoods as a matter of course. Most reports came directly from Detroiters. Weekly city council meetings usually included at least one public comment from a city resident listing empty buildings they hoped to see torn down in their neighborhood. Once the commenter had finished, councilors made a point of audibly requesting that the addresses be sent to Mitch's department for further examination. Similarly, consider what happened when Mitch participated in a career panel at one of Detroit's public high schools. Before he could begin speaking, students presented him with lists of the empty buildings they passed each day on their way to school. When the school principal attempted to stop their presentations, Mitch intervened. In a booming voice, he stated, "Don't apologize. We're responsible for fixing the blight in our city. For making it safe for residents. It's our job. But we need your help to know the city. Thank you for that." Mitch then walked through the steps his department would take to decide whether each building should be demolished. This mode of engagement was typical whenever Mitch and others in his office were met by Detroiters who wanted to make sure empty buildings on their block rose to the attention of demolition administrators.

When inspectors arrived to assess empty buildings, nearby residents sometimes peppered them with questions about when the structure might come down or why it was still standing. In one such instance, Mitch arrived on an eastside block to find a pile of rubble where he expected to find a two-story wood-framed dwelling. Ropes connected to a still-intact porch made it appear as if someone had pulled it over on purpose. An elderly woman waved Mitch over from the porch of a neighboring house, where she sat with a man around her age. Mitch's frame filled the narrow stoop as he inquired about what happened to the building. The woman gave a full body shrug. "It was empty a long time and you all didn't do anything about it. Just rotted and fell over, I guess," she quipped. As Mitch completed his report, both elders took him to task for the years their neighbors had complained about the building without receiving a response. Mitch nodded along respectfully. "Ma'am, sir, my division has [a few] of us for the whole city—138 square miles.[30] We can't know every street like the people living on it. That's why I really appreciate your persistence in bringing this blight to our attention. We'll get it out of here for you." The man sitting on the porch replied, "We'll believe it when we see it." When the debris was removed some six months later, neighbors mailed a thank-you card to Mitch's office.

The skepticism with which two elders greeted Mitch is indicative of how many Detroiters became frustrated by the experience of municipal offices struggling to even know where empty buildings were, let alone do anything about them. Consider how, in 1989, Detroit's mayor's office increased demolition funding in the municipal budget to $15 million, up from an average of $10 million each year in the preceding decade. The increase came in response to a weeklong series of articles by *Detroit Free Press* journalists reporting on their "census of blight" in the city.[31] The series included an interview with the head of what would become Mitch's department, in which he estimated Detroit had between five thousand and six thousand empty buildings at the time but also admitted, "The city really doesn't have a definite number of vacant buildings. The only way you could is to drive every mile of every street. We've never done that."[32] Two dozen journalists drove every street in Detroit (2,814 miles), spoke with the people who lived on them, and identified 15,215 empty buildings. Not included in that number were piles of debris marking where Detroiters had already knocked down structures on their own.[33] Reporters chronicled stories of city residents who had reported empty buildings to city offices a decade or more before. Tired of contending with places that became hazardous playscapes for young people on their blocks, neighbors gathered with chainsaws, prybars, and towing cables to topple empty dwellings themselves.

To be sure, austerity-driven downsizing of Detroit's municipal government has deprived city employees of the resources necessary to perform their jobs.[34] As Mitch intimated, his division relied on city residents' reports to keep tabs on the changing conditions of their blocks. Since the middle of the twentieth century, city employees welcomed the results of empty-building surveys submitted by block clubs, social services agencies, and university students. Like Motor

City Mapping—which reprised the *Detroit Free Press* blight census's methodology twenty-five years later—city residents were operationalized to fill the gaps left by budget cuts that hollowed out capacities in municipal offices. This came as decades of incremental belt tightening transformed public services like park maintenance, streetlighting, and emergency response from something all Detroiters could access in equal measure into scarce resources available only to residents who demanded loudly enough or implemented themselves. For example, following cuts to public works staff, administrators encouraged Detroiters who reported flooded roadways or broken streetlights to clear blocked storm drains or install solar-powered lights along sidewalks as an alternative to waiting for permanent fixes.[35] But demolitions could not be so entirely bootstrapped, as the resources necessary to transform a building into a grassy lot exceed those of even the most intrepid organizer. Neighbors could physically tear down buildings by cutting through support beams, but they were left with a pile of wreckage. Fully removing the debris still required making the structure legible as blight in the optic of municipal administration.

Before public resources could be mobilized to respond to Detroiters' demolition requests, staffers in those offices needed to formally categorize empty buildings within legal definitions of blight. City agencies could not make this categorization on their own. Even when Detroit's public services were more robust than they had been in the wake of municipal bankruptcy, departments like BSEED have not had sufficient resources for the municipal government to develop its own knowledge of the city on a building-by-building scale. Instead, inspectors like Mitch were attuned to the ground-level view other people had on Detroit's neighborhoods. Sometimes this knowledge came in the form of citywide surveys like Motor City Mapping, but it more often arrived as individual complaints of empty buildings submitted by people who lived nearby. This meant that the power to name a structure as "blighted" and with it, the power to have that building demolished, was not something that descended unilaterally from administrators in city hall. On the contrary, such definitions were built up from reports submitted on the ground. And yet, as Detroiters scaffolded local knowledge of empty buildings into reports to municipal departments, they confronted prolonged demolition timelines caused by the same threadbare budgets that left those departments reliant on city residents to begin with. Inspectors like Mitch could express appreciation for Detroiters bringing empty buildings to their attention, but they could not always shake city residents' frustrations that they were filling in for municipal employees who lacked the resources to know the city for themselves.

RESIDENT PRIORITIES

Tensions surfaced between Detroiters' knowledge that classifying buildings as blight was integral to demolitions and their lived experiences of the same classification being an engine of racist displacement. Recall Dorothy's pursuit of Claude and Andy's Motor City Mapping car through the snow with questions about whether their images could result in her once again being "blighted" from her home. Dorothy was not alone in taking this action, nor was she the only Detroiter who was keen to offer a list of structures that they thought should be "blighted" and torn down. The simultaneous apprehension and enthusiasm that greeted projects like Motor City Mapping reflected how contemporary logics of blight elimination driven by Detroiters' knowledge of empty buildings emerged from earlier models created to separate people from their homes. This earlier model played out across the United States. By classifying buildings and entire neighborhoods as "blighted," planning departments cleared the way for expressways, university buildings, factories, and housing developments. In Detroit, the people sent packing by these endeavors were almost always Black and, on occasion, impoverished white people. The racialized and classed skew of displacement was surgical and was enabled by block-by-block photographic surveys conducted by nonprofit organizations and researchers who fed them into municipal databases.[36] To distinguish contemporary efforts to locate empty buildings from the explicit racism of previous rounds of blight elimination, organizers emphasized how their understandings of whether buildings should be demolished would be based in the knowledge of people who lived closest to them.

Consider what happened when several hundred people packed into a stifling west side community center for the first of dozens of "public engagement meetings" about the Motor City Mapping project's suggestion that 40,077 buildings in Detroit needed to be torn down. Alicia, a Black urban planner in her forties, had just finished welcoming attendees when another woman's voice rang out from the back of the packed room, "You want to do to Detroit what they did to Black Bottom!" The speaker was invoking how, in 1947, Detroit's white politicians and civil society leadership unveiled the "Detroit Plan: A Program for Blight Elimination," which envisioned replacing thousands of buildings in a neighborhood then called Black Bottom with rows of glassy townhouses and highrises. In their words, "We present here the Detroit plan for the solution of this problem of urban blight . . . the increased ratio between tenants and homeowners, and the growth of slums." White business leaders prioritized this site—the center of what was then Detroit's Black-owned business district—for "renewal" based on 90 percent "non-white occupancy." By 1963, almost one hundred acres, the entirety of Black Bottom and several adjacent neighborhoods had been flattened, and 43,096 people, more than 30,000 of them Black Detroiters, lost their homes. Owners of demolished buildings—overwhelmingly white landlords—were paid for their "losses," but tenants were displaced without compensation. Often, they had nowhere to go.[37] Newly constructed housing was restricted to white residents.

Alicia seemed prepared for this interaction. She described how her parents had been displaced from Black Bottom, as well as how her desire to become an urban planner had emerged from hearing about family homes lost due to other midcentury urban renewal projects. While recounting her autobiography, Alicia flipped to a slide with photo of dark-skinned hands with acrylic nails grasping one of the tablets that surveyors like Claude had used to photograph buildings across Detroit. The tablet was photographing a two-story house with white siding whose the front door and windows were missing. Alicia asked, "Raise your hand if you think this is blight." Every hand in the audience shot up. Alicia continued, "We're going to do blight elimination that is led by the knowledge of residents and accountable to them." In the dozens of public engagement meetings I attended, I observed Alicia and her colleagues use similar photos and personal accounts to quell unease among Detroiters packed in to learn more about how Motor City Mapping data might be used. In addition to underscoring their understanding of how blight had been a critical infrastructure for white elites to level majority-Black neighborhoods during the twentieth century, they centered the question of what blight was at present in the hands of city residents, especially Black people. With commitments to amplifying Black Detroiters' knowledge, Motor City Mapping organizers like Alicia worked to draw stark contrasts between their efforts and prior blight elimination efforts steeped in explicit antiblackness.

More than simply giving voice to an aspiration to centering Detroiters' knowledge and priorities, public engagement meetings around Motor City Mapping were places for enacting them. With a crowd of several hundred people, I joined Mavis,

Dorothy, and a handful of their neighbors around tables in the stuffy fellowship hall of a westside church. Most people in attendance were, like Mavis and Dorothy, Black women between the ages of fifty and eighty. A handful were younger Black people in their twenties and thirties. Several children ran in and out of and adjacent nursery, mostly to pick from the dinner spread of chicken and lamb shawarma. After we listened to Alicia's historical account of blight and description of the Motor City Mapping undertaking, project staff distributed tablets that resembled those Claude and other surveyors had used to document Detroit's landscape. A brief tutorial oriented us about how to pinch and zoom our way around the digital map of the city. Homing in close enough revealed outlines of parcels—most of them were rectangles but others had more facets—listed in municipal property records. Once we zoomed into the scale where one square mile or so filled the screen, each shape shifted from faded blue to one of a range of color codes. Green indicated that the surveyor marked it as "good," yellow represented "fair," orange was "poor," and red meant "suggest demolition." Tapping a parcel pulled up the photograph and brief description created by one of the project surveyors.

Project staff asked attendees to corroborate or contest the survey designations of the blocks where we lived. With people like Alicia circulating to offer patient guidance to elders unfamiliar with the computational interface, they requested we tap on any of the red parcels that we would encounter on a regular basis. Sheets of paper listed the questions we should ask ourselves when viewing these locations:

Do you think this building is blighted?

Do you think this building should be demolished?

Is this building actually empty?

If someone lives here, do they need help? What kinds?

By adding responses to such questions to the Motor City Mapping entries, attendees contributed to what information and media studies scholars discuss as "thick data."[38] In contrast to "big data," thick-data approaches aim to predicate decisions on deep understandings of local contexts rather than computational aggregates without foundations in lived realities.[39] In some respects, the Motor City Mapping project was already an exercise in thick data. Computational scientists initially pitched that it would be possible to identify empty buildings by cross-referencing survey photos with information scraped from utility databases, tax offices, and postal service delivery records. But their models proved unreliable at predicting whether buildings were empty, let alone suggesting what nearby residents might want. Instead, comments appended to survey entries corralled Detroiters' situated experiences to flesh out information produced by people who photographed every building in the city.

People who panned around digital, color-coded maps of Detroit did not limit themselves to clicking on red boxes; they also tapped into entries coded in other colors. Consider how Mavis and her neighbors pulled up the orange-colored entries on their blocks—buildings classified as "poor." With features like droopy gutters, chipped paint, and slanting porches, these structures all looked like they could use some care, but intact windows and doors kept surveyors from knowing whether they were empty. Together, Mavis's group worked through whether people lived in each building. In some cases, they wrote, "This is a vacant, blighted building. Check if vacant, please demolish." In others, they described how people living there were dealing with a landlord who refused to make repairs or difficulties paying Detroit's notoriously inflated tax assessments. For instance, "The man who lives here, Mr. Jefferson is 88 years old. A very nice man. His wife passed last year. He might lose the house to the taxes. Not blight. Do not demolish." Within the next few years, most red-coded structures had been demolished around Mavis's house. So had most orange-coded ones appended with requests for removal. Following requests from Motor City Mapping project staff, housing-justice organizers visited people like Mr. Jefferson to assist them in navigating predatory landlords, contract-for-deed arrangements, and paperwork for municipal property tax abatements. The toolkit developed to gather Detroiters' localized visions of blight also served as an infrastructure for people to keep neighbors in their homes.

Amidst the highly publicized rollout of Motor City Mapping cars across Detroit, scholars and activists voiced concerns that the concerted effort to identify blighted buildings in Detroiters' neighborhoods would once again serve as the procedural mechanism for displacing city residents. Many feared that labeling buildings as blight would create the conditions of possibility for pre-ordained demolitions that evicted Black and working-class Detroiters from their homes, much as it had during twentieth century urban renewal projects.[40] This did not happen.[41] Indeed, people like Alicia who organized Detroiters to build and refine the Motor City Mapping database positioned their catalog of blight in opposition to previous rounds of blight elimination designed to serve the desires of Detroit's white business and political elites to remove Black and impoverished people from districts adjacent to the downtown core. To do so, they framed Motor City Mapping as guided by city residents, especially Black people who called the city home. Indeed, as Detroiters annotated database entries from places like community centers, church basements, and the sidelines of block parties, they encountered a platform that explicitly asked them to revise administrative classifications of blight based on their understandings of what was happening on the ground in their neighborhoods. Keying in responses provided opportunities for city residents not only to articulate which buildings they thought should be demolished but also to identify people who might benefit from supportive resources to maintain their homes.

DETROIT STREET VIEW

The 40,077 empty buildings identified for demolition through the 2014 Motor City Mapping survey process served as a measuring stick for subsequent administrative efforts to address blight in Detroit. Consider how municipal officials proclaimed that the 20,000th demolition following the survey, completed in 2019, marked the halfway point to a "blight free" city.[42] And yet, as city residents could see, the conditions on the ground in their neighborhoods were not static. In some cases, buildings that were unoccupied when Motor City Mapping crews photographed them gained new residents in the following years.[43] More often, new structures became empty through a confluence of systems discussed in chapter 1—especially tax foreclosures. Sometimes building occupants passed away or just moved on. No matter the reason, the absence of routine inhabitants was marked on structures that bore signs of fire damage, where trees and vines grew through windows, whose roofs had collapsed. When Detroiters brought newly vacated buildings to the attention of municipal administrators, they made apparent how failing to address the systemic production of empty buildings ensured that the path to a blight-free city was longer than the one presented in official declarations. At the same time, to proactively identify new empty buildings, elected officials directed municipal staff to survey the city for blight at least once per year. Though perhaps not intended, the SUV-mounted cameras rolled out for this purpose created the conditions of possibility for intervening in Detroiters' lives.

Motor City Mapping was never intended to be a one-time effort. Over a late afternoon coffee around a year after the project had concluded, Alicia explained to me how the coordinating team of planners, community organizers, and data scientists she worked with had proposed their work as a continuous undertaking. "The city is always changing," Alicia projected over the din of the shop. "Somebody could move into an empty building tomorrow, renovate it, start a business, or whatever. Even if our survey found the building was blighted, it's not blighted anymore." Alicia and others imagined making such changes legible through annual updates that reprised the model they had piloted in 2014, especially conducting public engagement sessions for Detroiters to provide the kinds of granular details and recommendations that Mavis, Dorothy, and others contributed for buildings in their immediate neighborhoods. But even funding promised by philanthropic and corporate capital to sustain a second citywide survey never materialized. As a result, the project went dormant shortly after Alicia and her coworkers transmitted their final report to various government offices and nonprofit agencies. A publicly accessible repository of project data lingered online where, for a few months, visitors could click through a map of the city and pull up any of the 377,602 entries. Prompts encouraged viewers to provide updated images and descriptions of places they knew well. When no funders chipped in to renew the domain registration, even this portal disappeared.

The temporal limits of Motor City Mapping data became apparent to public agency staff responsible for identifying empty buildings for demolition. Following the survey, Detroiters canvasing their neighborhood continued submitting thousands of petitions for demolitions each year. By 2018, demolition administrators had flagged more than 19,000 empty buildings where open windows and doorways easily met municipal definitions of blight, but the structures were classified in public agency databases as "unlikely to be blighted." Facing critical media coverage in which Detroiters questioned whether demolitions alone would eliminate blight in their city,[44] elected officials tasked municipal staff with imaging every building at least once each year. The stated mission of this program would be "to continuously observe and document Detroit's changing physical environment through remote sensing, resulting in freely available data that empowers effective city operations, informed decision making, awareness, and innovation." Shortly after, the municipal IT department launched Detroit Street View. Named for its resemblance to Google's Street View service, the platform involved two full-time staffers driving SUVs equipped with cameras and mapping equipment up and down city streets. While similar systems operated by tech companies produced images of parts of Detroit every few years, municipal staff driving through the city every day could drive every block three to four times each year. Image-processing software and drivers' input flagged conditions like fire damage or a building that increasingly leaned toward others, making it possible for municipal offices to tap funds available for emergency demolitions.

Detroit Street View came into being as an alternative to expanding police surveillance. At a meeting convened to discuss how municipal classifications of buildings as "unlikely to be blighted" conflicted with city residents' understandings on the ground, a representative from the mayor's office suggested expanding the municipal CCTV network to include at least one lamppost-mounted camera on every block of the city. At the time, the network was already streaming thousands of live feeds directly to Detroit's police department, where officers could track people through facial recognition. Demolition staff pushed back on this suggestion, noting demonstrated antiblack biases in the design and operations of facial recognition.[45] As one analyst put it, "We're trying to address blight for residents, not build a police state." They then offered an alternative proposal for mobile mapping rigs that would focus on Detroit's built environment while anonymizing the people who made their lives in it. When these rigs became a reality, the operational team articulated the following core value:

> Detroit Street View takes personal privacy seriously. Images are captured in publicly accessible spaces (primarily streets) and personally identifiable information is carefully anonymized through blurring of faces and license plates. Also, because the program is focused on observing stationary physical assets, the frequency of data collection at any one location is generally too low to gain insight into individual human behavior.[46]

Put simply, Detroit Street View promised to bridge the gap between the standpoints Detroiters and municipal employees had on their city's landscape. In so doing, municipal employees aimed to see buildings as residents did without subjecting them to blanket surveillance.

Like Google's Street View platform, Detroit Street View's mobile mapping rigs still raise thorny concerns about surveillance. It is well-established that corporate promises to make on-the-ground views of the world accessible to anyone with an internet connection are predicated on computer-vision programs that simultaneously fail to distinguish between Black people and subject them to heightened scrutiny.[47] For example, Detroit's municipal CCTV network feeds the police department's "real time crime center" where rows of agents face banks of computer monitors and a thirty-two-foot video wall. Established in 2016 with the ostensible purpose of keeping Detroiters safe, the real time crime center has set the national record for wrongful arrests due to cameras and software that have difficulties distinguishing people with darker skin.[48] The broader computational apparatus that knits together imaging and geospatial software also sits at the core of corporate and state-backed efforts to track and enclose vulnerable people while obscuring systems that create those vulnerabilities to begin with.[49]. Within this apparatus, practices that make certain people and landscapes illegible are not necessarily a bulwark against systemic harm[50]. This matters because commitments to protecting an individual's privacy by obscuring them from publicly accessible data feeds does not remove them from those data feeds entirely. Blurring out "personally identifiable information" sidesteps questions of whether people's neighborhoods should be monitored, the purposes for which it might be acceptable, and what it would look like for people to consent to such a project

To be clear, Detroit Street View was not created to harm Detroiters. Far from it. Building inspectors who frequently interacted with city residents frustrated by empty buildings were among the city employees incorporating Detroit Street View into their work routines. Over video chat, an inspector demonstrated navigating through the city without leaving their office. They panned around, ticking off blocks on a paper map. When they came across structures that appeared empty—places like a two-story house with a four-story tree growing through the roof or a stretch of fire-damaged warehouses with loading-dock garages yawning open—they made note of the location. If those possibly empty buildings were not already subject to demolition orders, this inspector or one of their coworkers would visit them in person to see if they were empty. If possible, they would confirm their understandings by asking neighbors what they knew about the building. In their words, "This lets us do something about blight even if neighbors are too busy to complain about it." In a similar vein, others across Detroit's municipal bureaucracy were plying through Detroit Street View captures to identify blocked storm drains, missing road signs, and broken sidewalks. They compiled lists of locations where maintenance crews could be deployed for preventative maintenance. As intended, Detroit Street View allowed public employees to stitch across digital and actual world versions of Detroit's neighborhoods to proactively address well-known matters of concern of city residents.

At the same time, with regularly updated Detroit Street View data available freely on the internet, implementation grew beyond its initial-use cases. For example, it made it possible for police department staff to comb through captures in search of inoperable vehicles parked on lawns and unpaved lots. Technically, it has been illegal to leave a car parked on a lawn in Detroit since the formalization of parking restrictions in the 1960s, but enforcement had been basically nonexistent for some time. Across the city, it was easy to spot cars parked on grassy lots created by previous building removals. Residents used these lots to park closer to their home, to have spaces to complete repairs, and to avoid tickets for blocking street cleaners or snowplows. Citywide data feeds brought these practices into the view of municipal employees tasked with enforcing parking restrictions. Splicing together computational and physical terrain, officers located and ticketed more than seven thousand vehicles in a few months.[51] Notices stuck to windows informed readers that $100 fines would escalate with a second offense and could lead to towing the vehicle if it was not moved into a street or driveway. City officials saw the penalties as encouraging Detroiters to leave cars in their proper place, a position that reflects how such restrictions enact a white, middle-class aesthetic of residential propriety.[52] As city residents noted when contesting tickets and towing fees in municipal court proceedings, paying off the tickets sapped them of resources they otherwise needed to fix up aging vehicles.

Systems like Detroit Street View highlight fraught feedback loops created by city residents' attempts to raise empty buildings to the attention of Detroit's municipal state actors. Deploying city staff to roll cameras and mapping equipment through Detroit's streets provided public agencies with routinely updated knowledge of what the city looked like on the ground. Routing this information into computer screens for city building inspectors made it possible to more quickly identify empty buildings, categorize them as blight, and mobilize resources for demolition. In this sense, constantly refreshing city offices' street-by-street vision of Detroit appeared key to restoring city residents' confidence that the municipal government had the capacity not only to know where empty buildings were but also to do something about them. The public employees who implemented Detroit Street View approached it as distinct from the burgeoning CCTV surveillance apparatus operated by the municipal police department. In a moment where surveillance systems were tracking people across the city in real time, Detroit Street View's focus on bringing the city's buildings into view a few times each year appeared comparatively low risk. Moreover, obscuring identifying information seemed to mitigate the possibility that survey images could be used against Detroiters. But even as Detroit Street View did not stream directly into the municipal real time crime center, the data it made available for the purposes of addressing Detroiters' complaints about blighted buildings also made it possible to scrutinize and patrol city neighborhoods in new ways.

GOVERNING THROUGH BLIGHT

On a brilliant summer day nine years after Dorothy clambered through the snow to request that Claude, Andy, and I "blight" certain buildings, demolition crews toppled twelve structures in the blocks around her home. Dorothy and I video-chatted as the crews tore through the burned-out brick house she had named as blight when we first met. Through the feed, I watched the excavator bucket gnashing through shingles, bricks, studs, plywood barricades, and other components while Dorothy recounted the years through which she had anticipated these demolitions. Like many Detroiters, Dorothy had expected that excavators would arrive promptly after Motor City Mapping surveyors came to photograph her corner of the city. Such expectations had been heightened by public workshops in which she expressly noted her support for possible demolitions identified by surveyors. In Dorothy's summation, "The city took its sweet time, but they finally came and took care of this blight." At long last, she felt the municipality had made good on its obligations. Nevertheless, in the same conversation, Dorothy also detailed how people in her neighborhood had been hit by waves of fines for parking cars on the grass, as well as for having delivery vans, food trucks, and other commercial vehicles they drove for work parked in a residential neighborhood. Dorothy's son regularly parked the panel van he used to deliver packages in her driveway. After ignoring the initial $100 ticket, he paid the second one for $500 that came with a threat to impound the vehicle.

Dorothy's views are indicative of how blight is a political concept that guides engagements with the landscape. In particular, when Detroiters labeled empty buildings as blight, they articulated expectations that doing so would compel their municipal government to dispatch demolition crews. Within neighborhood discussions and administrative procedures alike, blight is a biopolitical project to be sure. It enacts the landscape as a terrain to be governed and as a tool to govern through.

When blight emerged in the early twentieth century it was in the context of legal segregation in which Detroiters racialized as other than white contended with limited housing options, especially ones owned by landlords who refused to repair broken electrical, heating, or plumbing systems. In Michigan and elsewhere, state statutes codifying ostensibly blighted environments as threats to public well-being also responsibilize municipal staff with preventing their spread. Detroit's landscape bears the marks of twentieth-century blight-elimination projects that leveled majority-Black neighborhoods to make way for housing, expressways, and other structures desired by wealthy white stakeholders. The surgical precision with which corporate capital and municipal planners targeted these neighborhoods was made possible by photographic surveys that mapped the locations of collapsing buildings alongside the racialized identities of people who inhabited them. For Detroiters with personal connections to the waves of displacements precipitated by alleged blight removal, observing people engaged in the act of photographing buildings was enough to raise the expectation that a demolition crew would tear those structures down.

Over the past eighty years, the sorts of places classified as blight have seemingly inverted, from buildings home to too many people in the early twentieth century to places without documented residents altogether. Across this transition, the same administrative powers to uproot alleged blight from Detroit's landscape have remained in place. For most Detroiters I met, including but not limited to those named in this chapter, asking administrators to address empty buildings was central to their interactions with the diffusion of organizations that govern their city. At the same time, however, proposals to demolish tens of thousands of allegedly blighted buildings, among them the proposal to raze 40,077 structures following Motor City Mapping, raised concerns that blight designations would once again be operationalized to evict Black and poor people from their homes. When demolitions targeted only empty buildings, they confirmed hopes of leveraging city residents' knowledge to guide the removal of structures they understood to be empty and blighted. As demolition administrators and planners like Alicia explained to a crowd of uneasy Detroiters, "We're going to do blight elimination that is led by the knowledge of residents and accountable to them." Talk is easy, and it is well documented how planners and administrators will solicit input from city residents without ever enacting their desires.[53] In this case, however, state actors tasked with assessing whether Detroit's buildings constituted blight took pains to align demolition designations with those of proximal neighbors.

In explicit and implicit ways, Motor City Mapping raised the question of whether using residents' perspectives as the basis of administrative decisions facilitates outcomes that are accountable to those residents. Detroit's twentieth-century blight-elimination projects are emblematic of planning processes that intentionally and unintentionally operationalized municipal planning decisions to displace Black, Brown, and impoverished people.[54] In Detroit and elsewhere, it is evident how definitions of blight determined by interests of wealthier, whiter elites and their administrative collaborators positioned neighborhoods where Black people lived as a threat to the municipal body politic to be removed by any means necessary. In the aftermath of racist displacement, upholding the visions that people have of and for their neighborhoods over those of elite outsiders has been the hallmark of participatory planning interventions.[55] Such interventions have sought to move the locus of control over the built environment out of government offices and into the hands of city residents.[56] Building from these interventions, urban studies and media studies scholar Shannon Mattern identifies how "*city making* is always, simultaneously, an enactment of *city knowing*."[57] The point, Mattern summarizes, is how administrative actors and planning institutions face critical choices when they decide whose perspectives they look from when deciding what constitutes a problem and whether to act on it. From this vantage, it certainly appears that centering ground-level understandings of neighborhoods rather than outside generalizations would make for decisions that better support people who call those neighborhoods home.

But the end results of administrative searches for blight in Detroit complicate the notion that projects aiming to see landscapes as residents do necessarily support the interests of those residents. To be clear, nonprofit workers and municipal employees aimed to enact blight designations in ways that reflected the understandings and desires people had for the buildings in their immediate vicinity. For building inspectors like Mitch, this included scaffolding Detroiters' requests to classify empty buildings as blighted and mobilize resources for demolition into incremental updates to municipal databases. Meanwhile, planners like Alicia initiated projects like Motor City Mapping with the intention of creating a speedier, publicly accessible conduit for Detroiters to request resources from municipal offices, including but not limited to demolitions. Detroit Street View mapping rigs created a routinely updated survey of Detroit's built environment for the purpose of eliminating the yearslong process between when neighbors notify municipal offices about empty buildings and when public employees can route them toward demolition with a formal classification of blight. And yet, this effort to anticipate Detroiters' concerns of empty buildings made a ground-level view of the city available to every municipal office—and, indeed, to everyone with an internet connection. The very system of surveying Detroit's landscape to make empty buildings legible for removal as blight is also the system that made the cars city residents parked on the grass or commercial vehicles people kept at their homes legible as objects of mounting fines.

A $100 ticket may seem small, but in a city where seven in ten households live paycheck to paycheck,[58] the unexpected expense could prove consequential. The ways surveys for empty buildings made it possible to enforce arbitrary aesthetic norms embedded in the city code also point to the ways securing assistance with blight has routinely required Detroiters opening their homes up to scrutiny by the municipal state. This has remained the case even as the meaning of blight has changed significantly. In a moment of legal segregation, Black Detroiters sought support from city offices with accounts of how antiblack restrictions made it possible for landlords to charge higher and higher rents on unsound buildings. Photographic surveys made it possible to label those buildings as blighted and unsafe for inhabitation in the fine print of municipal records. But the ultimate result was flattening majority-Black neighborhoods and displacing residents from their homes. In the decades to follow, as the meaning of blight shifted to account for buildings emptied out by racist disinvestment, Detroiters conveyed the locations of such structures to public agencies in hopes of securing demolitions. With empty buildings visible in neighborhoods across the city, keeping tabs on blight entailed rolling out survey crews and mapping rigs citywide. And yet, despite the transformation of what blight means, the power relations it entails remained consistent. At each juncture, administrative interventions in Detroiters' lives were not myopic, top-down decisions. They rode atop projects that made the material conditions of racial capitalism visible from the ground up.

In summary, for administrative staff and Detroit residents alike, recent demolitions demonstrate the possibility for blight removal to work in the service of the city's majority-Black populace. Given the origins of blight as a tool for engraining white supremacy, feedback loops winding through front porches, meeting halls, and digital platforms shifted what the term embraced and guided wrecking crews to topple only empty buildings. They also enacted guard rails around Detroit Street

View to recognize buildings rather than human faces. Together, these protocols sought to undercut antiblack outcomes facilitated through earlier administrative actions to image and map blight. That is, by homing in on empty buildings that adjacent residents wanted leveled, contemporary iterations of blight removal reorder the city's landscape without displacing its population. But correction orders like the one delivered to Dorothy's house—the ones warning of increasing financial consequences if cars were not moved off lawns or out of the neighborhood entirely—troubles the conclusion that placing Black Detroiters' perspectives at the center of administrative programs was sufficient to ensure that those programs always upheld their interests and desires. At stake here are the ways projects of mapping so-called blight are surveys of how racist processes accrue in the landscape. Even with Black Detroiters' perspectives anchoring what counts as blight, making their desires actionable relied on making their neighborhoods visible. Doing so subjected people grappling with the consequences of antiblack disinvestment to examination by the administrative state with its attendant consequences.

PART TWO

MACHINERIES

THREE

ALGORITHMS

For almost six decades Daisy had lived in the same brick house on a shady street in Northeast Detroit. The dwelling was a family home passed down from relatives who had been among the first Black residents on the block in the 1950s. Daisy shared the home with her younger sister, Melissa, and Melissa's great-grandson. When we met, he had just started grade one, and a bright blue tarp stretched over the roof of their home. It kept some of the rain and melting snow from trickling through the ceilings of upstairs rooms. Contractors estimated it would cost around $15,000 to reshingle the leaky roof, shore up water-damaged rafters, and patch damaged plaster. Daisy and Melissa worked as housekeepers at a downtown hotel. Together, they earned just under $40,000 that year, more than the typical Detroit household.[1] But the pair could not afford such a large bill. Daisy's hearty laugh filled her kitchen when she recalled how a nonprofit staffer had suggested she could take out a bank loan for the repairs. Several banks refused, citing the dozens of empty buildings on her block. One loan officer explained to Daisy, "Your credit and income are OK, but there are too many empty buildings. Our system won't approve the loan. If you can get the city to tear down those buildings, we can get you the loan." Eight years passed before demolition crews leveled buildings on

Daisy's block. In the intervening years, the household had scraped together funds to repair the roof on their own.

Daisy's roof was not the only tarp-covered one on her block. Procured from hardware stores and online retailers, tarps were a relatively low-cost tool that people in neighborhoods across the city relied on to mitigate leaky roofs until they could afford more permanent repairs or landlords could be compelled to make good on their legal obligations to tenants under state housing codes. In 2021, university and community researchers identified almost forty thousand inhabited dwellings with serious roof leaks, nonfunctional electric or plumbing infrastructure, and broken heating systems.[2] Nearly half of all Detroiters lived in a dwelling with at least one of these conditions, and approximately one in six city residents contended with all of them simultaneously. Conservative estimates of the cost of addressing deferred maintenance issues in occupied dwellings projected that it would take around $1 billion to ensure all Detroiters lived in structurally sound homes with watertight roofs, solid foundations, and functional utilities. As researchers found, public funds allocated to home repair grant programs were insufficient to meet this need. They also noted that financial institutions frequently denied city residents' applications for the kinds of fixed-interest home repair loans that households in the United States conventionally rely on to shore up their dwellings. Even when Detroiters like Daisy could afford monthly payments, they experienced their application being turned back due to their home's proximity to empty buildings.

Neither Daisy nor Detroit's municipal administrators received consistent explanations about why bank systems rejected home repair loan applications based on nearby empty buildings. One loan officer explained to Daisy that the empty buildings reduced the appraised value of her home to below the cost of the roof replacement. Another suggested that it was the increased prospect of fires. Some just referred to "the system" without explanation. Reports on the topic from municipal and nonprofit offices detailed their own discussions with loan officers who provided similarly inconsistent explanations of exactly why empty buildings were such an impediment to people living nearby being eligible for home repair loans.[3] Detroiters were not alone in this regard. In conferences and webinars, I observed Detroit-based activists and administrators in conversation with their peers in cities across the country where people also encountered empty buildings as obstacles to the approval of home repair loans for which they would otherwise qualify.[4] It was not lost on folks that buildings emptied out by processes of racist disinvestment were being raised as a criterion to exclude the predominantly Black and Brown people who lived closest to them from accessing the resources they needed to make their dwellings habitable. Loan officers present for these conversations insisted that this was based in actuarial calculations required as part of the loan process, not a case of firms refusing to lend in communities of color.

It is well established how data-driven decisions can routinize racism and intersecting forms of injustice—processes visual artist and technology critic Mimi Onuoha names "algorithmic violence."[5] The point, as Onuoha and scholars of technology and inequality explain, is that computational systems give a veneer of legitimacy to decisions that can routinize racist outcomes in ways that make it difficult for human actors to intervene.[6] As a system, home finance in the United States has long enacted white supremacy through technical gatekeeping.[7] For example, in the run-up to the Great Recession, automated underwriting systems tended to route high-income Black and Latine applicants into high-interest subprime loans and low-income white applicants into low rates.[8] Those systems did so because areas where banks had previously not done business were coded as "riskier investments."[9] Because majority-Black and -Latine neighborhoods had been historically excluded from mortgage eligibility, applications from them were sorted into more costly financial products. Meanwhile majority-white neighborhoods appeared as the best fit for low rates. Financial institutions were largely not held accountable for racist algorithmic outcomes because race was not an explicit variable. To quote legal scholar Frank Pasquale's analysis, "As they dole out opportunities for 'prime' and 'subprime' credit, automated systems may be silently resegregating racial groups in ways that would be clearly illegal if pursued consciously by an individual."[10] Put plainly, algorithmic violence does not require biased individuals. It occurs because computational systems reinscribe already existing conditions of inequity.

As an administrative project, demolitions were explicitly an effort to make home finance eligibility calculations work a little differently. Requests for public funding to level empty buildings—to the tune of more than a half billion dollars between 2014 and 2024—hinged on the promise that leveling empty buildings would make it possible for Detroiters to repair their dwellings by leveling algorithmic barriers that blocked them from accessing conventional home financing.[11] With thousands of empty buildings being leveled every year, teams of demolition administrators and university researchers alike kept watchful eyes on data streams of loan applications, approvals, and rejections for signs of whether this promise would come to fruition.[12] As banks increasingly approved loans, especially for home repair loans, in the vicinity where empty buildings were coming down, they confirmed hypotheses that changing conditions in the physical world could indeed shift the outcome of algorithmic underwriting processes. Across a decade in which austerity measures shredded public services in Detroit, funding for demolitions remained robust. Public dollars continued to tear down empty buildings even as municipal grants for city residents to patch roofs, replace windows, and complete other essential projects to physically stabilize their homes became increasingly scarce. To justify funding demolitions rather than direct assistance for home repairs, city officials and public administrators pointed to data demonstrating how Detroiters living in majority-Black neighborhoods where empty buildings had been removed could access home financing on the same terms as people living in majority-white suburbs.

At a time when algorithmic violence is impossible to disregard, sitting with Detroiters like Daisy as they work to address leaking roofs, busted plumbing, broken foundations, and other structural issues surfaces how the appearance of equal opportunity in computational outputs can conceal the endurance of unequal conditions in the actual world. Demolition administrators parsed administrative datasets to target demolitions in places that would level antiblack barriers to home finance based on a faith that doing so would make it possible for Detroiters to access safe, secure housing. But demolitions that made Detroit neighborhoods eligible for conventional home mortgages and repair loans did not necessarily trickle down into physically stable homes for Detroiters. From the standpoint of administrative data, the increasing value ascribed to Detroiters' homes and the availability of home finance that accompanied demolitions certainly seemed to be a sign of financial uplift for the city's majority-Black populace. However, as empty buildings came down and housing values went up, city residents navigated increasingly constrained access to homes in good repair. Rather than evening out barriers to safe housing, demolitions ultimately reencoded racialized and classed systems in which access to a secure, well-supported home is contingent on household resources. This outcome illustrates how well-intended, data-driven efforts to enact race-neutral algorithmic decisions can leave the political economic calculus of racism untouched. Doing so furthers already existing inequities while obscuring possibilities for changing them.

PERFORMANCE METRICS

A few times during my research, I joined a dozen or so of Detroit's self-styled "public data professionals" at networking events that built relationships between people who worked as data analysts and program managers in nonprofit or government agencies. After attendees clustered around tables or piled into booths at various downtown bars, they would discuss ongoing projects in their offices. At one of these gatherings, I was seated at a table with Sam,[13] a demolition program employee at the Detroit Land Bank Authority (DLBA),[14] as they discussed how their work involved splicing together data streams about demolitions, property sales, home repair loans, and other indicators. Almost immediately, a municipal data analyst visiting from Cincinnati asked Sam, "So, how do you make sure you're allocating resources in ways that benefit everyone? Like you're not just demolishing buildings in the wealthiest neighborhoods or around where white people live." Conversations tapered off at other tables as everyone in attendance turned their head to hear Sam's response. This was a timely question. In recent public meetings, city residents had wondered aloud if the DLBA was passing over impoverished Black neighborhoods to demolish buildings elsewhere. They asked for confirmation that public funding for building removals was not being prioritized for use in the city's wealthiest, whitest neighborhoods rather than the rest of the city.

Sam fished a laptop out of their bag and, over the buzz of activity happening around the bar, responded to the question. "We were afraid of doing that," they stated as they pulled up a digital map locating all the buildings torn down in Detroit in the previous few years. Tens of thousands of dots filled the screen, and although they nearly blanketed some parts of map, other areas were visibly sparer (map 3.1). Sam began explaining how their office had used public data to "more or less" prioritize demolishing empty buildings that were adjacent to but not necessarily on densely populated blocks. Administrative records showed that empty buildings on densely populated blocks stood the greatest chance of being used again. Those elsewhere tended to remain empty for years or decades until excavators knocked them down. With a few clicks and keystrokes, Sam made circles around each demolition site to indicate to indicate their "impact areas." Each circle represented a little over 200 yards in diameter, the average size of one of the city's blocks. With a few more keystrokes, Sam incorporated demographic information. According to Sam's calculation, around 70 percent of Detroit's residents

MAP 3.1. The one-block "impact areas" of demolitions completed between 2014 and 2020.

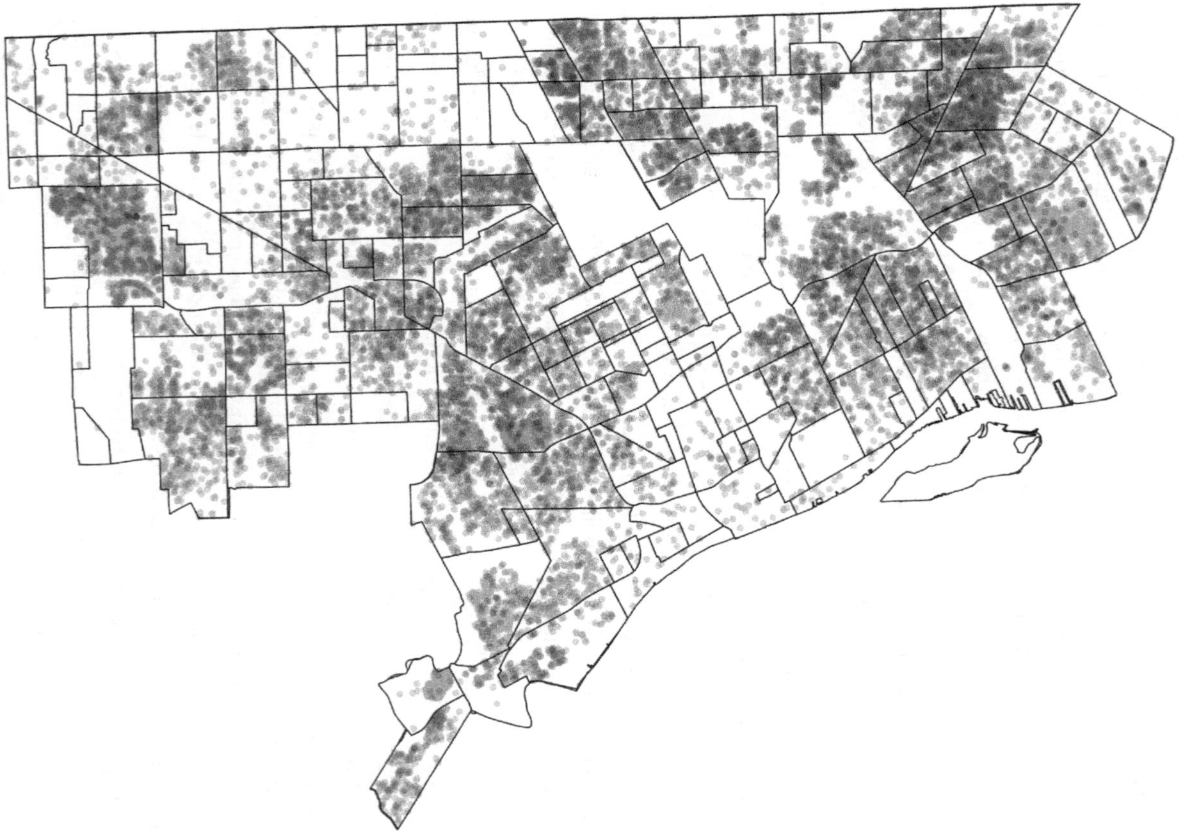

Source: City of Detroit. Image by author.

lived within 200 yards of at least one demolition. Switching to another window, they pulled up an analysis showing how the people living in each area were relatively similar on metrics of racial identity.[15] Median household income within the demolition impact-area bubbles and outside of them hovered close to the citywide median at the time.

The data Sam presented surprised me. It is not difficult to find instances in which administrative decisions that appear to be made based on indicators other than race have racist consequences. For example, consider eligibility algorithms commonly used in affordable housing lotteries in the United States that prioritize people who live closest to new developments and render people who live outside that target area ineligible. Because racial and economic segregation is the status quo in which decisions happen, the result of prioritizing proximity is to reinforce existing segregation.[16] Majority-Black, -Latine, or -white places remain majority-Black, -Latine, and -white, respectively. Places of concentrated poverty—sometimes but not always communities of color—remain places of concentrated poverty. Places of concentrated wealth—most typically but not always majority-white communities—avoid building affordable housing altogether by suggesting that nobody living nearby would be eligible. Scholars of the social dimensions of data-driven systems routinely identify how algorithmic decisions reproduce prevailing distributions of privilege and vulnerability. Mary Madden and her colleagues put it nicely: "While data analytics is touted for its ability to reduce human biases, it often merely replicates them."[17] Because the intersections of racism and economic inequity are already structured into the world, they cannot be removed from computational decisions by simply claiming color blindness or class neutrality.[18] To this end, I had always assumed that the DLBA's practice of prioritizing demolitions adjacent to the most densely populated blocks would create disparate outcomes. Sam's data suggested otherwise.

Detroit's municipal and nonprofit planning offices had their own recent histories of creating proxy variables that projected antiblack distributions of public resources. In 2010, local agencies contracted with consultants to develop a computational toolkit that would shape future investments in municipal infrastructure—including things like transportation, waste management, and street lighting. Dubbed the Detroit Works Project, on its face, the toolkit was race neutral. Service improvements would happen in "high-value" neighborhoods identified by their high volume of property sales and average sales prices. Neighborhoods with low property values and few residents would have services withdrawn. The ultimate result was that districts targeted for upgrades were home to the greatest concentrations of white residents in the city, whereas people living in areas targeted for service reductions tended to be impoverished and Black.[19] Geographer Sara Safransky observes how the project became indicative of the ways "racialized orders of value and risk are revitalized through new types of data-driven urban planning . . . making it possible for the disconnection and disinvestment of neighborhoods to be cast, at least rhetorically, as objective economic calculations that have nothing to do with race or politics."[20] In the United States, real estate markets remain predicated on assumptions that the most valuable places are homogenously white ones.[21] When real estate indicators, especially property value, become a central metric for allocating limited public resources, they reproduce the racist logics that are always already embedded within constructions of property value.

City officials publicly distanced themselves from the Detroit Works Project toolkit after Detroiters packed public meetings to protest the idea of uneven access to municipal services. All candidates in the following year's municipal elections panned the project, with the winning mayoral candidate campaigning on a platform that "every neighborhood has a future." Despite this public image, following decades of austerity budgets, unevenly distributed municipal services are still very much a reality in Detroit—as they are in many cities.[22] In their own ways, most people who identified as Detroit's "public data professionals" were tasked with ways to make public service delivery more "efficient," knowing that "efficiency" was code for retrenchment. At the same networking event where Sam made a presentation about the geographies of demolition, a transportation data analyst described being troubled by their recent assignment to comb through rider data to identify which parts of Detroit's municipal bus network were the most and least utilized. Nominally a project to "reimagine" the city's bus routes, it seemed likely that the information they gathered would provide ammunition for concentrating services along highly trafficked thoroughfares by ending routes that wound across city neighborhoods. While this would speed commuters in and out of the central business district, it would eliminate services that were essential for the mobility of impoverished city residents, especially Black, working-class Detroiters. Put simply, municipal and nonprofit technologists were acutely familiar with how their daily work routines could shape the lives of city residents, especially the most vulnerable, even if it did not make news headlines.

From the closing decades of the twentieth century into the twenty-first, consistent federal, municipal, and state funding for empty-building demolitions in Detroit contrasted with routine cutbacks in most other publicly funded services. For example, during the 2010s, municipal officials enacted draconian cuts to accommodate declining property tax collections and reductions in state and federal revenue sharing. These cuts included eliminating dozens of bus routes, shuttering libraries, privatizing waste management, slashing public retiree benefits, and temporarily closing the public health department, among other measures. During these same years, budgets for demolition agencies like the DLBA grew larger each year. With each budget and grant cycle, administrators projected that eliminating empty buildings would touch off a cascade of actions that would ultimately stabilize the municipal budget. Specifically, clearing empty buildings from Detroiters' neighborhoods would make it increasingly likely that financial institutions would approve repair loans. This, in turn, would make it possible for building owners to maintain buildings rather than continually deferring maintenance. Better structural conditions, especially in Detroiters' homes, would stem the ongoing trickle of people—and with them, tax revenues—out of the city. The complex calculations of this prospective domino effect were persuasive in securing significant public funding for demolitions.[23] During the same years, when most public employees in Detroit were tasked with identifying how to further gut service delivery, demolition administrators like Sam were focused on where to expand the reach of their programs.

In truth, I combed through DLBA records anticipating that demolitions would reflect the same triage that pervaded most publicly funded activities during my time in Detroit. As community researchers documented, the city's few upper-income neighborhoods, which were also its whitest neighborhoods, tended to receive targeted attention and most everywhere else was ignored.[24] Like Detroiters who peppered the public comment section of DLBA oversight meetings, I wondered if the agency's focus on spiraling out from densely populated blocks would skew who lived in the neighborhoods where empty buildings came down when compared to who lived in the neighborhoods where they remained standing. With a few keystrokes, Sam could check how building removals performed on these metrics.[25] In so doing, they forced me to grapple with the reality that Detroit's most densely populated neighborhoods are not always its whitest or wealthiest. Ample funding for demolitions contrasted with the broader paradigm of municipal austerity. With each new year bringing the resources for demolition offices to tear down more empty buildings, the scope of who lived around those buildings shifted a little bit further. As a result, the logic of moving building removals incrementally outward from Detroit's most densely inhabited blocks resulted in structures coming down around people who, at least from a demographic perspective, resembled the majority-Black, lower-income city.

MARKET PARTICIPATION

I regularly met up with Sam for a coffee on the afternoons when I came to the central business district to attend the monthly meeting of the DLBA's board of directors. Sometimes they squeezed into the narrow conference room where members of the agency's several-hundred-person staff presented on their ongoing work. Sam's department compiled highly anticipated reports that mapped the locations of demolitions alongside those of home finance transactions. Federal demolition funding was contingent on the agency demonstrating that removing empty buildings would stabilize Detroit's home financing market and increase the number of transactions. During one such meeting, one of Sam's coworkers described a report that showed an uptick in home finance transactions in Detroit over the past year, saying, "We're seeing loans happen in places that've been shut out of the home finance market for decades. Loan officers are saying that having empty buildings come down is making it possible for residents to participate in the market." Whoops rang out from the two dozen people crammed into the conference room. After the atmosphere settled, a member of the board who lived on the west side responded. "I just want to say thank you to all of our staff," she beamed. "I know how hard you all work. It's important work. We know building these opportunities is crucial for supporting long-term Detroiters." DLBA staff assured board members they had submitted news of increasing home finance transactions to federal agencies.

For DLBA administrators, including agency staff and directors, building opportunities for longtime city residents was explicitly a project of making home finance mechanisms accessible to Black Detroiters. Around half of Detroiters own their dwellings and the other half rent theirs.[26] This is somewhat different from the country as a whole, where approximately one-third of people rent their homes. In the United States, people who purchase their primary residence typically do so using fixed-rate financial products that spread out costs over decades, with cash purchases tending to come from only the wealthiest individuals and speculative investors.[27] Sam and their coworkers created graphs and maps of home finance transactions in Detroit beginning in 2013, the year the DLBA assumed control of the municipal demolition program. In that year, most of the 26,286 Detroit dwellings that changed hands did so in cash sales among investors. By comparison, the 529 fixed-rate bank loans banks approved in 2013 were clustered in the handful of neighborhoods ringing the central business district and a few of Detroit's wealthiest blocks on the far northwest and east sides. In a moment when eight in ten Detroiters identified as Black, more than half of loan recipients identified as white. The DLBA's routine reports resonated with arguments from progressive housing-justice organizers and centrist social welfare organizations alike.[28] Together, they sought not only to increase the availability of home finance in the city but to ensure that home financing was accessible for Black Detroiters.

By routing building removals in ways that would connect Black Detroiters with home finance, demolition administrators were attempting to recalibrate a system that originated as a project of white supremacy. Between 1933 and 1968, national policies that created long-term, fixed-rate loans as a means of supporting homeownership and repair among moderate-income Americans enshrined a system that marked nonwhite people as "adverse influences" to property value. Color-coded "redlining" maps designated homogenously white neighborhoods as the only secure locations for investment and rendered neighborhoods with Black residents of any income ineligible for financial products that were easily available in impoverished all-white areas. Like Black, Latine, Asian, and other nonwhite people excluded from federally supported low-interest loans, nonwhite Detroiters who purchased homes during this period did so in cash or through high-interest financial products. Examining redlining in Detroit and its suburbs, David Freund historicizes how the practice "helped give birth to a market that created more wealth for whites while providing a state-sanctioned platform for housing experts to argue that racial discrimination was simply a by-product of impersonal economic processes."[29] Though legally codified redlining practices became nominally illegal, racist policies that make whiteness a credential for accessing the lowest-interest loans and highest-value neighborhoods remain a decisive feature of racial wealth gap calculations in Detroit and across the United States.[30] Put simply, redlining made the disparate conditions of racial capitalism explicit, with white supremacy legally encoded in statutes and administrative guidebooks. As a matter of wealth and capital accumulation, those conditions roll forward even after their legal alibis and frameworks have been pulled away.

Racialized access to home finance continued after the end of legally sanctioned white supremacy because rejections based on antiblack circumstances were superficially race neutral. Consider the home finance applications from Detroiters that banks and other lending institutions rejected based on proximity to visibly empty buildings. Insurance and loan underwriting algorithms that flagged such structures as fire risks or detriments to property value did not include information on why those buildings were empty to begin with. As chapter 1 describes at length, Detroit's empty buildings are the cumulative products of racism, especially antiblack disinvestment. Divorced from this context, financial systems that screened out Detroit addresses from eligibility for home purchase and repair loans based on the empty buildings around them appeared unhooked from racism altogether. Like Daisy's experiences detailed at the beginning of this chapter, loan officers were sometimes frank with Detroiters that their individual incomes and credit histories would qualify them for a home repair loan or mortgage somewhere else, just not in the place where they lived. When this happened, people contended with the same circumstances that Daisy's household confronted. They could either pick up and move somewhere that credit was available, or they could stretch tarps over leaking roofs, wedge bricks under sinking joists, and implement other stopgaps until they could pull together the cash necessary to afford more permanent repairs. And yet, because none of the systems that put Detroiters in such positions used "race" as an explicit decision-making category, disparate outcomes were legally permitted.

In testimonies and gatherings, housing-justice activists in Detroit routinely called out institutional refusals to fund home financing in Detroit. One such action occurred during a city council hearing on Detroiters' home repair needs. Dozens of people packed into the small hearing room to detail their roof leaks, faulty electrical systems, rotting porches, wobbly beams, and other issues. Many described how they had unsuccessfully sought bank financing for repairs. They requested that city officials overrule financial institutions that denied loans because applicants lived near empty buildings. A woman who identified herself as a lifelong westsider in her seventies distilled their common sentiments when she said:

> On paper they can say it's not about race. In reality, it's redlining all over. It's Black folks getting denied loans. It's Black folks who can't fix our houses. In reality, it's Black folks leaving the city because we can't get the money to repair our homes here—but we can get it out in Southfield.

A councilor thanked the woman for her contribution and apologized that the municipality did not have the legal authority to compel action from banks. A representative from the housing department chimed in to share information from the DLBA that showed increasing approvals for home purchase and repair loans in areas where crews had recently toppled empty buildings. Much of the hearing turned around cautious administrative optimism that demolitions would help shift Detroit's landscape so that the physical conditions of Black residents' neighborhoods did not impede their home finance applications.

Expanding the footprint in which Detroiters were approved for home repair loans held critical meaning for demolition administrators in Detroit. Longtime residents sometimes applied for bank mortgages to facilitate moves from one neighborhood to another within the city limits. However, most mortgage applications for dwellings in Detroit came from people who were relatively new to the city, and longtime residents mostly applied for mortgages to move to the suburbs.[31] In contrast, home repair loan applications typically came from people who had lived in their dwelling for some time. Regulatory data that Sam and others at the DLBA scraped from disclosures made by financial institutions suggested that most repair loan applicants were Black Detroiters who had grappled with the realities of empty buildings in their city for years. In a conference training that used this data, a DLBA administrator clicked through administrative datasets where color-coded dots mapped the ways home repair loan approvals followed the paths of demolitions into new neighborhoods. Detailing how eight in ten Detroiters approved for home repair loans identified as Black, the administrator noted, "Home repair loans connect Black homeowners with the funds they need to fix roofs, get new windows, replace their electrical, and do all the things they need to stay in their homes." With demolitions framed as preceding nearby Detroiters being approved for home repair loans, administrative data provided evidence to support arguments that building removals expanded the territory in which financial institutions would approve credit.

Data analysts employed by Detroit's demolition program carefully tracked the ways home repair loan and mortgage transactions followed the paths of building removals, ticking up from a few hundred in 2013 to thousands each year by the end of the decade. Reports from Sam and their coworkers provided datapoints necessary to justify hundreds of millions in federal demolition funds during that period and laid the groundwork for future allocations. Expanded transaction locations suggested that removing empty buildings shifted the ways financing applications appeared within underwriting programs such that applicants for home mortgage and repair loans in Detroit were increasingly likely to be approved for credit. For local administrators, increasing existing city residents' access to home repair loans was particularly important because the system of conventional home finance has routinely discriminated against Black Detroiters. Even when legal statutes made racist lending decisions nominally illegal, Detroiters experienced how empty buildings created by antiblack disinvestment enabled "redlining all over." Whereas twentieth-century redlining projects made their racism explicit, the antiblack contours of home finance rejections due to the presence of empty buildings were obscured behind seemingly race-neutral decisions about the physical conditions of neighborhoods. To this end, as demographic indicators about people approved for home repair loans reflected those collected about Detroiters as a whole, they served to assure demolition administrators that building removals were not simply leveling barriers for newcomers to buy into a majority-Black city. Rather, they also leveled barriers that Black Detroiters faced to accomplishing much needed maintenance on their homes.

"YOUR HOME IS AN INVESTMENT"

In many ways, Carlos offered an ideal case to confirm administrative arguments that demolishing empty buildings helped to build up possibilities for Black homeownership in Detroit. An outgoing Black man in his thirties who worked as an automotive maintenance technician, he had lived in Detroit for his entire life. Carlos also held an ownership deed to a duplex on Detroit's west side. Carlos had grown up in the building and had inherited it upon the passing of his grandmother, the previous owner. At the time she passed, Carlos was living with her in the downstairs apartment, and nobody had lived in the upstairs apartment for years. Despite multiple layers of tarp over the roof, water dripped through the ceiling and into that apartment when it rained. The boiler and plumbing service for the upstairs were also inoperable. But the neighborhood where Carlos lived was included in the first wave of demolitions funded by the DLBA, and excavators tore down empty buildings up and down his block during the summer of 2014. Shortly after, a bank approved Carlos's application for a $20,000 home repair loan to replace the building's roof, as well as fix the heating and plumbing in the upstairs apartment. After paying off the initial loan with revenues generated from renting out the upstairs apartment, Carlos received a further $30,000 loan to cover the cost of heating, electrical, and plumbing upgrades to the downstairs apartment where he lived.

Carlos regularly detailed his renovation experiences as part of a "homebuyer education" workshop series hosted by a nonprofit devoted to supporting Black Detroiters' financial security. Every month, a dozen or so Detroiters arranged themselves around a conference room table for a Saturday filled with discussions about the process of buying a home in the city. The workshops filled quickly, since participants qualified for subsidized down payments and rate reductions on future loans. Nonprofit staff opened with a presentation on the loan underwriting process, highlighting the different ways that loan applicants could document their various income streams and past rental payments. Loan officers would walk through the unique complexities of mortgage and home repair loan applications at their respective employers. While the financial institutions represented varied between meetings, loan officers consistently underscored how the changing contexts of Detroit's neighborhoods, especially demolitions, facilitated increasing loan approvals in the city. Attendees tended to stare quietly forward during presentations about credit agencies, debt-to-income ratios, the legacies of redlining, and other minutiae of home finance. But they grew animated when Carlos gave advice on ongoing maintenance routines and emergency repairs. Everyone in attendance tended to nod vigorously to his declarations like "Remember, your home is an investment. If you take care of it, it will take care of you." As other presenters gathered their belongings to leave, Carlos was usually fielding questions from Detroiters interested in learning about how they too could amass the resources necessary to acquire and fix up dwellings of their own.

Even within workshops designed to propel Detroiters into loan eligibility, presenters did not offer homeownership as an unimpeachable good. Facilitators and participants spoke candidly about friends and kin who had been displaced from their homes by mortgage and tax foreclosures.[32] They also described how buildings, no matter how solidly built, need almost constant maintenance to remain in good repair—gutters cleaned, hot water tanks flushed, leaks sealed, heating filters changed, and so on. And yet, despite the financial obligations and ongoing labor associated with taking on owning a building, Detroiters routinely foregrounded how owning their home would provide them with a sense of security that they could remain in Detroit. Meanwhile, eviction cases for lease and land contract holders churned through local courts by the tens of thousands annually—even when tenants were withholding payments because landlords did not address municipal code violations.[33] By comparison, Detroit activists successfully used the procedural conditions of mortgage foreclosures to keep neighbors in their homes.[34] Scholar of land struggles Jessi Quizar contends such actions are emblematic of the ways Detroiters, especially Black Detroiters, "assert a logic around rights to a place that centres use value—the house as a home rather than the house as a property."[35] Like Quizar, I found many (though certainly not all) Detroiters who attended homebuyer workshops excited about the use values of a home, even if they were ambivalent about the exchange value transactions of buying a house.

I first met Carlos at an evening "housing assistance fair," organized by staff at a community agency and various municipal offices. Carlos had driven straight from work to the east side high school cafeteria where the event took place. His blue jumpsuit still bore traces of grease from that day's labors and his short locs were tucked under a cap as they had been for most of the day, but Carlos's hands were meticulously scrubbed clean. In them, he held a manila envelope that contained his recent paystubs and a copy of the probate court documents transferring the duplex into his name. Alongside a hundred or so other Detroiters, Carlos wound his way between the handful of tables arranged around the perimeter of the room. Carlos's salary that year qualified him for a partial property tax exemption available to low-income Detroiters. He was not poor enough to qualify for reduced water and sewerage bills. A home repair grant program had exceeded its cap of twenty-five applications that year. But a loan officer employed by a bank headquartered in Detroit's suburbs reviewed Carlos's documents and listened as he described his desire to fix up and rent out the upstairs apartment in his home. Keying Carlos's address into a search bar, the loan officer informed him that his home fell within one of the Detroit neighborhoods where the bank was issuing loans. The outlines of those districts corresponded to areas included in early waves of the DLBA's demolition program.

The next week, Carlos drove to a suburban bank branch to file a formal loan application. He returned to the same branch a month later to sign loan paperwork that committed him to repay the loan at a rate of $396 each month for five years. Within a few months, the upstairs apartment was ready for tenants. Contractors had reshingled the roof, installed a new heat and hot water service, laid wall-to-wall carpeting, as well as replaced broken pipes and a couple shattered windows. On evenings and days off from work, Carlos had painted the walls and moldings in the same light beige and white he used downstairs. Soon after, someone Carlos knew from high school, her mother, her partner, and two children lugged their belongings up the stairs and settled in. The $600 they paid each month covered the cost of Carlos's repair loan, as well as half the building's tax and utilities. Once he had made the final installment payment on the first loan, Carlos received a second loan to cover the costs of upgrades to the downstairs apartment. Though it had certainly been in better condition than the upstairs apartment, its core systems had seen better days. Drains ran slowly, lights flickered, and radiators barely warmed in the winter. Contractors quickly ran new plumbing and electrical lines and stuffed exterior walls full of insulation before covering them back over with drywall. They also replaced the boiler. In return, Carlos agreed to pay the bank $438 each month for seven years.

Close relations can cushion against structural precarity, but they can also facilitate its grind. In a moment of ever-rising rents, knowing someone who knew someone who had access to an affordable place to stay, even if just for a little while, was often critical for longtime Detroiters to find a place to live. Globally, chains of social relationships—what urban studies specialist AbdouMaliq Simone terms "people as infrastructure"—have been essential for Black peoples to make and keep homes in contexts where the political economy of housing is defined by white supremacy.[36] Consider how the people who rented the upstairs apartment from Carlos moved there after being evicted from a central city building being renovated into a hotel. Six hundred dollars was as much as they could initially afford each month, and Carlos increased rent only when tax and utilities rose. All the same, settling into a newly updated apartment, which was finally cozy inside despite a bitter chill outside, Carlos ruminated about the position he found himself in as a landlord. "Honestly, I'd like to charge them less," he said, pausing. "But I can't do that and pay the bills." To be clear, Carlos was not sweating his upstairs apartment for maximum gain. Yet the payments he collected each month distilled how landlord-tenant relations are always structural relations. Making good on obligations he had taken on to physically repair his house prevented Carlos from sharing his home with others without demanding payment in return.

Carlos was one of many Detroiters who shared their home repair financing experiences as part of workshops organized to support others in navigating the same process. Like Carlos, other participants encouraged their fellow city residents to take advantage of the increasing availability of home repair loans and mortgages, especially in the vicinity of recent demolition sites. In many ways, their accounts of recent renovation projects funded by home repair loans provided credence to administrative hopes that tearing down empty buildings would create different conditions of financial possibility for Detroiters—ones in which financial institutions would lend Detroiters the funds they needed to make repairs so that the places they lived were structurally sound. With their fixed interest provisions, payments on conventional financial products like the loans Carlos took on to fix up his two-unit home were meaningfully more stable than the escalating rents and land contracts with which Detroiters were deeply familiar. And yet, these loans still emplaced dwellings as financial products in which debts needed to be repaid each month with interest. This set conditions around who exactly could share in a newly repaired home. To reprise Carlos's words, making Detroiters' dwellings eligible for bank financing meant opening them up to a calculus in which "your home is an investment." Within that calculus, leak-free roofs, functional heating systems, and secure foundations were not things that could be freely given to people who needed them. The benefits of structural integrity were constrained to people with the ability to pay.

STABLE DWELLINGS

Daisy and I met at a resource fair like the one where Carlos received encouragement to apply for a home repair loan. In a community center gymnasium, Daisy went first to the table where nonprofit staff distributed information about home repair grant programs that promised low-income Detroiters resources to complete major structural repairs. Once she turned 65, Daisy's age gave her priority standing for a grant that would cover the costs of replacing her home's leaking roof. But as the staff from organizations who distributed the grants told people who stopped by their table, the organizations had only enough funds to award a few hundred grants each year. Waiting lists were thousands of people deep.[37] Daisy and I stood next to each other in the queue that circled from the home repair grant table to the one where another agency helped Detroiters file applications for utility assistance. We chatted as the line inched forward, and I learned she had been attempting to save fifteen grand to fix the roof for several years. Unlike Carlos, when loan officers plugged Daisy's address into search bars, their systems usually indicated that her home was unlikely to be deemed eligible. Even when Daisy made it further in the process, approval for the funds never came through after an appraiser photographed her house on a block full of empty buildings.

In anticipation of addressing her roof leak, Daisy made regular calls to the DLBA's main office line to request the demolition of buildings on her block. On one of those occasions, we stood on the front porch as Daisy smoked and made the call on speaker. After thanking the staffer for taking her call, Daisy provided an address, winking to me as she asked for a possible demolition date. The staffer paused and we could hear keys clatter as she entered the address in the land bank's property database:

> DLBA staff: OK, ma'am, so I do see that address in the demolition pipeline. But we don't have a date yet.
>
> Daisy: OK. But do you know when you will have a date?
>
> DLBA staff: I'm sorry, but that's all the information I have in the system. We've got a lot of structures to knock. We'll get those buildings down as soon as we can.

Daisy thanked the staffer for her assistance and ended the call. Pointing toward the tarp-covered roof, Daisy asked me, "You know what that means?" I shook my head. "We better plan to get that leak fixed on our own dime." Indeed, like many in the city, when Daisy heard DLBA officials' breathless 2014 announcements kicking off "the nation's largest demolition program," she imagined excavators rolling down her block in droves. When they did not, she began to wonder if they ever would.

Despite the barriers that limited home repair grants and constrained prospects for home repair loans posed to maintaining dwelling structures that had sometimes been standing for a century or more, Detroiters found ways to keep their homes in working order. Sociologist Claire Herbert discusses how "appropriation" in which Detroiters "use, take from, deconstruct, trespass across, or otherwise engage with real property they have no legal right to" has been a key aspect of this process, including for people who inhabit dwellings as owners, renters, or without formal tenancy.[38] For example, consider what happened when the twenty-year-old water heater in Daisy's basement rusted through and sent a cascade across the concrete floor. A new heater alone would have run almost a thousand dollars. Instead, members of the household asked friends and neighbors if anyone knew where they could find a used one in working condition. Later that week, someone from down the block dropped by with a five-year-old model he had recovered from an empty building on the other side of town. It landed with a thud in the yard and I helped him lug the tank inside. We swapped it in, following step-by-step videos posted to online home improvement channels. Daisy and I then carted the old heater to a scrap dealer along with some broken window air conditioning units that had been gathering dust in the attic. She pressed a few of the $20 bills we received from the scrapper into her neighbor's hands as thanks.

It was not possible to appropriate a leak-free roof. Hot water heaters can be moved from one building to another, but shingles need to be installed new. Daisy and her sister spent five years socking away enough cash to pay a roofing team to complete the job. Critically, the son of someone they knew from Sunday worship services worked as a roofing contractor. He agreed to take on the job for a price that was thousands lower than any other bid Daisy received. Over a chilly but clear week in early November, a crew began by sistering new beams to some rotted attic timbers and replacing others entirely. They then continued by stripping off three layers of tarps, old shingles, and rotted wood decking. Finally, they built up new decking and a waterproof layer of asphalt shingles. I arrived at the house just as the crew wrapped up their final day of work. Roofers loaded massive ladders onto the top of a truck as Daisy looked up at the new roof with joyful tears on her cheeks. She insisted that the four men who completed the job gather on her porch so I could take a picture of them with the new roof. In the image, a beaming smile fills Daisy's face as the jet-black color of fresh shingles on her roof contrast with the weathered grey ones on the empty buildings that abutted her home.

After the new roof went on, Daisy's calls to the DLBA stopped. A few years later, demolition crews did show up on her block in the peak of summer and remove thirty-seven empty houses. On one of the afternoons when Daisy was free from work, we sat on the front porch as a pair of excavator operators chewed through each structure. Once one building was broken into parts and the debris loaded into a truck-mounted dumpster, the excavator would clatter down the street to the next waiting structure. At one point, a man in a neon hi-vis walked up to the porch and identified himself as a demolition program supervisor. He carried with him administrative documents that included Daisy's name, address, and phone number—records of the many calls she had made to demolition offices requesting the buildings come down because they were blocking the approval of a home repair loan. While Daisy's calls did not bring forth excavators in a timeline that she might have desired, they had evidently created a feedback loop. Pointing to the white metal siding that wrapped around all four sides, parts of which had yellowed over the years, the supervisor remarked, "Sure will be great to get that home repair loan so you can get things fixed up around here." "Mmhmm," Daisy replied, chuckling to herself. After the demolition staffer departed, Daisy made clear she had no intention of taking on a loan for siding that still had decades of useful life left.

On an autumn evening after dozens of empty buildings were flattened around her home, I joined Daisy back in the same community center gym where we first met. Another housing assistance fair, it was once again filled with a "one-stop shop" of tables from a dozen social services agencies, municipal offices, and private financial institutions. Daisy began at a table where workers from one agency helped her complete an application for winter heating assistance. She skipped over tables focused on tenants' rights and stopped at one for a municipal office where workers made sure she had filled out paperwork necessary to receive a reduced property tax rate. Daisy moved down the queue to a table where volunteers reassured her that she was still on the wait list for a home repair grant. She then made her way to the table where bank representatives provided information about home repair loans. Flyers greeted people with color photographs of a Black woman with greying hair standing in a newly renovated kitchen. Spotless white cabinets, granite countertops, black appliances, and other upgrades had been paid for with a $22,000 loan from the program. A representative keyed Daisy's address into her laptop and smiled, "It looks like you're living in an eligible neighborhood! With a home repair loan, you can make your house just like new." Daisy declined the offer to complete an application. In her words, "We just did the roof and got the house stable. We're good." After that, we left.

Daisy's path through that resource fair is illuminating. In earlier years, she had applied for a home repair loan in hopes of being able to stop her roof from leaking. But empty buildings on her block had prevented the loan from being approved.

Having incrementally saved up enough to make the roof watertight before demolitions brought those structures down, Daisy was no longer interested in taking on debt, especially for cosmetic upgrades like new siding or a kitchen renovation. This is not to say that others did not do so—the woman featured on bank advertising certainly did. However, in gatherings frequented by Detroiters who qualified for income-based support on their housing and utility bills, home repair loans were a tough sell unless Detroiters had exhausted all other prospects to temporarily patch up their homes while waiting for more permanent fixes to come through. Journalists who attended resource fairs sometimes profiled people who lived with water cascading through roofs, busted porches, and backed-up plumbing for more than a decade.[39] Even when their neighborhoods qualified for home repair loans, including ones with low-to-no interest, those loans require paying hundreds of dollars a month that the average Detroit household did not have on hand. As people like Daisy appropriated secondhand hot water heaters or slowly accumulated the resources necessary to fix leaky roofs, they made legible how Detroiters were not necessarily clamoring for access to home improvement loans. What they wanted were structural repairs and stable homes.

HOMES, NOT LOANS

During the COVID-19 pandemic, Detroiters Zoomed into public meetings where municipal administrators solicited priorities for $826 million in federal relief funds earmarked for the city. In addition to a universal-basic-income program pilot and improvements to spotty internet infrastructures, the number-one shared priority was home repair grants. During this time, a set of Detroit-based foundations allocated $20 million to make Detroiters' homes structurally sound. Initially, program officers anticipated it would take a year to identify 1,000 dwellings in need of roof replacements, foundation support, and other costly repairs. Within twenty-four hours, the program's application line received more than 125,000 calls and closed with a wait list of 14,000 households. It was in this context that municipal officials ultimately allocated $30 million in relief funds to home repair grants and $95 million to demolitions. Staff from multiple city departments attempted to justify the limited repair grant funding in videoconferences filled with hundreds of incredulous city residents. Administrators seemed to grow frustrated when audience members' positions were unchanged by evidence that empty building demolitions were linked to expanded access to home finance—the same data that was integral to demonstrating that federally funded demolitions had met their statutory goals.[40] Audience members appeared equally unimpressed when administrators touted a repair loan program where the municipality would backstop Detroiters who could not access credit through private financial institutions. "We don't need loans," someone wrote in the chat. "We need to fix our homes." Dozens responded affirmatively to the comment.

From the standpoint of administrative data, tearing down empty buildings contributed to addressing long-standing inequities encoded in home finance. As thousands of buildings came down, data analysts like Sam tracked their removals alongside home finance transactions. Their reports provided indicators that demolitions could secure access to financial products that had long been denied to city residents, especially Black Detroiters outside the city's wealthiest, whitest neighborhoods. On the surface, this was a meaningful change to the status quo of algorithmic racism. Recall how the early-twentieth-century origins of contemporary home finance in the United States relied on explicit calculations of white supremacy in which nonwhite people, especially Black people, were a categorical "risk" to property value. Even when explicitly racist access to home finance became illegal, racist risk assessments remained operational. Actuarial calculations categorizing empty buildings as risky neighbors facilitated the continued exclusion of places that contended with the material residues of white flight and capital disinvestment. Because race was not an explicit criterion within these systems, neither individual Detroiters nor housing-justice advocates nor municipal administrators could challenge these systems using antidiscrimination policies. Instead, administrators turned to demolitions as a means of leveling physical and computational barriers that city residents, especially Black Detroiters, faced to receiving loan approvals on the same terms as people living in majority-white suburbs.

It is worth emphasizing how demolition administrators and data analysts saw their work as removing barriers standing between city residents and safe and stable homes. In a context where antiblackness and white supremacy are purposefully reinforced through computational systems, this intent is notable.[41] It resonates with what scholar of the social dimensions of engineering Aurora Zhang discusses as a program of "algorithmic reparations for housing justice" that dives into the data created by discriminatory systems to make them work otherwise.[42] Rather than merely assigning a dollar value to damages, Zhang builds from broader intellectual and political insistence that reparative projects must construct the possibilities for equitable futures.[43] In so doing she argues that efforts to remedy historical and ongoing routines of algorithmic violence from housing systems, especially antiblack discrimination, "should focus on bringing about a social structure that ensures that all will have safe, well-maintained living conditions."[44] It is here that administrative suggestions that demolitions trickled down into a more just housing system for Detroiters break down. Demolitions were targeted to cascade across algorithmic systems in ways that increased the value assigned to Detroiters' homes within the optic of financial markets. Rather than housing justice, demolitions reinvigorated an inequitable system that enacts dwellings as financial instruments in which profits should be maximized at all costs. Within this system, safe, well-maintained living conditions are a commodity in which access is available only to people who can pay.

The refrain of "We don't need loans. We need to fix our homes" illustrates just how changing the algorithmic calculus of eligibility for home finance did not eliminate the structural barriers Detroiters navigated in pursuit of stable homes. In some cases, doing so exacerbated them. Carlos's experience receiving bank loans to repair the two-unit home where he lived is demonstrative of how the financial resources made possible by demolitions made access to structurally secure dwellings conditional on Detroiters' household finances. The obligation to make hundreds of dollars in payments each month prevented Carlos from opening his home to people who could not help him make good on that obligation. Meanwhile, Detroiters who made do with leaky roofs, faulty electrical systems, and sagging floors were not necessarily waiting around for conventional financing to appear. Consider how neighborly relationships helped Daisy's household locate a working hot water heater. Or how layering hardware store tarps made it possible to hold out on a roof replacement for as long as possible. Even when subsequent demolitions unlocked the possibility of a home repair loan to pay for cosmetic upgrades, Daisy declined. Her refusal is indicative of how city residents sometimes saw beyond the promised inclusion in home finance. Rather than a world in which structural repairs were contingent on rendering the places they lived into collateral, they sought to build a city in which access to physically stable homes was broadly shared.

Detroiters who navigated increasingly unaffordable living conditions in the wake of demolitions bring into relief how the appearance of equality or even racial uplift in algorithmic outputs is not the same as constructing conditions of racial justice in the actual world. Demolition administrators meticulously tracked how demolition funding flowed across neighborhoods, looking for evidence that removing empty buildings shifted home finance algorithms such that Detroiters could receive credit on the same terms as they might in majority-white suburbs. Computational evidence of expanded access to conventional home finance markets helped sustain public dollars for demolitions through years when most other public services were gutted. But seemingly colorblind outcomes are not a guarantee of just systems. Consider how computational evidence that demolitions unlocked access to bank financing for Detroiters also helped rationalize reducing the availability of home repair grants that provided direct assistance to city residents. Instead, demolitions stabilized a racialized political economic system in which access to safe and stable dwellings is limited by design. Predicating the structural integrity of Detroiters' homes on the logics of financial markets crowded out other possible methods for stabilizing city residents' homes—including visions people like Carlos and Daisy had for the places they lived. Like many who Zoomed into meetings with requests that municipal administrators fund home repair grants, they imagined a world in which access to stable and secure homes was decoupled from the financial calculus of qualifying for a loan entirely.

FOUR

EXCAVATORS

When examining the technical means necessary for demolition, the excavator literally and figuratively dominates the scene. Consider what happened during the highly anticipated removal of a long-vacant parts foundry in Southwest Detroit. Four members of the demolition crew were on site from the early hours of the morning. Two laborers connected hoses to nearby fire hydrants and began wetting the building's brick walls to minimize dust. A pair of operators unloaded two excavators from their flatbed trailers and maneuvered them into position. Each of the machines weighed around twenty-five tons, and they shook the ground when they hit the pavement. The fifth member of the demolition crew—a truck driver who would drive fifty miles round-trip to ferry loads of crushed building components to the nearest landfill—arrived just before nine. When he did, nearby residents and representatives from the mayor's office were already massing in the road in front of the site. An administrator kicked off the proceedings by shouting into a bullhorn, "Excavators, start your engines!" The crowd roared as one of the excavator operators extended their machine's hydraulic arm and began pounding the metal scoop against the foundry wall. They roared again when the wall and ceiling above it collapsed in a shower of bricks. Administrators left after twenty minutes and members of the crowd dispersed soon after. Members of the demolition crew chipped away at the massive building for ten hours each day for more than two weeks until no trace of it remained.

It takes a team of a dozen people using power tools at least ten working days to disassemble a two-story, detached house. By contrast, a three-person demolition crew—one laborer, one excavator operator, and one truck driver—can knock down a similarly sized building in less than thirty minutes. Even with the driver making repeated landfill runs, the entire structure and foundation can be gone in less than one workday. Though differentiated by brands like Volvo, John Deere, and Caterpillar, excavators are mass-produced machines and the general architecture of each is effectively the same. A diesel engine, hydraulic pumps, machine arm, and a hefty counterweight rest atop a continuous-track undercarriage. Operators sit atop the machine and guide its operation from an enclosed cabin that contains a pair of joysticks, pedals, and a set of control switches. In most respects, the excavators that chewed through Detroit's buildings resemble those you might see digging into the ground on a construction site. A key difference, however, is that demolition excavators are typically equipped with a hydraulic "thumb" that closes over the standard-issue construction bucket. This "grapple bucket" allows operators to level buildings more quickly by grasping onto key structural supports and wrenching them free. They are also essential for maneuvering the tangled mass of building components from the demolition site into dump trailers. In a matter of seconds, operators could shift entire sections of brick walls or concrete foundations that would have taken hours to pick apart in the absence of heavy machinery.

To keep a swift pace, demolitions required a coordinated division of labor. Operators could pilot excavators to knock holes in buildings, pull apart their foundations, and lift heavy loads of components. These movements tended to produce cascades of debris, especially drywall and plaster, that rained down under the bucket before reaching the waste hauler. Laborers aiming fire hoses and water mists were essential to keeping demolition sites in compliance with clauses in municipal demolition contracts that required contractors to take certain dust suppression measures. When excavators paused to wait for the return of a truck-mounted dumpster, laborers moved to other tasks. They commonly spent this time brooming up scattered components so they could be shoveled by hand into the waste hauler. Laborers were also typically the people who climbed up dozens of feet on top of truck-mounted dumpsters to force in stubborn components like wooden and metal beams that were preventing their closure. Despite this ongoing flurry of activity, media reports about demolitions typically focused on the excavators, with descriptions of multi-ton machines ripping buildings to shreds, crowding people out of the scene, including the operators who deftly flicked joysticks to make this action possible.

Demolition worksites were acutely racialized and gendered workplaces. The people who worked as general laborers were almost always Black and Latine, whereas those who worked as excavator operators and truck drivers tended to be white. The people working in all three positions were almost always men. Exceptions existed and workplace demographics varied somewhat between the various companies that public agencies contracted to level buildings. Between 2010 and 2023, white-owned firms completed a slight majority of Detroit's publicly funded demolitions. These firms tended to employ excavator operators trained by a local union specializing in operating heavy machinery. Similar circumstances shaped the workforce of commercial truck drivers who transported demolition waste. Reflecting racist and sexist structures that have constrained what counts as "labor" in the United States, as well as discrimination that has been constitutive of trade union organizing in this context, most union-trained excavator operators were white men living in Detroit's suburbs.[1] Firms owned by people of color, which completed the balance of demolitions during this period, sometimes employed union-trained operators. However, many employed operators and drivers trained in nonunion programs that focused on routing Detroiters into demolition employment. The operators and drivers working for these contractors tended to be Black men who lived in the city. A few firms, including white- and Black-owned companies, hired laborers through a union local that organized laborers. Many laborers employed on demolition worksites were nonunion.

It is helpful to keep in mind that relations of racial capitalism are expansively structured in ways that complicate simplistic readings of the hinge between race and political economy. Cultural theorist Stuart Hall and those building on his legacy note how the interwoven system of race, sexuality, gender, and sex "is the modality through which class is lived. It is also the medium through which class relations are experienced."[2] Gendered experiences are particularly diagnostic of the ways racism makes capitalism possible.[3] For example, sociologist of struggle W. E. B. Du Bois and others historicize how the racialization of whiteness as freedom in contrast with Blackness as eligibility for bondage that codified chattel enslavement continued to fracture nascent solidarities between European and African-descended men laboring for wages in the century following the nominal abolition of slavery in the United States.[4] In Du Bois's words, "It became easy to say and easier to prove that these black men were not men in the sense white men were, and could never be, in the same sense, free."[5] At the same time, policy commitments to familial units in which a masculinized member labored for a wage outside the home and a feminized member labored unwaged within it reflect gendered experiences of whiteness.[6] Meanwhile, women and nonbinary people of color, especially Black, Indigenous, Latina, and Asian women, have been consistently enrolled to labor, waged and unwaged, within and beyond their homes, in ways that sustain whiteness as a racial formation.[7] Put simply, white supremacy and heteropatriarchy go together in creating the conditions of possibility for racial capitalism.

Detroit is an epicenter of Fordist racial capitalism, in which Fordism as a political economic model is inextricable from Henry Ford the man.[8] Ford built his first assembly line in Detroit.[9] Getting a job "down at the plant" is still a sensical statement, including for operations that produce metal, watches, clothing, cars, and automobile parts—though none of them crank out Ford Motor Company products. Detroiters who work these jobs can support extended relations, sometimes with the stability of pensions and working conditions negotiated in union contracts. Nevertheless, the decomposing hulks of defunct factories that dot the landscape in Detroit and other so-called postindustrial centers mark how waged labor—to say nothing of dignified wage labor—is increasingly scarce in North America.[10] Yet the promise of broadly distributed welfare through industrial capitalism was only ever a whitewashed mirage.[11] Consider how the high wages paid to keep cars rolling off Detroit's twentieth-century factory lines relied on the low and sometimes unwaged labors of colonized peoples working on rubber plantations.[12] Bosses and workers alike policed gendered color lines within the Fordist metropole. They routed Black men into the "hardest job on the line" and white men into the highest-waged industrial positions for most of the twentieth century.[13] This is to say that the industrial workplaces that made Detroit a household name were ones that propped up people who fit the mold of white masculinity at the expense of others.

Multi-ton excavators clawing through buildings and moving around Detroit's metropolitan region provide a vantage on how the political economy of demolition reproduces some of the very inequities that typify Fordist mass production.

Demolition work is cyclical, meaning laborers, excavator operators, truck drivers, and firm owners alike—most but not all of them men—all encountered annual ups and downs in the availability of work leveling buildings. But people contended with these cycles in racialized ways, reflecting the racialized breakdown of roles on demolition worksites. For the mostly Black men who earn their livelihoods performing odd jobs as "general labor," the end of demolition employment meant transitioning into low-waged service jobs or harvesting components from empty buildings for sale to architectural salvage warehouses. Meanwhile, the mostly white men employed as unionized excavator operators could easily transition to work in other unionized operating sectors, including construction and waste management. Even for Black Detroiters who owned demolition firms, their claims on the means of production were never as secure as those of more established firms owned by white suburbanites. Overall, building-removal worksites ensured the security of white men, even when people wanted otherwise. In this regard, demolition crews that physically leveled the remains of Fordist mass production marked not a departure from the inequities of industrial racial capitalism, but their endurance.

Yet the uneven configurations of people, machinery, and profits enacted through the demolition of Detroit's buildings also present a meaningful disjuncture with Fordist models. Industrial projects deliberately constructed systems to uplift white men above others as people moved through recruitment centers, assembly lines, and labor-management agreements. Decades of purposeful struggle to enact equal opportunity in the workplace succeeded at removing explicit discrimination from job classifications, hiring protocols, and other locations—though such stratifications remain apparent in who does what work and under what conditions. Consider how unions of excavator operators constructed heavy-machinery training centers in the periurban fringe of Detroit's metropolitan region during the mid-twentieth-century moment when white Detroiters were leaving the city to avoid the prospect of integrated neighborhoods and workplaces. This literally and figuratively placed footholds to secure employment in the backyards of white suburbanites, especially the descendants of longtime union members. Even as union members explicitly sought to bring Black Detroiters into their ranks, significant distance posed a barrier to city residents wanting to reach training facilities, reinforcing disparities in who could access the most stable, well-compensated positions on demolition sites. In this way, paying attention to the traffic of people and excavators as they contribute to mass disposal makes clear how scrubbing explicitly unequal employment conditions does not end structurally unequal distributions of economic stability associated with mass production. Those inequities endure, embedded as they are in regional and institutional landscapes forged by earlier efforts to provide opportunity to some while foreclosing it to others.

CYCLICAL EMPLOYMENT

Demolition work in Detroit followed the seasons. It ramped up in the spring when the ground thawed, continued rain or shine through the summer and fall, and tapered off just as the ground froze again toward the end of the year. Technically, it is possible to level a building in the dead of winter, and demolitions typically happened during this period. But their numbers paled in comparison to those knocked down every month during warmer parts of the year. Freezing conditions turned demolition sites into hazardous ice rinks, with laborers who directed fire hoses to tamp down dust created with every crash of the excavator bucket risking hypothermia even if they bundled up. Winter also increased the likelihood that demolition crews—who needed Detroit's fire hydrants to source water for dust suppression—would render emergency systems inoperable. The municipal fire department requested limits on cold season demolitions after fire crews repeatedly encountered hydrants that were frozen solid after demolition crews failed to properly flush them at the end of their workday. Even when buildings were knocked down in freezing temperatures, completing the process, especially removing utility connections, grading the site with topsoil, and covering it with grass seed, had to wait until the ground was no longer solid. People who worked in demolition as laborers, excavator operators, and waste haulers were accustomed to this cycle. It was one in which they could anticipate a consistent paycheck for ten or so months of the year.

Wages that came for only part of the year were among the promises demolition firms made in recruiting prospective laborers. Consider flyers that hung at bus stops outside the offices where Detroiters queued up in search of formal-sector employment. Postings for work on demolition sites were pinned up alongside ones from landscaping and other service-oriented firms, with flyers seeking demolition laborers signaling higher pay rates than most other positions, for which starting pay usually hovered around the state minimum wage. Between 2010 and 2020, the hourly pay rate advertised for general laborers rose from just over $8 to just under

$15. Pull tabs at the bottom of each flyer provided company contact information and specified the cyclical contours of the work. For example, a tab might read "$13/hr, 30+ hrs/wk, March-Nov, Start Now," with a phone number for interested applicants to call. Though income and benefits ended with each demolition season, their existence was notable in a city where residents increasingly relied on unbenefited odd jobs and app-based gigs to make ends meet.[14] When waiting for the bus at one of these locations, I usually found demolition contractors' tabs picked clean, even if those for other positions were not. People waiting with me often noted that hourly pay rates posted for demolition laborers would be the highest they ever earned. Potential employers did not hide that demolition labor offered time-limited wages for time-limited work. Temporary though they were, such positions still promised greater security than other options available to Detroiters who queued up looking for work.

Most every person who worked directly on demolition sites, including laborers, excavator operators, and truck drivers, occupied a cyclical position. This designation reflected a built-in expectation that people would regularly move in and out of paying work over the course of a year. Cyclical or seasonal work contrasts with the types of waged labor associated with the Fordist mass production model for which Detroit is known.[15] In the Fordist archetype, workers keep all manner of production humming along—whether in factory lines, schools, restaurants, office buildings, and elsewhere—in exchange for a regular wage. At least in theory, production (and with it, wages) is understood to be continuous under this model, making periods without work (and without wages) an aberration.[16] By comparison, cyclical work is such that the promise of work and wages always comes alongside the promise of the end of work and the end of wages.[17] Cyclical work, especially as it occurs through agricultural, household, and reproductive labors, makes the hum of production lines possible.[18] In the United States, such positions, which tend to be the domains of people who are not white and not men, also tend to be excluded from most state unemployment benefits.[19] To put it directly, even in its Global North metropoles, the imagined security of Fordist production has never been guaranteed.[20] Such political economic conditions have always been tuned to provide stability to some and deny it to others.

Centering the differential treatment of cyclical work emphasizes how those of us who experience the twenty-first century as a moment of increasingly precarious economic conditions in places like United States do so from a position of relative privilege. To be clear, because of offshoring, subcontracting, gig work, and eviscerated social safety nets, the number of people who draw regular wages and secure benefits has decreased in North America and other parts of the so-called postindustrial world. Anthropologist Anna Tsing identifies how "the economy is no longer a source of growth or optimism; any of our jobs could disappear with the next economic crisis."[21] The ever-expanding reach of "post-Fordism" or "late capitalism" is one that dissolves implicit and explicit contracts that linked the security of living wages and modest social welfare to the structural position of alienating labor for a wage. For those who reaped material benefits from those contracts, their erosion is painful.[22] And yet, it is essential to avoid presenting this transformation of racial capitalism as a flattening or generalization of precarity, even if those conditions are more broadly experienced.[23] Between 2010 and 2020 the documented unemployment rate in Detroit averaged 15.4 percent. This was double the statewide average and almost three times the rate in the suburbs surrounding the city. Jobs disappeared across the region, but they disappeared quickest and in greatest numbers for residents of the majority-Black city.

As places where Detroiters could be relatively well-compensated, albeit only for certain parts of the year, demolition worksites are characteristic of the economic promises of waste work. After all, the bulk of building components landed in the same gigantic landfills where trucks dumped household refuse around the periphery of Detroit's metropolitan region. Asbestos and other toxic hazards ended up in specialized facilities. Most concrete was deposited at plants where it could be crushed into road fill. Whatever copper and precious metals workers could find got picked out for the scrap yard. In his ethnographic account of life and labor around a rural Michigan landfill, discard studies scholar Joshua Reno tracks how routing materials into waste streams offered consistent work that financially buoyed towns and preserved Fordist ideals in a moment when plant closures shook other parts of the industrial Midwest.[24] As a "workforce readiness specialist" at a nonprofit that supported Detroiters in finding formal sector employment put it in a presentation to unemployed city residents, "Demolition is a 21st-century growth industry here in Detroit." Detailing how her grandparents had moved to Detroit in search of better economic prospects during Great Migration, she also noted that between 1950 and 2010, Detroit had shed 70 percent of its waged jobs, including more than 300,000, or 90 percent, of its manufacturing jobs.[25] By contrast, as demolition programs scaled up in subsequent decades to level thousands of buildings each year, employment on demolition sites was apparently easy to come by.

At the same time, not all demolition employment was the same. Truck drivers who shuttled materials and equipment to and from worksites and excavator operators were classified as having "skilled" roles. Their pay rates were significantly higher than those of people classified as "general labor" and considered "unskilled." Experienced operators sometimes earned more in a year than firm owners.[26] Reno observed from that Michigan landfill, "A significant division of labor between the more skilled machine operators and mechanics and the slightly lower-paid, easily replaceable truck drivers" tended to impede collective action in waste workplaces.[27] Indeed, no worker-initiated strikes or slowdowns occurred during my decade of research, nor could anyone recall one in the past. Across global disposal chains in which people pick, sort, compact, store, and repurpose materials, technical work that is identified as more "skilled" is usually more secure, while "unskilled" labor is more precarious—no matter how difficult.[28] In the United States, this division of labor is deeply racialized and gendered. Like mass production, more reliably waged positions are typically occupied by white men, whereas positions with more irregular wages and higher potential for bodily harm are the occupations of men of color.[29] With few exceptions, demolition worksites reflected this division. Most but not all people working as demolition laborers were Black men or Latinos. Most but not all people working as excavator operators or truck drivers were white men. Most but not all people who owned firms that drew profits from building removal were white.

Working demolition, no matter the role, meant riding a cycle. For operators, laborers, and truck drivers alike, winter slowdowns meant entering an annual process of layoffs or terminations with the expectation of being called back to work in a month or two. And yet, sometimes this expectation was not met, including when delays in funding availability or federal investigations into bidding practices shut down demolition sites for more than six months at a time. Acutely and structurally, the people who labored on demolition sites had to contend with paychecks and benefits that were always going to end—at least for a little while. In some respects, this routinized evaporation of work may seem to mark the continued unraveling of Fordist social contracts that, at least as some people experienced them, seemed to guarantee regular and ongoing support to anyone willing to alienate their labor. But, in Detroit and other showrooms for racial capitalism that bear Henry Ford's imprint, greater levels of comfort and security have at times been reserved for people who fit specific racialized and gendered molds. Stability for some has been made possible by the significantly more precarious labors of others. To this end, the cyclical promises of demolition work—things like pull tabs reading "$13/hr, 30+ hrs/wk, March-Nov, Start Now"—do not necessarily mark a shift from one set of racial political economic routines to another, but a continuation of conditions in which whiteness in general and white masculinity in particular offered priority access to stability.

GENERAL LABOR

Typically, people working as "general laborers" were the only people visible when I pulled up to demolition sites. Excavator operators and truck drivers were enclosed in cabins. Meanwhile, laborers moved about lugging hoses, directing sprays of water, and shoveling debris too small to be grasped by the excavator bucket and emptied into the back of the waste truck. Nominally classified as unskilled because their work did not involve specialized machinery, laborers were the lowest paid members of demolition crews. Like any labor classified this way, it was still essential to the process. When excavator operators had loaded their machines onto flatbed trailers to move on to another building or return home for the day, laborers were commonly still sweeping up piles of components and washing dust off sidewalks. Joel, a middle-aged Black Detroiter, worked on and off as a demolition laborer for the same demolition firm for more than a decade. At first, Joel started out earning $9 an hour as a demolition laborer. A decade later it was $16.50. Between lugging hoses and shoveling up piles of components, his joints ached at the end of every day. Medicated patches helped dull a neck twinge whenever he grasped a fire hose under his arm to ensure the angle of the spray matched the moving excavator bucket. Still, at least as far as Joel told me, demolition labor took less of a bodily toll than the winter he spent shoveling snow for a landscaping company.

After a decade, Joel was accustomed to an annual cycle where paychecks stopped coming in December or January until he received a phone call to come back to work in February or March. During that time, Joel, in his words, "ate bricks." He did not literally eat bricks. But he exchanged red and brown bricks he recovered from the walls and foundations of Detroit's late-nineteenth and early-twentieth-century buildings for cash (figure 4.1). Filling the bed of his small Ford Ranger—which held around 750 bricks—would fetch around $100 if Joel delivered

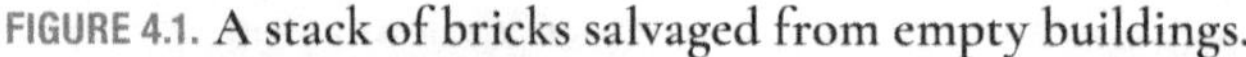
FIGURE 4.1. A stack of bricks salvaged from empty buildings.

Photo by the author.

it to a suburban garden center that resold them as patio pavers. He could make double that if he delivered them to an architectural salvage warehouse. There, a dealer would stack Joel's bricks on pallets with thousands of others. When I asked where they went, the dealer said he loaded them on a flatbed and trucked them south to Atlanta, Nashville, and Dallas. In those growing metropolises, antique bricks were evidently in high demand as a material for constructing new custom-built dwellings.[30] Between regular work during the demolition season and salvaging bricks outside of it, Joel usually cleared around $25,000 each year. It was enough to complete repairs that kept his pickup creaking along, as well as to pay his share of the taxes, utility bills, and maintenance in the house he shared with his mother, her partner, and other relatives on occasion.

I spoke with laborers who worked for most of the dozen or so firms that regularly won contracts to knock down empty buildings in Detroit. A few of them were employed on demolition sites year-round, since even when the pace of building removals slowed, they did not stop entirely.[31] But like Joel, most laborers had to find other ways to pay their bills outside the demolition season. Some took on other seasonal, formal-sector employment, especially shoveling snow and salting sidewalks for the duration of Michigan's bleak, gray winters. Laborers commonly harvested materials from Detroit's empty buildings before selling them onward to scrapyards and architectural salvage dealers—practices commonly referred to as "scrapping."[32] A trunk full of aluminum siding might fetch 55¢ per pound. A cast iron radiator might bring in 7¢ per pound. Copper materials commanded around $3.00 per pound, but this premium price was only once copper roofing tiles, wiring, and pipes, and other components were free from other materials. Demolition laborers were not alone in scrapping, with many empty buildings bearing telltale signs that someone had wrenched pipes, appliances, and other materials free. Yet laborers also found themselves with easy access to beams, conduits, and other metals that only became accessible once structures were run through by heavy machinery. When laborers picked through components, they could move metals into recycling-and-reuse networks as a means of smoothing over inconsistent wages from demolition work.

Joel made a point of telling me that he did not deal with metals. "I don't do that scrapping stuff," he said as we drove a load of bricks to a suburban architectural salvage dealer. "They've got the police all out at the scrapyards checking IDs and asking where folks got stuff. It's too hot." Indeed, after a 2013 spike in the disappearance of streetlight wiring, catalytic converters, and coils of metal fencing, the state government enacted regulations that required scrapyard operators to document transactions and restricted cash payments. Prior to these rules, it was common to find people clustered near scrapyard entrances performing small moves that increased what they could earn from their hauls, including burning away plastic insulators from wiring and hacking open appliances to break apart brass components and copper condenser coils. Metal scrapping continued apace after state regulation, with people taking additional steps to obscure the origins of their scrap hauls. As one scrapyard owner put it to me while weighing bundles of aluminum siding, "People don't have work, they're hungry, and the buildings are there." When municipal police began hassling people who lit fires or hacked open appliances near scrapyard entrances, those processing steps moved further afield.

Bricks, as Joel intimated, did not carry the same level of state scrutiny as precious metals. Whenever we met up, Joel usually had a pile of bricks in the bed of his pickup. They were reddish orange to brown ones, common materials for constructing Detroit's foundations, chimneys, and walls in the late nineteenth and early twentieth centuries. During that time, workers in the city's brickyards dredged up clay deposits from beneath the city's surface and fired them into thousands of bricks each day.[33] A century later, Joel and others gathered up those same bricks on demolition sites where they worked. When the excavator operator stopped swinging at the end of the day, he would wander around demolition sites looking for bricks that were still intact. Sometimes, excavator operators would gingerly set sections of wall to the side so it could be broken apart more carefully by hand. When Joel passed a partially collapsed building in his drives to jobsites across the city, he would pull to the side of the road to scour it for any bricks that he could safely gather, piling anything he found in the yard behind his house. On weekends and during slowdowns in demolition work, he spent days carefully chiseling each brick free from mortar. Inspecting each piece to ensure the corners were relatively square, he then stacked the intact bricks along the back fence. The neat rows could be converted into cash whenever Joel's regular paychecks stopped coming.

Notwithstanding the distinction Joel drew between metal scrapping and salvaging bricks, both practices extracted economic value from the material stuff of empty buildings. Scrapyards moved copper, aluminum, cast iron, and other metals pulled from Detroit's buildings into global supply chains in which they could be refashioned and resold in new commodities.[34] Landscaping companies and architectural salvage warehouses moved bricks into somewhat less broadly distributed supply chains in which they could be refashioned and resold as luxury building material. In Black feminist scholar Marisa Solomon's ethnographic research with people who recover furniture, moldings, and doors from condemned buildings in Bed-Stuy, she identifies how those materials travel along "racialized circuits" in which the dispossession of Black people is obscured as materials are incorporated into dwellings built for mostly white gentrifiers.[35] To borrow words from one of Solomon's interlocutors, Sal, "As pieces of the projects come down and housing for white people go up, our homes are turned into junk. But really, the ghetto is a gold mine." In Bed-Stuy, that "gold mine" includes the returns developers generate by evicting longtime Black residents, demolishing their homes, and replacing them with new, luxury buildings in the space of a few years. In the twenty-first century, demolitions did not typically clear way for new construction in Detroit, but Sal's words are still instructive. They make evident how the same relations of racial capitalism that devalue places where Black people live simultaneously render the material components of those places into an extractive frontier.

People who worked as general laborers on demolition sites described the work as backbreakingly hard. And yet, like Joel, they tended to return to their roles day after day and following each annual slowdown. They did so because, by comparison to most other jobs available in Detroit, heaving around equipment to ensure excavator operators could knock down as many buildings as possible as quickly as possible was relatively well compensated. Demolition labor pay rates exceeded those in Detroit's service sectors and even matched some entry-level office jobs that required advanced educational credentials. This is to say that in the context of the most impoverished large city in the United States, Detroiters like Joel who showed up as demolition labor could eke out a greater modicum of financial security than a significant number of their neighbors. That security was contingent on the cyclical ups and downs of employment on demolition sites. Joel provides a helpful vantage on the ways demolition laborers made it through anticipated downturns. Some got by shifting into other labor-intensive, seasonal employment that peaked in the winters. But many turned to the components of empty buildings as a source of subsistence. Here and there, they generated a few hundred dollars by extracting metal, bricks, and other materials from structures that were already slated to be knocked down. Routing these materials away from landfills and toward other avenues—particularly scrapyards and architectural salvage warehouses—stabilized demolition labor paychecks that were always guaranteed to come to an end.

UNION OPERATORS

When I visited him on demolition sites, Joel was sometimes working alongside an excavator operator named Billy. A white man in his thirties who lived in one of the majority-white suburbs north of Detroit, Billy had been demolishing buildings since he finished high school. Like other operators, Billy could punch through buildings and send them crumbling down upon themselves with a few moves of the excavator joysticks. In a few more nudges, he could balance the machine on the precipice of a basement cavity while swiveling back and forth to drop debris into a massive truck-mounted dumpster. Every few hours, after a driver had left on a landfill run, Billy would climb down from his excavator to smoke a cigarette or take a meal break with Joel. After sitting in his rig for hours at a stretch, Billy would signal a pause in work by shutting down his excavator and taking a seat atop the tracks of the excavator or on the tailgate of someone's truck. Like other demolition work teams, Billy and Joel filled these pauses with stories about their children or commiserated about how Detroit's various professional sports teams had fared in recent games. From time to time, Billy attempted to persuade Joel to apply for the paid apprenticeship training program organized by his union local. Billy's father, who also worked as an excavator operator, had made sure Billy submitted his apprenticeship application the year he turned eighteen.

Membership in the heavy equipment operators' union smoothed over the cyclical booms and busts of demolition work. The demolition company that employed Joel and Billy hired excavator operators trained through the union's apprenticeship program. In so doing, they agreed to pay union-scale wages, contribute toward the union's health insurance and pension plans, and fund one week of paid training for union members each year. Union members like Billy typically timed their week at the union's training center for sometime between December and February, when few demolitions happened. There, they completed safety courses, learned to pilot new equipment, and updated state-mandated certifications. After a few weeks at home, union operators counted on receiving a "call to work." Sometimes this was for demolitions approved to move forward during the winter. More often, it was from companies who needed short-term workers to use heavy machinery for other purposes. One rainy winter, Billy spent a few months digging trenches for underground utilities at a suburban office development. In another, he drove an end dump truck, making runs between gravel pits and a utility plant construction site. The truck was identical to the ones that drivers used to ferry demolition debris to landfills. In Billy's experience, "Same machines, different jobs, same pay." To emphasize, he pantomimed how the joystick nudges he used to tap an excavator bucket against a building to knock it down were same ones he used to pack soil into a vertical wall.

The union's training facility was in a rural township some sixty miles northwest of Detroit. The local opened the facility in the 1960s, a dozen or so miles from the exclusively white suburbs where its members increasingly lived. Aerial photos of classroom buildings showed the extent of the property, especially the acres of flattened earth where dozens of excavators, loaders, cranes, grading apparatuses and other equipment were typically visible. From the air, the yellow machines resembled children's toys in a sandbox—a comparison people at the training center eagerly made for me. Through courses, trainees learned the basics of excavator operation and maintenance, with days of classroom instruction complemented by longer periods of hands-on practice. During these trainings, experienced operators patiently coached trainees as they haltingly moved excavators around and made their first attempts at digging into the ground. The yard was typically filled with people in neon safety gear who were learning to use various machines. After gaining more experience on paid jobsites, work that beginning apprentices completed under the supervision of a more experienced operator, union members could return to the training center for a further course in more advanced excavator operations. Although trainees practiced digging trenches and moving soil, none of the trainings were centered on demolition. Nevertheless, as trainers emphasized and excavator operators knew well, the pedal and joystick movements they practiced could earn them as large a paycheck building new things as tearing them down.

To Billy's frustration, Joel declined his repeated requests to submit his name for the union's apprenticeship program. From Billy's standpoint, Joel should have applied without a second thought. Apprentice operators earned salaries that more than doubled what Joel earned as a laborer; they also accrued pension benefits and vacation time that Joel did not. On a union-sponsored fishing trip, Billy had heard that the local was particularly interested in recruiting Detroiters to be new apprentices. Contractors who employed city residents could earn preferential credit toward bids on municipal contracts, including ones for demolitions, but there were few Detroiters in the union's existing ranks. Billy made the pitch to the half-dozen laborers he regularly worked with, all of whom were city residents. All six thanked him for the information and ultimately declined. Joel explained to me one evening, as we cleaned masonry from bricks, stacked, and counted them in his backyard, that the location of the union's training facility made Billy's offer a non-starter. The increased pay and relative job security were enticing, but Joel doubted that his truck would make it very long if he had to travel some one hundred miles round-trip each day for a week at a time. Even if he could get a new car by earning higher wages, the training facility was in a town well-known as home to prominent members of white nationalist organizations.[36] Like Joel, other laborers noted that the distance to the training center and the reputation of its neighbors made it a difficult proposition.

Joel and his coworkers' hesitance to apply for heavy-machinery apprenticeships reflected the uphill battle operating engineers faced in recruiting Detroit residents. In conjunction with unions organizing electricians, plumbers, masons, carpenters, line workers, and other skilled trades, the union representing heavy equipment operators participated in programs designed to build "pipelines" from Michigan's cities into unionized ranks. The explicit goal of these programs was "opening up of skilled trades to Detroiters."[37] For decades, union-based recruiting practices had tended to exclude city residents from apprenticeship consideration, focusing on suburban and rural vocational programs. People employed in skilled trades were disproportionately white and overwhelmingly men. To compensate, unions brought busloads of students from Detroit's vocational high schools to tour their training facilities. In the remote operating engineers' facility, students watched in rapt attention as trainees demonstrated their knowledge of various cranes and earth-moving equipment. As students looked on, union members encouraged them to apply for the next cohort of paid apprenticeships. Though Detroiters made up significant numbers of apprentices in carpentry, electrical, and plumbing training centers located in the city's inner-ring suburbs, they were few and far between at far-flung heavy-machine operating courses. Indeed, when the same union convened trainings for HVAC specialists and other mechanical trades at a facility just west of Detroit's city center, participants of color, especially Black Detroiters, were well represented.[38]

Eventually, Billy stopped asking Joel to consider training to be an excavator operator. Billy's dad, Bill, also worked as an excavator operator at the same demolition firm. Soon after Bill retired after thirty years of heavy-machinery operation, the company brought on an apprentice excavator operator. The person who filled the role was a white man in his early twenties who was the son of one of the company's truck drivers and had recently completed an initial excavator course organized by the operators' union. I watched Bill and the newcomer work together on a job demolishing an empty west side school complex. It was a brick structure with stone archways. Over a radio, Bill shouted encouragement and advice to the new operator about which pedal to tap when, as well as how to rotate the joystick just so, to ensure the excavator bucket burst through solidly built walls rather than glancing off them. Elsewhere on the site, Billy swiftly tore through what remained of classrooms and the gymnasium in ways that demonstrated his decade of experience. One of the truck drivers signaled his relationship to the new excavator operator by yelling a version of "Let's go, son!" each time he pulled back in from a run to the landfill or concrete crusher. Joel moved between them all. He shifted the direction of water cannons to keep them trained on excavator buckets, clambered up onto the waste truck to release a snagged dust netting, and scooped unbroken bricks into his pickup bed.

Excavator operators who were trade union members were the most securely employed people on demolition sites. Despite the cyclical availability of demolition work, they continued to draw wages through paid training and calls to jobs in other fields. Overwhelmingly, the people who labored as unionized excavator operators were white men. Many—Billy and his father among them—came into their profession at the recommendation of close relations, including fathers, uncles, neighbors, sons, and friends. At first, I took this as indicating the endurance of explicit gatekeeping in which membership in skilled-trades unions tended to pass through families of white men across the twentieth century and into the twenty first.[39] When Joel and his colleagues declined Billy's invitation to enter the apprenticeship program, they helped me see this somewhat differently. To be sure, heavy-machinery operation is a masculinized profession within the prevailing social imaginary of the United States.[40] But even as white women were increasingly visible in the ranks of heavy equipment operators, nonwhite operators remained relatively few. Detroiters like Joel were attracted to the possibility of employment that could bring stable wages and benefits. But the remote location of the heavy-machinery training facility posed a barrier to making this a reality. Difficult for Detroiters to reach and in a place known for white supremacist activities, its location made becoming a union excavator operator relatively inaccessible to some who might have otherwise desired it.

BLACK OWNED

At a press conference convened to mark the approval of another round of demolition funding, representatives from Detroit's demolition agencies gathered in front of an active demolition with news cameras rolling. Behind them, an operator punched holes in the roof of a frame dwelling, and a laborer diligently soaked the excavator bucket with a firehose. Administrators were there to mark how "minority-owned business enterprises" were increasingly winning bids to tear down the city's empty buildings.[41] As part of the gathering, a middle-aged Black Detroiter who owned the company completing the demolition that day spoke at length about how federal funding for demolitions in Detroit was essential for his firm's ongoing operations. A dozen nonwhite men and women who owned companies that specialized in various aspects of the demolition process were also on hand to speak. They collectively emphasized how they employed city residents—many of them Black Detroiters—at living wages. As one contractor phrased it, "When one of our companies wins a contract, Detroiters win a contract." Later that day, after a demolition administrator posted an image from the event to their personal social media feed, a profile belonging to someone who identified as a union excavator operator replied, "Why are you celebrating with companies that hire scabs?" Other union-affiliated operators liked the reply. The firms employing these operators were owned by white suburbanites and had won more than half the contracts for demolitions in Detroit that year. By the end of the day, the post was gone.

To be clear, some of the firms pictured in the social media post were signatories on union contracts covering heavy-machine operations. It was also the case that some firms owned by white suburbanites demolished buildings using nonunion excavator operators. This said, the deleted social media post helpfully brings to the fore how predominantly white, union-affiliated excavator operators advanced a casually racist assumption that firms owned by nonwhite people, especially Black Detroiters, did not employ union operators. It also underscores how companies demolishing most of Detroit's buildings tended to be white-owned firms whose owners did not live in Detroit. In the year before demolition administrators gathered to feature the contributions of companies with nonwhite owners, those firms had completed fewer than one thousand demolitions combined. Firms with white, suburban-dwelling owners had knocked down more than three thousand.[42] Several white-owned companies employed fifty or more people each and could deploy dozens of excavators to level thousands of structures each year. Few Black-owned firms approached this size, and those that did employed union workers. By comparison, most Black-owned firms were significantly smaller. They employed only a handful of workers with one or two excavators and averaged a hundred or so demolitions annually. According to people who owned these demolition companies, eschewing union affiliation helped them ensure they could employ Detroiters. Nevertheless, their small size also left both workers and owners in precarious positions when spigots of federal demolition funding were unexpectedly turned off.

Ken, a Black Detroiter owned a demolition firm that did not employ union-affiliated excavator operators or truck drivers. Instead, he recruited people identified through an employment training program. The program parked a massive excavator and heavy-duty waste dump truck on an expansive stretch of gravel created by the removal of a factory. After weeks of classroom safety training, trainees took turns practicing with joysticks to reposition the excavator bucket and gouge holes in the site's gravel covering. Stacks of pallets stood in as mock-ups for the structures of buildings to be demolished. When I participated in the training, it took me numerous tries to get the hang of punching the excavator's auxiliary hydraulic switch to release the thumb closed over the excavator bucket. Until I did, the load of pallets I had managed to pick up refused to drop into the open top of the truck-mounted dumpster. With my exception, the other nine people I completed the month-long training with were Black or Latino Detroiters drawn to the possibility of work as commercial-waste drivers or excavator operators on demolition sites. During the closing days of the training, Ken and owners of other small companies who employed nonunion operators came through our lunch break to recruit. Most of the people I spoke with during the program's early years landed full-time jobs as excavator operators and truck drivers. Over time, with fewer open positions, the program's trainees tended to find work as demolition laborers or on asbestos abatement teams.

During one of our conversations in his small office adjacent to the yard where company equipment parked at the end of the day, I pressed Ken on why he refused to hire union operators and drivers. Like other nonunion firms, Ken's response framed his resistance as an effort to employ Detroiters rather than as a wholesale resistance to unions. "I'm from a union family," he said. "My dad is UAW. That put food on the table, clothes on my back, college on my résumé. But these union guys, when you sign up with them, it means you have to hire their guys. Their guys aren't my guys. They don't live in the city. You know what I mean?" Ken then pointed to how everyone who worked at his firm was a Detroit resident, all of them men of color, most of them Black. The hourly wages paid to employees at Ken's company and other nonunion firms matched those paid by firms that were signatories to union contracts. To retain employees from year to year, the firms' health insurance coverage also typically extended through any seasonal lulls. This is to say that Ken's opposition to bringing on union-affiliated excavator operators or truck drivers did not appear to be grounded in an ideological opposition to collective bargaining or to undermining workers' material interests. Rather, it was based in a commitment to shaping who those workers were, especially to prioritizing Black Detroiters who were not typically rank-and-file union members.

Workers at demolition companies like Ken's may have drawn similar pay and benefits to people whose labor conditions were shaped by union contracts, but they did not have the passbook of union membership that facilitated moves into other sectors during periods without demolitions. For excavator operators and truck drivers who lived in Detroit, their wages over ten months exceeded what the typical Detroit household earned in an entire year. Many took winter slowdowns as time to work on household maintenance projects that took weeks to complete—sanding floors, replacing roofs, and painting were common. Laborers at Ken's firm faced the same need to supplement wages from demolition work with other income sources as people who worked at large firms. Like Joel, some of them salvaged bricks. Some scrapped metals. Others found seasonal snow removal work or took on app-based gigs to pay bills until spring. Meanwhile, like most firm owners, Ken drew a twelve-month salary. He justified this to me by noting how he spent the winter getting caught up on processing invoices and other paperwork. Like most firms, he also attempted to time significant equipment maintenance and upgrades to periods when it would not disrupt revenues. In most respects, this was a typecast example of capitalist production in which person who owned the means of production—Ken—was most secure and workers assumed to be most replaceable—demolition laborers—were the most precarious. Workers who held specialized knowledge about the means of production—operators and drivers—appeared to occupy a middle ground between them.

Unanticipated slowdowns scrambled this status quo. For example, in summer 2016, federal agencies pulled funding for demolitions in Detroit as part of an investigation into allegations of bid rigging by a white-owned demolition contractor.[43] Because the investigation did not conclude until the late fall, it put the bulk of demolitions on hold for more than six months. As Joel described it to me, "Boss just called us to say, 'There's no work. Don't come in.' Didn't call us back till spring." For Joel, the prolonged work stoppage was a period when he made more frequent trips to out-of-state architectural salvage warehouses to sell bricks for higher prices. Other laborers returned to routines they had already honed during previous periods without paychecks. Union-affiliated excavator operators and truck drivers like Billy could answer calls to work in other fields. But nonunion workers had few readily accessible avenues to find alternative work arrangements, even for machines for which they held deep knowledge. A few found work in nonunion construction crews. Some joined laborers in scrapping buildings for metal, bricks, and other components. A few picked up and moved hundreds of miles to places where they could find work as excavator operators on demolition sites. The differential routes people took through an extended period without readily available demolition work were not simply configured by their position within demolition work regimes as laborers or heavy-machine operators, but by the conditions of their labor as unionized or nonunion workers.

Difficulties receiving public demolition contracts contributed to Ken's company going out of business. Procurement processes limited small firms like his—many but not all of them Black owned—to a few municipally funded building removals at a time.[44] When federal demolition funding stopped flowing to Detroit, Ken found his bids for private and municipal work in Detroit undercut by larger firms. In an effort to pivot, he looked beyond Southeast Michigan and submitted bids to publicly funded demolition programs in Ohio, Indiana, Illinois, and Kentucky. Despite Ken's attempted inroads, potential clients outside Detroit declined his bids, citing apprehension about the capacity of an out-of-state firm with limited equipment. By late winter, Ken did not know how he would make tax payments on the small yard where he stored excavators and other equipment. He was also starting to fall behind on the mortgage for the home where he lived. In his view, "We were so far in the red, it was sell out or go bankrupt." To balance his books, Ken sold the entirety of his business—excavators, transport trailers, waste truck, and equipment yard—to a much larger firm. That company shipped the excavators south, where they had won a bid to tear down several hundred buildings. Profits from the sale kept Ken's bills paid until he landed a job as a construction manager. But as the new firm scraped Ken's name from an excavator, they materialized how owning the means of production is no guarantee of keeping it.

FORDIST CONTINUITIES

Let's conclude by way of a former steel mill along the Detroit River. For a month one spring, Joel worked alongside Billy and a half dozen other operators and laborers to level the mill's buildings. A team of truck drivers cycled through to load out the wreckage and return with piles of crushed gravel for laborers to spread over the site. On a few occasions, I watched the operation from a small rise adjacent to the metal fencing that encircled the site. For a few hours, I was joined by an older white man who stepped out of a dusty sedan to sit next to me. Without initially giving his name, he detailed decades of work as a machinist in the plant prior to its closure in the early 2000s. We sat together for an afternoon watching excavator operators and laborers jam various pieces of his former workplace into waste haulers. The man described how his retirement pension had been cut when the company that previously owned the plant declared bankruptcy. He supplemented social security payments with part-time work at a big box store and had planned one of his days off to come watch. At one point, he said, "This place, that life, it's gone," followed by a long pause. The statement crystallized the observed disappearance of the end of the steel plant as a physical building alongside an existential feeling about a moment in which the end of dignified work seemed close at hand.

During the demolition of factories and other large production facilities, I frequently found myself watching alongside people who previously labored in them. Most were men. Many, but not all of them, were white. Unlike nearby residents who came out from their homes to watch the removal of long-empty structures, these men were not in celebratory moods. Like the man at the steel mill, they reminisced about their previous work lives.[45] A common theme was their sense that demolition crews were not only leveling buildings, but in so doing they were snuffing out a world in which hard work brought with it predictable pay and decent benefits. Those are the ostensible promises of Fordist capitalism, and from the vantage of these observers, such a conclusion seems almost reasonable. It is true, after all, that since the 1980s, former industrial capitals have shed manufacturing-related jobs. Some credit the increasing scarcity of well-compensated, industrial labor as a reason for white America's rising support for right-wing populisms based in explicit white supremacy.[46] Yet Fordism, including but not limited to the models Henry Ford prototyped in Detroit, was always already racist and patriarchal by design. To long for Fordism as a secure past is to long for security that was only ever available on unequal terms.[47] Racialized and gendered distributions of demolition work with more or less precarious conditions mark the ways contemporary racial political economies resonate with inequities built into the very structures of Fordism that excavators tear down.

Excavators, tractor trailers, skilled-trades unions, and other equipment that is essential to leveling empty buildings came into being as technologies of mass production. When demolition crews pick apart empty buildings, they push against assumptions that empty buildings signal a generalized decline in the availability of decently compensated work in the present conjuncture of capitalism. To quote one of my interlocutors, "Demolition is a 21st-century growth industry here in Detroit." So, to be clear, demolition worksites do not mark the end of industrial racial capitalism. On the contrary, they distill just how such relations endure through the transformation of technologies of mass production to the work of mass disposal. Consider how union-affiliated excavator operators—a group composed predominantly of white men—related to demolitions as places of consistent, well-compensated work. Even when such work was unavailable, knowledge of heavy-machine operation combined with union membership made it possible to answer calls to work using similar machinery to dig utility channels, excavate foundations, and engage in construction activities. Meanwhile, demolition laborers—a group largely composed of men of color, especially Black men—experienced the same worksites in meaningfully more precarious ways. Not only were laborers significantly lower paid than operators, but accommodating slowdowns in demolition usually meant living without wages entirely. As people differentially made livelihoods in relation to the cyclical movements of excavators, they contended with the ways demolitions invigorated systems in which occupations most typically filled with white men were reliably secure, even if others were not.

To follow the sometimes interrupted motions of excavators on Detroit's demolition sites is to grapple with the mutual entanglements of race, gender, and capital. Specifically, it is to grapple with white masculinity as a durably profitable subject position. Consider how firms owned by white suburbanites have leveled most of Detroit's buildings, profiting from every structure their workers knocked down. Workers from these firms were publicly hostile to efforts to route demolition funds to firms controlled by people of color, especially Black Detroiters. As part of their resistance, they suggested that these firms would cut demolition costs by employing nonunion workers at lower wages, even when this was not the case. It is true that firms owned by Black Detroiters tended to employ nonunion excavator operators, but they did so with union-scale wages and benefits. Ken's explanations are emblematic of how demolition contractors knew that hiring union-affiliated operators meant constraining their potential employees to a pool that was overwhelmingly filled with white men who lived in the suburbs. Eschewing unionized operators made it possible to provide city residents with a shot at well-compensated work. Firms like Ken's that pursued this route tended to be owned and staffed by Black people. Making it through expected winter slowdowns was not a problem for any firm owner. But the unanticipated absence of demolitions created conditions in which nonunion workers and firm owners alike found themselves meaningfully less secure than the mostly white cast of unionized operators and their employers.

As people differentially made livelihoods in relation to demolition excavators, they navigated political economic systems that were always racialized and classed. The constitutive inequities of these systems are not identical to the structures of Fordist racial capitalism for which Detroit is well-known—but they are connected. When Henry Ford built his first production line in Detroit, the racist and sexist structures of industrial employment were purposeful components. To the extent that people who were not white men gained entrance to employment on production lines, it tended to be for more strenuous work at lower pay. Antiblack, misogynist disparities could be attributed to biased employers and workers. Biased employers and workers certainly still exist a century later, but uneven distributions of economic security and precarity on building-removal worksites cannot be uniquely attributed to them. Recall how the heavy-machine operators' union took purposeful steps to recruit Detroit residents into their ranks as a means of expanding their unit's membership beyond established pipelines that reliably turned out white men. While a few Detroiters responded to this call, the hundred-mile round-trip journey to the union's training facility made it inaccessible to many. A location chosen out of convenience for the union's membership in the 1960s, a group that was almost entirely white men, remained most convenient for them decades later. The lesson at stake here is that, even in cases when individual sentiments and institutional policies change, the systemic inequities of industrial racial capitalism can remain quite literally in place.

PART THREE

AFTERMATHS

FIVE

ASBESTOS

For many Detroiters, the sight of workers taping plastic sheeting over the windows and doors of an empty building was the point when they became certain the structure would come down. It was the moment they began to believe the removal of an empty presence they had navigated for years (or sometimes decades) was imminent, rather than one in a long line of deferred promises. Signs attached to the plastic informed people who read them:

DANGER
ASBESTOS
MAY CAUSE CANCER
CAUSES DAMAGE TO LUNGS
AUTHORIZED PERSONNEL ONLY
WEAR RESPIRATORY PROTECTION
AND PROTECTIVE CLOTHING
IN THIS AREA

Written in multiple languages, the signs helped explain why workers arrived with respirators,[1] Tyvek coveralls, and other gear. For a few days, the drone of generators, scraping, grinding, and sawing would be audible to people listening in the vicinity. Workers would emerge on occasion, often carrying opaque plastic bags and drums plastered with warning signs of their own. Only after workers departed a final time could outsiders see evidence of what they had taken with them. Sometimes the pieces removed were limited to patches of floor, siding, and pipe insulation. In many cases they included the layers of plaster that had once covered walls and ceilings. Buildings in the latter category had the appearance of being in a stage of construction—simply timber frames with floors awaiting finish work. Nevertheless, within a few weeks, these shells were usually gone, collapsed by demolition crews who loaded them out to landfills.

Signs announcing the presence of airborne carcinogens in Detroit neighborhoods also marked the implementation of safer demolition practices. In 2010, State of Michigan Department of Environmental Quality (DEQ)[2] staff brought building removals in the city to a halt with a report that municipal demolition programs leveled buildings without first removing asbestos. Environmental Protection Agency (EPA) regulations have nominally required "asbestos abatement" (the technical term for the process of identifying and removing materials containing carcinogenic asbestos fibers) in advance of large-scale demolition projects since 1973.[3] Employing specialized abatement workers increases removal costs by around 30 percent, leading local governments and demolition contractors to chafe against expectations for asbestos removal.[4] Despite challenges, DEQ and EPA staff have maintained regulatory controls on asbestos in demolition, noting that sidestepping abatements unleashes plumes of hazardous dust into neighborhoods that tend to be inhabited by Black, Latine, and working-class people.[5] Nevertheless, in Detroit, these regulations went unenforced for years, with residents and contractors easily recalling plumes of dust emanating from demolition sites, likely distributing asbestos into surrounding neighborhoods. When the Detroit Land Bank Authority (DLBA) assumed responsibility for demolitions in 2014, its staff insisted, "Nothing matters more to us than the health and safety of our residents."[6] Signs posted at demolition sites and flyers distributed to nearby addresses explained asbestos abatement as integral to demolition practices that supported rather than imperiled human and environmental well-being.

Concerns around asbestos are heightened in Detroit, where upwards of 90 percent of buildings were constructed between 1930 and 1959. This time span corresponds with the peak period when asbestos fibers were mixed into building materials sold in North America. Weaving tiny threads of asbestos into insulation, plaster, drywall, flooring, siding, roofing, pipes, adhesives, and other products makes them extremely durable and heat resistant. This adds a certain degree of safety and longevity to buildings, so long as they remain standing. But it also means demolitions carry toxic potential. To allay the fears of skeptical regulators and environmental health advocates, DLBA staff submitted new demolition protocols to the regional EPA office for review. The protocols promised that contractors would need to submit photographic evidence that buildings had been inspected for asbestos-containing materials, that those materials had been removed, and that they were deposited in a specialized landfill. Limited exceptions were allowed for structures so precarious that asbestos inspectors and abatement laborers might fall through the floors. In such cases, contractors were required to treat the entire structure as if it were made of asbestos and prevent dusty releases during the entirety of demolition. After reviewing the proposed protocol, EPA staff released a statement. In their words, "These practices may be applicable to other communities seeking to reduce the environmental impact of demolitions, comply with applicable environmental regulations, and ultimately leave sites better positioned for reuse."[7] The city that had previously stood out for sidestepping regulatory compliance now offered a model of best practices.

Detroit's municipal demolition website announces, "We are proud that the U.S. Environmental Protection Agency has recognized Detroit's demolition program as one of the safest in the country, due to the many steps we take to protect our residents and the environment." The statement rang hollow after investigations by journalists and state regulators found contractors were falsifying asbestos removal records, completing asbestos removals without first enclosing structures in airtight plastic sheeting, or leaving asbestos-containing materials in nearby garages rather than taking them to landfills.[8] Because the DLBA was still paying for demolitions, actions like this meant contracting firms could pocket several thousand dollars in abatement costs at the expense of majority-Black and -Latine Detroit neighborhoods being pumped full of aerosolized asbestos. Local organizers and residents made public statements in city council hearings, noting how contractors profited from channeling hazards into working-class communities of color. They presented this as a straightforward case of environmental racism in which contractors saw the majority-Black neighborhoods surrounding demolition sites as having what foundational environmental justice scholars Robert Bullard and Beverly Wright term "the wrong complexion for protection."[9] State regulators agreed.[10]

Yet following decades of austerity-driven cuts, their handful of inspectors found it impossible to keep eyes on the hundreds of abatement and demolition sites active each day.[11] As a result, contracting firms that Detroit residents observed flouting regulatory frameworks could not be suspended because violations were not personally witnessed by state actors.

Regulatory breakdowns make clear how important state-facilitated regulatory processes are. In Detroit, revelations that certain contractors were skirting asbestos removal requirements came alongside evidence that tearing down buildings with lead-painted walls made lead particles airborne, contributing to an uptick in lead-poisoned Detroiters.[12] Despite the plethora of latent toxicities woven into contemporary building materials, asbestos is the only material in the United States subject to environmental controls during demolitions.[13] So, at the same time as Detroit-based environmental justice organizers mobilized to demand that local agencies step up visits to demolition sites to enforce existing regulations around asbestos, they also called for the federal EPA to "regulate lead the way it regulates asbestos [in demolition]."[14] Such demands surfaced how demolitions that saddled neighborhoods with contamination merely transformed empty buildings into new forms of unevenly distributed burdens. They resonated with broader struggles to regulate industrial fence lines across the United States, where regulatory action is contingent on demonstrating harm. It is well-documented how protections that ensure breathable air and potable water arrive fastest to the whitest and wealthiest places and more slowly for everyone else.[15] Uneven rollouts invariably result in majority-Black, Indigenous, and Latine communities that are grappling with environmental violence engaging in intensive organizing to be treated on the same terms as wealthier, whiter communities.[16] In a context where the text of regulatory guidelines are key in separating people and places from harms, environmental justice struggles coalesce around shared commitments to enacting broader distributions of protection.

Specially trained laborers and inspectors who successfully stabilized volatile asbestos-containing materials within airtight enclosures demonstrate the embodied work that makes broader regulatory protection possible. The barriers they constructed include the sheeting that became the figure of an upcoming "safe" demolition, sample bags that seal samples of suspect materials for testing, and the personal protective equipment (PPE) provided to asbestos workers. The racially diverse group of upper-middle-class people employed to inspect empty buildings for asbestos-containing materials did so from within the enclosure of respirators and gloves that kept them at a comfortable remove from possibly harmful substances. For the group of mostly Black men employed as asbestos abatement labor, their work carried wages around three times the state minimum, with some channeled into it as a condition of release from incarceration. Despite knowing the protections offered by woven plastic coveralls and respirators, they described needing to remove them to complete worksite tasks. The swirls of hazardous particulates that abatement laborers inhaled from behind opaque barriers of plastic sheeting ultimately enabled demolitions that met or exceeded regulatory requirements. Following asbestos through regulatory trainings and worksite enclosures showcases how constructing even fragile barriers between Detroit's majority-Black populace and demolition hazards concentrated harm within the majority-Black workforce of abatement laborers. In so doing, it demonstrates how successful efforts to "protect our residents and the environment" from environmental violence can be made possible by racist distributions of toxic harm.

THE MAGIC MINERAL

During the several years I spent trying to understand how demolitions could happen in ways that kept environments and communities "safe," I attended trainings for people seeking work in asbestos abatement. A state-mandated forty hours in length, these weeklong courses culminated in a few days of hands-on activities where people donned respirators, disposable coveralls, gloves, and goggles to practice techniques for packaging asbestos-containing materials within plastic enclosures. The days before, however, were filled with lectures and quizzes about the histories of extracting, using, and suffering from this peculiar set of silica crystals. Some trainees found this section tedious. They stared out the window or fiddled with smartphones concealed under desks. To varying degrees of accuracy, some scribbled down quiz answers before instructors concluded their presentations. Nonetheless, as feminist scholar of technoscience M. Murphy reminds us, "toxicity is in the details."[17] Lectures chronicling the myriad ways tiny threads of asbestos have been woven into fireproof building components bring such details into focus, especially how a known carcinogen continues to permeate built environments in relative safety. But running buildings through with heavy equipment casts that safety into doubt. Because asbestos is in all practical sense of the term, indestructible, materials containing it cannot be eliminated, only managed. Asbestos-abatement trainings are geared to develop workers who can facilitate this management. Within the structure of these curricula, access to practical abatement skills requires reckoning first with the simultaneously protective and harmful characteristics of asbestos threads.

Though industrial hygienists tasked with leading asbestos-abatement trainings operated from a common curriculum and set of workbooks required by state occupational health regulations, their slide decks were relatively bespoke. One hygienist opened her first day with a slide emblazoned with "Asbestos: Miracle, Magic, Deadly." The text was superimposed over a collage showing samples of the six naturally occurring silica minerals that share the "asbestiform habit," in that they are composed of durable, easily separated fibers.[18] Subsequent slides would detail how crystalline veins of asbestos are distributed across all continents, with light pressure from human fingers being enough to pull them into arrays of threads no larger than a human hair. Further crushing results in spindly, microscopic crystals, with the first known human uses being pots and burial shrouds dating to around 2500 BCE. Clay and textiles enriched with inert asbestos fibers are practically impervious to fire, water, and chemical decay, leading to descriptions of asbestos as a "magic" or "miracle" mineral.[19] By the 1960s, asbestos was incorporated into almost every building, automobile, boat, airplane, and engine produced in the United States.[20] At the same time, microscopic asbestos fibers also gusted through mines, factories, shipyards, and construction sites, blowing into the respiratory tracts of workers and their relations.[21] Once lodged in lungs, the jagged edges of asbestos fibers cut through tissues like so many tiny knives. With passing years, the scars become progressively more painful, sometimes spurring cancers and other distinctive growths. Among workers exposed to high concentrations of asbestos for prolonged periods of time, 80 percent of workers developed respiratory problems and 40 percent died from asbestos-related diseases.[22]

It was against the backdrop of this information that I first met Rayshawn. In his early thirties when we met, Rayshawn was the father of two children. Like most asbestos-abatement laborers I came to know, he was Black and under the supervision of the criminal legal system. Among the trainees who filed into the drab conference room that morning, some, including Rayshawn, were present as a condition of early release from state prisons. Others were there as part of programs for recently unemployed people. The other was me.[23] As Rayshawn described it, a prison "reentry preparedness counselor" had offered asbestos as a peculiar sort of magic mineral, one that could secure him a livable wage and an early return to his family. Others reported similar conversations. Due to the volume of abatement work necessary to prepare buildings for demolition, state-certified abatement laborers could earn upwards of $18 per hour—almost triple the statewide minimum wage at the time. A shortage of certified workers also meant abatement contractors were eager to hire people like Rayshawn, even if employers in other sectors regularly refused to hire someone with a carceral record. Indeed, within weeks of completing the training, Rayshawn was working on an abatement site with a starting wage of $19.25. State officials cited the trajectories of people like Rayshawn as inspiration to enroll currently incarcerated people in asbestos-abatement trainings.[24] The hope was that people who completed carceral training programs could draw wages from the moment of their release.

The industrial hygienist leading our training, Brenda, was about five minutes through a historical account of asbestos when Rayshawn raised his hand. After Brenda called on him, he asked, "Miss, we all know asbestos is bad. We've seen the commercials. Wouldn't our time be better spent learning how to protect ourselves?" If you are reading this in the United States, you may have seen the commercials Rayshawn was referring to: the ones suggesting you call an attorney's toll-free number if you might have inhaled asbestos fibers suspended within insulation, flooring felt, baby powder, fertilizer, automotive parts, drywall, or other products.[25] Sometimes they feature first-hand accounts of breathing difficulties or masses growing in lung tissue. Brenda and other instructors routinely fielded questions like this from trainees who were eager to skip lectures and suit up in respirators. Ultimately, Brenda responded by asking us to join her on a field trip. As we filed out of the classroom and headed toward the training center basement, Brenda explained that the structure—built sometime in the fifties or sixties by her guess—had asbestos laced through it. Indeed, when we arrived in the basement, we were greeted by a massive, insulation wrapped boiler plastered with signs reading "DANGER: CONTAINS ASBESTOS FIBERS. AVOID CREATING DUST. CANCER AND LUNG DISEASE HAZARD" (figure 5.1). By way of this system, Brenda discussed how at that very moment, asbestos was keeping the scalding heat from overpowering the small basement. It kept us safe. Breaking open the wrapping, however, would turn this protection into a source of problematic dust.

Brenda's object lesson on the continued presence of asbestos was not the only

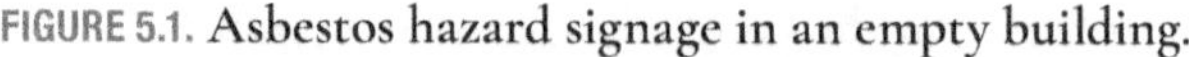

FIGURE 5.1. Asbestos hazard signage in an empty building.

Photo by the author.

one I encountered in an abatement training. But most industrial hygienists drew heavily on archival materials to make similar arguments. One common resource was a 1922 short film, *The Story of Asbestos*, produced by asbestos marketers.[26] First, bare-handed workers lug three-hundred-pound bundles of asbestos ore from tunnels in Arizona and New England onto train cars bound for manufacturing facilities in Illinois and New Jersey. Once there, factory workers crush and screen asbestos into piles of tiny fibers to be mixed into commercial products, including brake linings, cloth, cement, window glaze, paint, siding, clothing, and roofing materials. Finally, a manager applies the "blowtorch test" to a section of asbestos-reinforced roofing paper stretched over a wood panel. Subjected to flames for almost an hour, the paper blackens but the wood beneath it remains unburnt. In viewings almost a century later, abatement trainers discussed how asbestos manufacturers knew well that dusty conditions in mines and factories endangered occupational and environmental health. Harms did not accrue in error; they were the predicate to profit.[27] Processes that suspended carcinogenic fibers in paper, mastic, gypsum, and other matter created structures that were well-insulated and fireproof for the long haul. They also suspended carcinogenic fibers in human tissues, creating bodies would become riddled with mesotheliomas, pleural plaques, and scarred airways. Abatement instructors like Brenda insisted on specificities in which harm did not extend from the existence of asbestos, but from its incorporation into drafty work routines.

I was reminded of the warnings issued by abatement instructors when I was settling into the office where I have written large portions of this book. It is in an institutional building constructed in the 1950s. Allegedly, plans to demolish the structure were shelved due to the costs of abating asbestos-containing ceiling tiles. As part of my onboarding, a university staffer emailed me a notice about the tiles. She described how they made the building fireproof and cozy in the winter. The microscopic fibers were set in resin and would not drift off, but I should take care not to scrape against the ceiling (something known to happen when faculty were unloading books onto the top levels of bookshelves). The knowledge conveyed in this friendly email resonated with industrial hygienists leading abatement trainings. It also distilled cultural historian Arthur Rose's labeling of asbestos as a "modernist object" that encapsulates vexed promises of industrial life.[28] Bound up in my office ceiling tiles—and indeed, in all asbestos-containing materials—is the reality that technological promises of security through industrial progress ride alongside corporate obfuscation of environmental violence and terminal illness.[29] Those ceiling tiles may pose little threat to people learning, teaching, reading, and typing beneath their fireproof care. But mining and manufacturing them certainly generated toxic lineages.[30] Removing them would create new ripples of harm. Industrial hygienists like Brenda sought to ground abatement trainees like Rayshawn in these details. For them, asbestos was not something to be unilaterally feared. Rather, they framed it as a curiously protective substance that unleashed hazardous dust when torn out of place.

CRITICAL BARRIERS

Notwithstanding cautions from people like Brenda, highly public histories of corporate coverups of cancer, mesothelioma, and other injuries make asbestos a matter of popular concern. I was once walking up the entry steps to a community event center on Detroit's northwest side when the group of elders in front of me turned around abruptly at the door. They had been chatting about a standing card game, and as we crossed paths one looked to me and said, "Best not go in there, they've got asbestos work happening. Don't know why they are even open." Indeed, just beyond the glass entry doors, a handful of people were milling around in hooded Tyvek coveralls, hard hats, respirators, and goggles. They were arranged next to a pop-up asbestos decontamination area. The box, around eight feet in all directions, was constructed out of white plastic sheeting and PVC piping. It featured the DANGER ASBESTOS signage that adorned buildings where asbestos removal was in process. People built decontamination areas like this as part of the "practical skills" section of training courses that prepared people like Rayshawn to work as abatement laborers. For the plastic box to operate according to plan, it should have been partitioned into zippered airlock chambers and include a wash station. Gear like coveralls and respirators folded workers within plastic cocoons that buffered against airborne asbestos fibers. Decontamination areas offered portals for donning and removing that equipment while keeping asbestos within worksite spaces allowed by regulatory statutes.

But this was not an active abatement worksite. The pop-up decontamination area and protective gear were props brought in as part of an event organized to formally recognize Detroiters who had recently completed asbestos worker training courses. Newly certified workers, some of them wearing coveralls, respirators, and goggles, used the chamber as a backdrop for celebratory photos with family and supporters. When Rayshawn and I finished our course, Brenda handed out certificates of completion over a lunch from the nearby Szechuan takeout. In subsequent years, however, municipal, state, and federal funds for training abatement labor had swelled class sizes. So, this gathering had the mood of a graduation ceremony. A city councilor who had been instrumental in ensuring that people returning from incarceration were eligible for abatement training was on hand to present certificates of completion. In her remarks, she mentioned the decontamination chamber and PPE that sat in the hallway: "Knowing that demolitions could spread asbestos around our neighborhoods makes a lot of us nervous. You now have the knowledge to use all that gear to keep yourselves and our communities safe. Thank you." Reflecting the sentiments of many Detroiters, this city councilor saw the material evidence of abatement—gear for constructing barriers around buildings and bodies—as indicative of processes that kept people safe. Crucially, these items did not work on their own. Safety relied on knowledge held by abatement technicians, including the newly minted ones she had come to celebrate.

For many people enrolled in asbestos-abatement training programs, suiting up in a hard hat, hooded coveralls, gloves, a respirator, and goggles to learn how to build plastic enclosures around abatement worksites was a highly anticipated moment. After a few days of lectures about the magical dangers of asbestos, the open-air garages and equipment yards reserved for "hands-on learning" were a welcome break from classrooms. Ultimately, the goal of this learning was for trainees to construct a set of air-tight bubbles. The first was around our bodies—a fit-tested respirator, nitrile gloves, Tyvek coveralls duct-taped at our wrists and ankles, Tyvek boot covers duct-taped around our legs, goggles, hard hat, heavy-duty gloves. The second was around our worksites—double layers of plastic sheeting over any crack an asbestos fiber might escape through. In some jobsites, this involved creating a plasticated cube supported by the structure's walls, floors, and ceilings. But since pre-demolition abatements often involved removing those very things, at minimum we learned to place double layers of plastic over every doorway, window, and chimney that led to the outside. These "critical barriers," as we had learned during lectures, were part of federal requirements for legal asbestos abatements (figure 5.2).[31] Decontamination areas were also required. There were many more regulatory details, but they are beyond the scope here.[32] Apart from hard hats, goggles, and heavy-duty gloves that we were instructed to scrub vigorously in a field shower, everything else—critical barriers, coveralls, boot covers, respirators, nitrile gloves, duct tape, water—would be packaged up as and labeled as hazardous asbestos-containing waste.

If asbestos is the calling card for certain aftermaths of contemporary industrial life, plastic is certainly the calling card for others. Manufacturers spin the former into promises of enduring protection, the predicate to which is immensely hazardous conditions for workers and fence-line communities who shoulder the burdens of production, installation, and disposal.[33] Plastics, meanwhile, promise impervious flexibility and portability, the predicate to which is petrochemical violence visited unevenly upon lands, people, and their relations.[34] Within late-industrial worlds made of forever chemicals, there is no such thing as a clean break.[35] Struggling against them is a series of exercises in harm reduction.[36] Anthropologist of science Elizabeth Roberts chronicles such exercises in Mexico City's Colonia Periférico, where sewage runoff flooded residents' homes

FIGURE 5.2. Critical barriers.

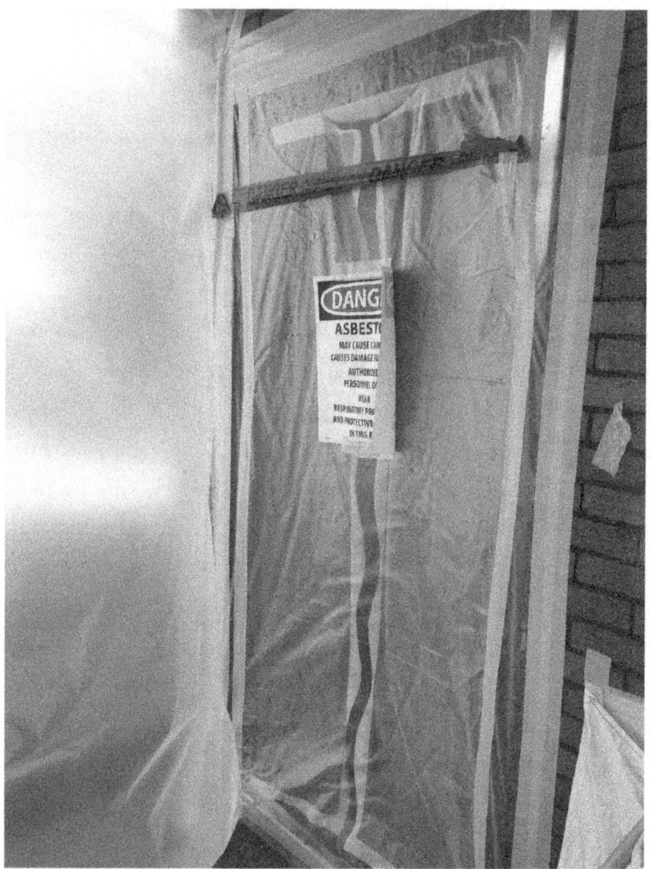

Photo by the author.

with putrid odors but also buffered against incursion by militarized police and organized crime. She observes, "Those living in the shit [often] seek boundaries between objects, as well as the stability that boundaried objects have to offer."[37] Detroiters watching workers pack out abatement waste (PPE and critical barriers folded up in yet another layer of plastic) sometimes had similar observations. I was making small talk with a man on his porch when his eyes widened at the volume of sheeting deployed in the abatement of the dwelling next door.[38] He mused, "I sure hate the thought of all that plastic going into our landfills. But I sure hate more the thought of all that asbestos going into our lungs." Like others, he reckoned with how tools for sealing out airborne asbestos brought their own harmful trajectories into being.

For state environmental quality and occupational health regulators, checks for airtight critical barriers and PPE usage were also encounters with the limitations of their protections. Double-layered plastic enclosures are easy to assemble in training yards. But taped-up seals come unstuck on flaking paint and chipped siding and after prolonged exposure to weather. Tyvek coveralls snag on nails and jagged lumber. State laws guided environmental quality inspectors to ensure asbestos dust remained within critical barriers enveloping worksites, whereas they guided occupational health inspectors to check for leaks in protective gear and unsafe working conditions.[39] Municipal field inspectors were tasked with ensuring demolition firms completed work on schedule. But people in these roles tended to look across their narrowed mandates. Consider what happened when a municipal demolition field inspector visited a site where Rayshawn and some colleagues were removing asbestos-containing plaster and pipe insulation. In the initial pass, the inspector noted that a corner of an outer layer of plastic taped to an upper-floor balcony flapped loosely in the breeze. In the inspector's view, this did not merit a formal report, as workers quickly retaped the sheet. The inspector was more deeply concerned upon catching a glimpse of Rayshawn's respirator as he stowed it in the decontamination area before hauling out a ladder to ascend the structure. The plastic head strap appeared broken. After offering all three workers disposable P100 masks, the field inspector left them with a strong suggestion to contact the occupational safety and health inspector assigned to their worksite.

Rayshawn and his coworkers did not call occupational health officers to request inspections. As one of Rayshawn's coworkers told me with a shrug, "He needs this job for his parole. I need this job for my rent. Would you call if you needed this job?" This comment reflects a sentiment I heard from many abatement laborers. During my time in Detroit, the front pages of local newspapers were filled for several days by investigative reporting that raised an issue that abatement laborers knew intimately. Certain contractors, including but not limited to several who bid on pre-demolition abatement jobs, encouraged laborers to work without protective equipment like respirators and Tyvek jumpsuits. Like asbestos manufacturers before them, contractors downplayed occupational health research showing that even low levels of asbestos inhalation is linked to cancer years later. Because regulatory spot checks were few and far between, on the off chance an inspector visited, laborers were instructed to shimmy into their protective equipment before the state agent could breach the airlock. Environmental justice activists and inspectors like the one who pressed a P100 mask into Rayshawn's hands implored laborers to report their employers. Few ever did. After all, for people with carceral records marshalled as a labor reserve for asbestos abatement, that work was one of the few better-than-minimum-wage jobs open to them. In the best case, giving state inspectors a peek into working conditions might fix broken jobsite safety gear. But, as asbestos laborers also feared, transparency could also spur contractors to make that job and its associated protections go away.

The plastic sheeting, high-filtration respirators, and other gear that enclose asbestos laborers and their worksites strive to carve out life-sustaining containers within hazardous terrain. Feminist philosopher of technology Zoe Sofia, as well as others extending her line of thinking, describes "container technologies" that hold and facilitate life as the building blocks of supportive care.[40] Nevertheless, containers can also be enclosures that serve as vectors for immense violence—private property, incarceration, nation-states, and settler colonies come to mind. Regulatory containments like critical barriers emerged from logics of industrial modernism that promise insurmountable barriers between bodies and their environments (say, barriers crafted from asbestos or plastic). Such logics routinize pollution and environmental violence by obscuring how even the most sophisticated boundaries are never hermetically sealed. Like the strap on Rayshawn's respirator, industrial containers tend to be flawed, leaky, and prone to break. But regulatory demands to wrap critical barriers around abatement worksites, as well as respirators and coveralls around abatement workers, are not foolhardy displays of modernist hubris. As workers, observers, and even regulators knew well, plasticated sheeting and protective clothing were imperfect. Their commitments to deploying plastics as barriers for containing asbestos fibers away from lung tissues were not evidence of faith in the unalloyed good of technical fixes. Quite the opposite. For those who inhabited them, critical barriers and PPE were shot through with compromise. They established fragile boundaries that routinely materialized how their protection was something other than absolute.

SUBURB LUNGS

Rayshawn regularly texted me with the location of his worksites. Every few weeks, I would accept his invitation to "come thru." This involved spending the day chatting with people who lived around abatements while Rayshawn and his coworkers periodically emerged from their plastic enclosure. Crucially, though, I never personally observed the physical labor necessary to pry asbestos components from their place. It was obscured behind milky plastic sheeting, with Rayshawn and other abatement laborers cautioning me against ever following them through the decontamination chamber. Once, I came prepared with protective coveralls, gloves, and a respirator. But Rayshawn placed a hand on my shoulder to ask, "Why risk those soft suburb lungs of yours?" When other workers discouraged me from entering their worksites, they tended to draw attention to my white skin and advanced degrees as evidence for why. Rayshawn triangulated these with the exurban location where I was raised. Comments about my "soft" hands, sensibilities, and lungs betrayed interpretations that I was ill-suited for the same work as the commenter.[41] Abatement laborers had similar discussions of soft bodies with respect to asbestos inspectors who mapped buildings to determine which components needed to be removed by hand to meet regulatory standards and which aspects of buildings to leave for an excavator. Unlike laborers, who were mostly Black and worked shifts behind critical barriers punctuated by limited breaks, the ranks of professional class inspectors drew higher wages for more flexible work routines. Seen through the prism of suburb lungs, following an inspector as she searches for the presence of asbestos-containing materials clarifies how racialized geographies that shelter people from toxic hazards become inhabited as characteristics of physical bodies.

Arguments predicated on innate, racially differentiated bodily capacities are the hallmark of racist science. The idea that African-descended people are least susceptible to pain or that European-descended bodies are most prone to environmental destabilization are two prongs enabling cruelty targeting Black people.[42] And such ideologies are not relics of the past. They pervade twenty-first-century medical science and with it, classrooms, clinics, court judgments, political economic systems, and routine conversations.[43] Historian of medicine Lundy Braun locates the origins of medicolegal faith in inherent, racially differentiated breathing capacities—with Black people assumed to have the lowest inherent lung capacities—within efforts to understand the vital capacities of workers in racially unequal industrial labor regimes.[44] Braun takes note of late-twentieth-century efforts by US asbestos manufacturers to require Black workers to meet higher disability thresholds to receive compensation for breathing difficulties, mesothelioma, and other injuries linked to asbestos exposure. When accused of a patently antiblack legal maneuver, attorneys for the manufacturers cited the medical standard of racializing breathing assessments, as well as current pulmonary research showing Black people had 10-15 percent lower lung function when compared to other racial groups. Braun details how racialized breathing is not based in natural abilities. Like other population-level measurements of racial difference in vital capacities, they are produced by unequal social conditions.[45] Racial disparities reflect racist environments—air quality, healthcare access, employment hierarchies, and so on—that protect whitened bodies at the expense of others.

Judges prevented asbestos manufacturers from requiring Black workers to meet higher standards of disability than their white counterparts. But "race correction" remains standard practice in some occupational health assessments of breathing capacity.[46] Federal and state regulations require routine pulmonary tests for workers exposed to asbestos on the job, especially for people like asbestos laborers and inspectors among whom asbestos is the matter of their employment. These tests are relatively straightforward. A technician clips your nostrils shut and instructs you in a set of breathing rhythms where you blow from your mouth into a measuring device. It all takes less than fifteen minutes, with the results reported to you, your employer, and a state regulatory office. I once observed a discussion among representatives from Michigan's occupational health and safety regulator and public health students considering careers in occupational health. In his presentation, one regulator commented that some disparities—such as the reduced lung function of asbestos laborers when compared to asbestos inspectors—might not result from increased exposure to jobsite hazards. Instead, he reasoned the difference stemmed from more workers in laborer positions identifying as Black compared to more inspectors identifying as white. Students and faculty nodded along in agreement. This interpretation was consistent with professional guidance for workplace lung-function tests, which reminds those performing assessments: "Recording the worker's age and race/ethnicity, as well as measuring exact height, is important because a worker's normal range of lung function is determined by these factors."[47] Cast in the technical minutia of regulatory standards, demographic categories explain away the possibility of disparate exposure to hazards.

Pulmonary function test results delivered to regulatory offices do not report information on the recipients' incomes. But if they did, regulators and others with access to the data might have observed that the salaries of some asbestos abatement inspectors worked out to around double what laborers were paid for their time. I got to know several asbestos inspectors during my time in Detroit. For the most part, we met on the sidelines of educational meetings that inspectors and other practitioners in "environmental services" attended to maintain eligibility for state licensure. Because common building components like asbestos-containing insulation, drywall, and plaster mixes did not carry bold-faced warnings, inspectors' work practices were necessary to bring their presence into view. Doing so allowed demolitions to meet regulatory standards for asbestos abatement. Maureen, a Black woman in her late forties, had worked for various firms as an asbestos in-

FIGURE 5.3. **Asbestos-containing materials removed from a single house.**

Photo by the author.

spector and management planner for almost three decades. She was the inspector who I came to know best and took days driving around Detroit to explain inspection processes to me. Maureen commuted to work from her rambling contemporary ranch in the same northern suburb where she grew up. Divorced, her wages were nonetheless sufficient to cover most of the college tuition for her children. In this way, even though Maureen's racialized and gendered experiences might not reflect many of her colleagues, as an upper-middle-class professional living in one of Detroit's suburbs, she was representative of them.

Maureen summarized her job as "a scavenger hunt to collect everything in a building that might contain asbestos" (figure 5.3). One scavenger hunt I accompanied her on was through a two-story house clad in yellow brick that had been built in 1949 on Detroit's west side. When we arrived, the structure was entirely closed up. Faded plywood covered where windows and doors once had been. Maureen carried a pry bar in her truck that helped us get inside. A damp, musty smell sprang forth as we peeled back plywood from the first-floor windows and entryways. With headlamps and respirators positioned on our heads, we shouldered our way through the front door and onto undulating wood floors that bounced with each step. Over the course of an afternoon, Maureen moved methodically through each room of the 1,300-square-foot dwelling. Among other things, she took core samples from each wall, pulled strips of insulation from behind them, scraped window glaze and various adhesives, pulled up tiles, and cut bits of pipe wrap. She folded each sample into a plastic sandwich bag, labeled it, and dropped it in a bin. Most of these actions generated little puffs of debris, hence the respirators. But with the afternoon sun baking the structure and the temperature pushing 90°F, sweat pooled in our masks. We regularly left the building for fresh air and a swig of water on the front stoop. At the end of her scavenger hunt, Maureen stacked the bin in her truck bed alongside ones from earlier jobs.

Like all inspectors, Maureen deposited her samples at a testing laboratory. The serrated edges of microscopic asbestos fibers embedded in the physical materiality of existing buildings are practically invisible to the human eye, something Maureen once demonstrated for me by laying plastic-sealed handfuls of asbestos-infused tile adhesive, plaster, and insulation atop her office desk. Alongside these packets she placed others containing seemingly identical pieces of products that did not contain the additive. The substances looked and felt the same, with the dry materials crumbling when I pressed them through plastic membranes. Nevertheless, breaking open one set of packages and breathing deeply from their contents would likely cause me to cough. Doing so to the other might provoke a coughing fit followed by cancers decades later. The distinction between harmful and benign materials had been determined in the same laboratory tasked with analyzing samples from the buildings I followed Maureen through. There, a technician would follow protocols involving tweezers, microscopes, chemical stains, and polarized light to parse which samples contained the telltale jagged outlines of asbestos fibers and which did not. Maureen correlated lab readouts with her walk-through notes to total the "regulated asbestos-containing material" present in a structure. For the yellow brick house, that included 2,747 square feet of wall and ceiling plaster, 141 linear feet of window glaze, and 25 linear feet of pipe insulation. Mapping colors, textures, and other descriptors onto a floorplan, she identified which walls, pipes, and windows to tear out and which to leave behind.

Seated in Maureen's office, I once asked her whether she worried about health consequences from her job. Like all the asbestos inspectors I asked, she said no.[48] Maureen also expanded on her response, noting how devices like plastic sampling bags and high-filtration respirators were quite effective at keeping even the tiniest threads of asbestos from getting through. As evidence, she pulled up the results of her most recent pulmonary-function test. The pair of charts showed Maureen's lung capacities measured in the upper tenth of those expected for people of her age and height, figures the interpretation guide considered excellent if she were a white woman and far exceeding the parameters expected for a Black woman.[49] For Maureen, pulmonary function tests confirmed the effectiveness of her worksite protective equipment. This is no doubt accurate. But respirators and plastic baggies were not the only things that sheltered Maureen's lungs from the cumulative effects of airborne chemicals and fine particles that scar lung tissue and impede breathing. Like me, Maureen had suburb lungs. The wealthy, majority-white polity where she had lived most of her life placed her a great distance from production lines, refineries, warehouses, factory farming, expressways, and other sites belching contaminants skyward. Racial capitalism, including but not limited to white supremacy, is atmospheric.[50] By design, such facilities were concentrated elsewhere.[51] The racist slant of exposure is not intended to support the well-being of people like Maureen—quite the opposite. Nevertheless, she inhaled protections that were cast in place.

CITY LUNGS

To warn me off ever crossing the critical barriers around an active abatement worksite, Rayshawn and other laborers described dusty conditions: plumes of fuzzy insulation and plaster grit that hung in the air despite the hum of portable air filtration units. Regulators and university environmental health staff gave me similar cautions. Not all worksites were like this—the dust produced in small jobs or those limited to heavyweight materials like tiles, glue, or window glazes could be sucked up into the plasticated folds of a high-powered filter, provided one was in use. But for someone with suburb lungs, Rayshawn reasoned it was never worth the risk. By contrast, he described himself and his coworkers as having "hard city lungs." If soft suburb lungs like mine or those of asbestos inspectors like Maureen were a sheltered inheritance worth protecting, city lungs carried signs of wear. In Rayshawn's case, that included a recurring dry cough he attributed to living most of his life at the margins of one of Detroit's still active industrial corridors. Abatement laborers tended to share this sort of origin story. They talked of living next to a refinery, growing up next to a steel plant, attending school near a sewage treatment spillway, and so on. Wearing high-filtration masks compounded breathing difficulties, meaning abatement laborers found themselves gasping for air as they ripped out asbestos-containing materials and packaged them for transport. To maintain their jobs, they surfed the threshold of personal exposure limits, removing respirators for the precise duration allowed under occupational health statutes. When workers tasked with cleaning up asbestos inhaled carcinogenic dust, they inhaled further layers of environmental violence entirely within the parameters of regulatory acceptability.

Abatement laborers perform the final work necessary to remove strands of asbestos from the scene to ensure they are not sent skyward during demolition. Following maps created by inspectors like Maureen, laborers rip, scrape, pound, pry, smash, and otherwise tear out any aspect of the structure identified to contain asbestos. Sometimes their work was so extensive that they stripped buildings back to the studs (figure 5.4). The yellow brick dwelling I walked through with Maureen offered a good example of such a structure. When Maureen completed her inspection of this building, it was fairly intact. Jagged slashes through the plaster walls and ceilings, as well as across some of the wood floors marked where people had removed most of the valuable metal wires, pipes, and radiators. Metal pipes

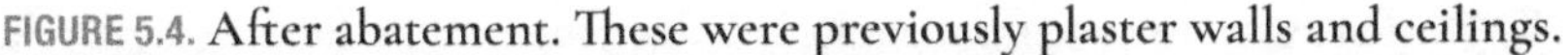
FIGURE 5.4. After abatement. These were previously plaster walls and ceilings.

Photo by the author.

remained in the basement, possibly left undisturbed due to stickers warning that the surrounding insulation contained asbestos. Whatever the reason, when I accompanied Maureen, there was still plaster on the walls, pipes in the basement, and cabinets in the kitchen, as well as tile and a toilet in the bathroom. After a week of work by abatement laborers, it was possible to see straight through the building. Getting at all the asbestos-containing plaster and insulation required removing many non-asbestos-based components too. Workers sealed everything into thick plastic waste bags or storage drums before stacking them inside a shipping container planted at the curb. The container would be carted off to a storage site that promised to keep debris in airtight suspension forever.[52] Arrival paperwork marked the completion of asbestos abatement "in compliance" with regulatory requirements.

Rayshawn's identification of city lungs as metaphorically harder than suburb lungs resonates with the physiological effects of inhaling asbestos, which quite literally hardens lung tissues. Pulmonologists describe healthy lung tissue like a sponge. When biopsied and placed under a microscope, its pink sacs provide evidence of membranes transferring oxygen from air into blood. Asbestos fibers are so small they easily travel deep into lung tissues, where their sharp edges refuse to be broken down by physiological processes that dissolve viruses, bacteria, and other airborne chemicals. As the fibers linger, the scars that build up around them impede oxygen transfer. In biopsies they stand out as black speckles that displace the expected pink field. Specialists associate these speckles with the audible crackling sounds of people attempting to draw breath through hardened lung tissues that have become brittle and will, even with care, stop functioning. As part of presentations to abatement workers seeking to recertify state licenses, occupational health and safety regulators would screen a clip of a retired asbestos insulation worker describing the sharp pain he experiences when inhaling into scarred lungs. Detailing how his former coworkers died from conditions that left them gasping for air, even when strapped to supplemental oxygen tanks, the man reflects, "I hope that some guy who's not driving a car very carefully hits me and kills me instantly, so I don't have to suffer."[53] He advises abatement workers to always wear respirators on the job and to report dusty conditions to regulatory offices.

The message of occupational health promotion materials appeared simple: wear a respirator to keep a breathable life. But this message took people with protected breathing as its starting point. For me—a person whose suburb lungs have been relatively sheltered by inhabiting geographies of racial privilege—breathing in the sort of respirators provided to asbestos abatement workers takes focused effort. Combined with physical exertion, drawing air through dense charcoal filters contained within layers of plastic fabric produces a dull ache in my chest—the kind of feeling I associate with an intense sprint up a hill. Yet other abatement laborers in training described unbearable sensations of pain and burning in theirs. During a training exercise that involved lifting bags packed with mock insulation and plaster above our heads, an instructor chided one member of our group, Chris, for moving slower than everyone else. A white Detroiter in his thirties who had a relatively trim physique, Chris tore his respirator off entirely. He wheezed, "Sir, . . . I know . . . we . . . need the masks to breathe. . . . But I can't breathe with the mask. . . . can't breathe. . . . You hear?" Others nodded and removed their own respirators, their chests heaving. It is easy to blame workers' "noncompliance" with workplace safety measures on workers not understanding the dangers of their jobs.

Chris's and his coworkers' strained breathing suggests other explanations. They point to workplace demands that push workers beyond the capacities of protective equipment.

"I can't breathe." When Chris sputtered those words, Eric Garner's phrase, had become the rallying cry of the Movement for Black Lives. It is an analysis of interwoven systems that unequally suffocate people to the point of death.[54] Taken expansively, it names how the same Black, Indigenous, and colonized places most subject to the violence of police brutality are also places that corporations and governments configure into sinks for the violence of chemicals, radiation, and other signs of industrial "progress."[55] White-skinned people uttering "I can't breathe" are often cosplaying at oppression.[56] But Chris was not. In casual moments, when he and other abatement trainees talked about where they lived or grew up, Chris plotted a life spent at the fence lines of a refinery and salt mine in Southwest Detroit. It resonated with others' trajectories between the radii of factories, steel plants, sewage processors, and other facilities that spew hazardous emissions into some of Detroit's neighborhoods. Carceral facilities, the institutions from which Chris and many abatement trainees were channeled, are also common locations that stitch the violence of industrial and criminal legal orders together.[57] Structural racism operates at scale, and being subject to the antiblack violence of these atmospheres did not require Chris to be a Black person.[58] Antiblack environments entered abatement trainings in the lungs of most every Detroiter. They peppered classrooms and training yards with throaty coughs, raspy wheezes, and talk about the impossibility of drawing breath.

Abatement instructors advised people who struggled to breathe within the protective confines of their respirators to cultivate different breathing practices. "Short breaths will not pull through the mask. Try for long inhales. In through your nose, out through your mouth. Slow down when you need to. Keep the respirator sealed." Well-meaning advice, but it was an individuated "solution" that collapsed on contact with systemic conditions. Counting inhales did nothing to slow the physical demands of heaving, pulling, and packing bags of asbestos on abatement worksites. Regimented breathing in a respirator is difficult to maintain under such strain, so workers found other rhythms. I sometimes heard watch and phone alarms ding at half hour intervals when sitting outside abatement worksites. In the United States, this marked the maximum time that workers could inhale clouds of asbestos-containing materials on the job while remaining in compliance with occupational health and safety regulations. Specifically, statutes carved out a "permissible exposure limit" of one fiber per cubic centimeter of workplace air for up to thirty minutes before requiring employers to provide respirators. Abatement workers described using their exposure limit to work flat out—lugging debris up and down stairs, ripping out walls, and other tasks requiring increased respiration. Afterward, they would slip respirators over their heads. The possibly hundreds of thousands of asbestos fibers filling their airways materialized the constitutive feature of exposure limits.[59] Even for substances like asbestos classified as having "no safe level of exposure," permissible limits open a space for subjecting people to harm before offering them protection.

Writing to Swedish factory workers suffering from asbestos-related conditions, public historian Sven Lindqvist suggests, "History is still living even in the bodies of those who took part in it. History is lying in wait till it finally kills them. When you open the dead body you will find history in the form of silvery fibres—the last remnants of the air people had to breathe in the factories."[60] Lindqvist argues that people coping with labored breathing through fibrotic lungs should follow silvery fibers from their bodies toward the assemblage of corporations, shareholders, and regulatory offices who downplayed evidence that asbestos harmed workers, their families, and adjacent communities. The facts of asbestos hazards that corporations purposefully concealed to maximize profits from asbestos extraction are now well-known. Some might say that people who remove respirators on abatement worksites are ignoring the potential consequences of their actions. But a singular focus on asbestos fibers obscures the conditions under which abatement workers like Rayshawn and Chris made such decisions.[61] Almost certainly, their lungs contain silvery fibers, with workers' respiratory systems enrolled as part of the apparatus that keeps asbestos from breaching the critical barriers around abatement sites. Yet as Rayshawn strikes at with his own diagnosis of city lungs, those silvery fibers do not wait alone. For people channeled into abatement labor, asbestos deposited under the legal cover of permissible workplace limits adds yet another layer alongside the already felt burdens of unequally restricted airways.

RACIST PROTECTIONS

By way of conclusion, a final encounter with airborne hazards. Consider how, at the end of March 2020, the State of Michigan, like governing bodies around the world, asked people to remain in their homes to prevent the spread of a novel respiratory virus. And yet, abatement laborers continued to show up to jobsites. Most abatement-firm owners notified their employees that their labor was considered "necessary to sustain or protect life" and, thus, exempt from stay-at-home protections. Rayshawn forwarded me updates from a WhatsApp group of abatement workers. It pinged with a debate over whether it was a good idea to wear respirators on buses to and from work. People chimed in with requests for extra masks and PPE for relatives working in hospitals, driving buses, stocking warehouses, delivering groceries, and in other places of "essential" labor. Soon after, however, state officials ordered abatement sites shut. They clarified that only infrastructure maintenance and construction projects that facilitated healthcare workers' movements were classified as essential. Demolition and asbestos-abatement contractors were livid, since closing worksites interrupted a steady flow of profits. In a videocall where abatement contractors tried unsuccessfully to sway public officials to restart abatements, one contractor managed to share his screen and show a video of a building toppling over—seemingly of its own accord. It unleashed a flood of dust.[62] The contractor grumbled that, absent asbestos abatement, "That's probably deadly dust flying everywhere. Our guys are essential to protecting life. People get mesothelioma from that dust." Officials stood fast in their decision that abatement laborers should remain at home.

Suspensions of airborne hazards are a perennial site for understanding how struggles for environmental justice come into being. Science and technology studies scholars Chloe Ahmann and Alison Kenner observe, "We find that it is often something in the air that prompts people to advocate for change."[63] For instance, charting connections between dust clouds, gritty residues, and painful breathing enabled people to galvanize successful calls for the closure of asbestos mines. This even happened in places like the United States where industrial actors slowed wholesale bans on asbestos use. Likewise, in a moment when people reached for bandanas, trash bags, plexiglass, and other improvised barriers, abatement laborers had high-quality respirators, gloves, Tyvek coveralls, duct tape, and plastic sheeting ready at hand. Put differently, laborers appeared among the most well-protected of anyone to face pandemic uncertainties. Contractors marshaled these protections and the specter of carcinogenic asbestos in their attempts to keep laborers on the clock and generating revenue. But as Rayshawn and his fellow laborers were intimately familiar, there are stakes to holding hazards at bay. The same plasticated boundaries of critical barriers that kept people on the outside safe from blasts of asbestos-laden particulate also concentrated those same fibers inside worksites. Working rhythms attuned to the regulatory insistence that not a single asbestos fiber pass beyond a decontamination chamber enrolled workers' bodies as release valves for making that possible. As ever, technological promises of protection were filtered through distinctively human relations.

Early pandemic waves crashed hard in Detroit. Like carcinogenic dust clouds on abatement sites, novel contagion cast into relief how privileged people are better insulated than most, even if we feel just as unprotected.[64] Detroiters filled hospital wards and morgue freezers while the residents of adjacent majority-white, wealthier polities emerged from periods at home relatively unscathed. Observers with credentials in public health and infectious disease blamed the city's Blackness for this disparity. Reflecting false claims made about majority-Black places in the United States and elsewhere, they suggested that Detroiters' racialized social values, genetic ancestries, skin pigmentations, and educational attainment made them uniquely "vulnerable" an emergent viral threat.[65] Of course, disparate infection and mortality rates were not produced by the mere existence of racial demographics. Rather, they reflected how those demographics have been—and continue to be—harnessed into stratified conditions of labor, housing, and environmental exposure.[66] Those of us who Zoomed into meetings from improvised home offices could do so specifically because of people whose face-to-face engagements kept energy, food, and other life-supporting systems operational. This relationship has a manifestly racist logic, one in which the comfortable well-being of the racially privileged is propped up by "essential" labor that subjects racially devalued people to harm. Demographically, there might be exceptions—people like Maureen and Chris whose positions and identities invert expectations. But their experiences serve to reinforce rather than contradict how racism shapes lungs by virtue of where they breathe.

Following processes of locating and removing asbestos-containing materials in advance of demolition highlights how antiblack outcomes become routinized within systems that also protect Black people from harm. Movements to address racist distributions of environmental contamination often begin with calls to better protect people and places who bear the brunt of systemic violence. Against the atmospherics of racial capitalism, this means fortifying the lifeworlds of Black, Indigenous, and colonized people.[67] While imperfect, state-mediated regulations have been crucial in bending hazards away from taken-for-granted sinks of chemical violence.[68] As Detroiters experienced, in the absence of regulatory scrutiny, demolition contractors flooded their neighborhoods with aerosolized contaminants, including but not limited to asbestos fibers. It was only under threat of regulatory enforcement that sheets of plastic were taped over windows and around door frames to protect the places where Black and Latine Detroiters lived from becoming the landing ground for asbestos particulates. But plastic barriers and regulatory procedures that promised to keep "our residents and the environment" safe during demolitions did not eliminate the antiblack skew of asbestos exposure. Protecting Detroit's majority Black residents was made possible by focusing those harms upon the majority-Black workforce of asbestos-abatement laborers.

Make no mistake, environmental health regulations do important work. In the absence of federal statutes and state enforcement, demolitions in Detroit would likely have distributed carcinogens through city neighborhoods in addition to the lungs of workers. But following how existing regulations channel the flight of asbestos threads brings into focus how technological systems that some of us inhabit as protective—regulations, respirators, plastics, and so on—are too often steeped in antiblack compromises. Regulatory processes and their associated interventions are always already political processes.[69] They shape who, what, where, and when is protected, as well as who, what, where, and when is exposed. Plastic pollution researcher Max Liboiron notes how evidence-based struggles to mitigate unevenly distributed environmental violence are shot through with compromises. Liboiron details how actions that seem necessary to preventing injustice can also serve to "reinforce and reproduce the structures of power and essentialism they are designed to resist."[70] In the case of regulatory controls targeted at asbestos, the very procedures that regulators implement in the hope of preventing building demolitions from compounding racially unequal health outcomes are also the source of racially unequal occupational conditions. Despite intentions to the contrary, asbestos protections still produce racist outcomes. They reproduce a status quo that pollutes city lungs while keeping suburb lungs protected. Asking who and where is made to contend with hazardous materials to make environments safe for the rest of us is essential to understanding whether regulatory procedures rework or reinforce structures of power.

In other contexts, asbestos-abatement worksites might have become places where people demanded changes to routinized environmental harm. Yet for abatement laborers like Rayshawn, choking down dust as a condition of their jobs did not spark a collective movement. Perhaps it was something workers discussed among themselves behind critical barriers. But workplace hazards did not provoke industrial actions or even complaints when beseeched by regulatory staff. Especially for people channeled into abatement labor by way of the carceral state, losing steady compensation at a living wage carried other significant risks. Despite the absence of public struggle, the rhythms of abatement—building critical barriers, putting on respirators, taking them off, ripping through buildings, inhaling, exhaling—did political work. Abatement laborers knew in detail how particulates gusting through worksites could harm them, and worksites became places where workers considered the stakes of inequitable exposures. Rayshawn's differentiation between sheltered suburb lungs in need of protection from asbestos and hardened city lungs that could bear the brunt of further damage captures what many saw from their experiences. They diagnosed fallout patterns that fortified privileged locations by routing harmful materials into places already too familiar with their burdens. Worker observations might not have bubbled into outward demands, but their views appraise how their own exposure made it possible for others to breathe freely. Doing so provides critical vantage on how regulatory barriers that materialized good-faith promises of protection were also structures that further entrenched antiblack conditions.

SIX

SOIL

Jay texted me the evening he found soil testing results in his mailbox: "You know people who deal w bad stuff in dirt? We got some." Attached to the message was an image of a laboratory analysis showing that soil Jay had submitted contained significant levels of lead, barium, and other hazards. A Black man in his thirties, Jay shared a large house with his partner, Aubrey, their two children, and few roommates. Grassy lots filled most of the blocks around their west side home—the cumulative results of decades of demolitions. That spring, the household had begun making plans to cultivate a vegetable garden on the lot immediately adjacent to their home. A handful of neighbors who were already growing food on the surrounding blocks eagerly chimed in with advice, as well as printed copies of gardening resource guides distributed by a nonprofit that provides technical assistance to Detroit's home gardeners. Following the first piece of advice from the guide, Jay and Aubrey had dug up palmfuls of soil from the two empty lots next to their home, sealed them in plastic bags, and shipped them to a university extension laboratory. When the laboratory staff emailed Jay their findings, they included a warning against planting directly in ground that contained elevated levels of lead and heavy metals. To avoid consuming contaminated fruits, vegetables, and herbs, it recommended planting in containers filled with less hazardous soils or finding alternate locations.

What Jay and Aubrey learned about the sedimented conditions around their home was hardly unique. Random soil testing following demolitions often surfaced evidence of hazardous ground, even when building removal contractors were found to have used "clean soil."[1] Yet the distribution of hazards was variable, with the ground containing different suspensions of materials from one lot to the next.[2] Sometimes, Detroiters who opened emails and envelopes containing laboratory reports received news that their samples "did not meet thresholds for concern" for any one of dozens of possible toxicants. But they sometimes did, most commonly for lead, a heavy metal linked to all manner of health difficulties for people who consume it.[3] To be sure, some aspects of leaded soils indexed the lingering effects of leaded gasoline, which circulated lead particles near roadways across the United States until it was phased out in the late 1970s and '80s. Yet the highly irregular and uneven distribution of lead in Detroit's soils following demolitions points to other sources too, especially layers of lead paint that had once covered walls and siding.[4] Excavators smashing through walls transformed paint into dust that settled into surrounding soil. Other industrial toxicants flagged in testing reports—materials like barium, PCBs, diesel, and vinyl chloride—most likely arrived suspended in the soil that contractors used to fill excavated basements before seeding sites with grass.

Simultaneously geographic and geologic archives, soils articulate complex, relational histories of place. People who work the ground to make plants grow know this well, including Detroiters who contribute to the city's long-standing practices of subsistence gardening.[5] In attending to the contents of soils, they learn how various qualities and suspensions do not reflect flattened understandings of territorial units—residential, commercial, industrial, and so on.[6] PCBs, for example, are industrial toxicants, but they end up in the soils of residential districts in the wake of demolitions. As environmental anthropologist Kristina Lyons learns through engagement with Amazonian soil specialists who contend with toxic fallout from a hemispheric war on drugs, soils "hold in tension and articulate the varied rhythms and intensities of geologic, human, microbial, and vegetal materials and temporalities."[7] Likewise, among geologists writing from the United States, soils are not backdrops of inert "nature" upon which "human" or "technological" activities play out; rather, they are "long-lived archival systems [that] accrue features over their lifetimes due to temporally variable soil-forming processes, natural and human forced."[8] Put simply, soil is an amalgamation of organic and anthropogenic matter, water, air, organisms, and weathered materials—which includes bedrock and other substrates to be sure, but also bricks, concrete, toxicants, wiring, and anything else buried beneath the surface.[9] Far from disrupting sedimentary processes, human-initiated processes like constructing and demolishing buildings are constitutive of them. Work crews and excavators add layers to records of inhabitation and disruption in which historical conditions are quite literally material.

Soil-testing reports like the one delivered to Jay trouble the conceit that demolitions produced a clean slate of grassy lots in the wake of racism and intersecting inequities. They also trouble the basic idea that demolitions sweep buildings entirely "away." As scholars and activists attuned to waste management practices know well, elsewhere is always somewhere.[10] For the most part, crews trucked off mangled chunks of empty buildings to sanitary landfills on Metro Detroit's peri-urban fringe.[11] Some particularly noxious elements pulled from factory grounds landed in industrial waste processing and storage facilities within the city limits. But the acts of ripping through structures with heavy machinery were also the mechanism through which hundreds of thousands of lead-painted walls could sediment into the ground.[12] Loads of topsoil and fill trucked in from supply yards across Southeast Michigan were themselves the vehicles for adding new toxicants into Detroit's neighborhoods (figure 6.1). The resulting landscapes made it apparent that demolitions could, for the most part, remove empty buildings from view. Yet parts of those structures remained. Empty buildings that indexed racist disappearances of people and industry had simply been transformed into contaminated soils that pointed to more straightforward conditions of environmental racism.

Aubrey and Jay had this transformation in mind as we walked a dozen lots where they hoped to build a garden—lots they now knew were all laced with lead, barium, and other hazards. Aubrey had lived in Detroit for almost four decades, practically her entire life. Most of it had been spent in a family home that relatives had purchased after relocating to Detroit from northern Mexico. Jay had grown up in a suburb just downriver from Detroit and moved to the city ten years before I met him, when he and Aubrey moved in together. Like most every Detroiter I spoke with, Aubrey and Jay knew well how their city's empty buildings had come into being. As we walked, they named how evictions, plant closures, and disappeared neighbors were bound up in processes that had extracted people and industry from Detroit and moved them elsewhere. What set the pair's historical

FIGURE 6.1. A sign warning that a demolition company "left toxic waste here."

Photo by the author.

narration apart from others was the way Jay brought it back to the soil. Grinning, he gestured widely at the grassy expanse and imagined: "They take down the buildings and we get a bunch of toxic dirt. I'd really like to be able to take this dirt and give it to the people who made it. Maybe trade it out with those folks living out in Livonia or Birmingham. Wouldn't that be some shit? Make it rain barium in the suburbs!" We all doubled over laughing at this prospect.

When Detroiters like Jay and Aubrey worked to cultivate gardens on lots opened by demolitions, they navigated unevenly contaminated soils. The conditions they encountered, ones of sedimented toxicities concentrated in a majority-Black and poor neighborhood, recall conditions that birthed the environmental justice movement in the United States and elsewhere. Hard-won legal protections against unequal environments mattered little in the aftermath of demolitions. In the limited instances when state actors could remove contaminated soils from Detroit neighborhoods, those sediments never traveled far before coming to rest in hazardous waste storage facilities on the other side of town. From one corner of the majority-Black city into another. More typically, toxic soils remained in the ground, with gardeners accommodating them by growing food in raised beds or piles of compost rather than directly in the earth. Eventually, after several years of planning and sampling soils from around Detroit's metropolitan region, Jay and Aubrey dug up the hazardous ground below their gardens and swapped it out with relatively cleaner soil they sourced from a majority-white, wealthy suburb. For the household, this meant being able to plant sweet potatoes and greens in the ground without fearing that they would become contaminated with lead or barium. Making it rain barium in the suburbs transferred those hazards into places where comparatively privileged people lived.

Demolitions that leave behind soils laced with hazardous materials point to how inequitable systems do not disappear with a few swings of the excavator. Removing physical traces of racist disinvestment can amplify the "racial and spatial politics that render certain bodies and landscapes pollutable" that environmental historian Traci Brynne Voyles calls "wastelanding."[13] At the same time, Jay's provocation to "make it rain barium in the suburbs" suggests how other spatial politics are possible. The work Aubrey, Jay, and their neighbors undertook to carve out less toxic growing conditions on their block provides an example of what it can take to bring those politics into being. Through extensive soil testing, they develop a granular understanding of where and for whom conditions of structural racism take hold, complicating taken-for-granted divisions between Detroit and its suburbs. In so doing, they also illuminate how commitments to fully insulating everyone from environmental burdens are not enough to shift material conditions of structural racism to produce something more equitable. Even when brought into force, those commitments do not disrupt the structurally unequal ways that protections and harms have already literally settled into place. As people like Jay and Aubrey transform contaminated soils into safe growing conditions, they challenge us to grapple with how, rather than protection, evening out inequities entails building up systems in which burdens are more equitably shared.

SOMEWHERE ELSE

The contemporary environmental justice movement in the United States was built from soil. In 1978, residents across North Carolina reported oily substances coating grassy embankments along state roadways. State investigators identified oils containing PCBs (polychlorinated biphenyls) at the edges of more than 240 miles of roadside. They also traced them back to a firm that used PCBs to make electrical equipment. In attempts to avoid the costs of disposing production wastes in compliance with recently enacted environmental regulations, the firm had hired contractors to spray more than 31,000 gallons of waste along state highways.[14] In people and other animals, consuming, inhaling, or even touching PCB-containing materials is linked to cancers and other serious health effects.[15] North Carolina state officials, with approval from the recently created federal Environmental Protection Agency, determined that the best course of action was to dig up contaminated soils and inter them in a specially constructed landfill. Without informing nearby residents, state actors acquired farmland in a majority-Black corner of Warren County, North Carolina, as the landfill site. When surrounding communities learned of the landfill plan, they began a multiyear campaign against dumping 60,000 tons of hazardous earth in their vicinity—what they termed "an unwarranted act of toxic aggression" on politically and economically disenfranchised towns.[16] Groups of activists held off the landfill with legal challenges and direct actions that blocked trucks ferrying PCB-laden soils.[17] After four years, police cleared activists from roadways to allow landfill operations to begin.

Warren County activists failed to block contaminated soils from being interred in their towns, but they succeeded in establishing a coalition that sought to understand whether conditions experienced in their majority-Black and poor county were of a piece with those occurring elsewhere. At the time, federal agencies like EPA did not track the demographics of people living around hazardous waste disposal locations, but in the years following the Warren County protests, researchers combed through datasets for themselves. They found that across income groups, Black, Indigenous, Latine, and Asian-identified people were significantly more likely to live near hazardous waste disposal sites than white-identified people.[18] Formal reports provided crucial evidence for naming "environmental racism" as such.[19] At the same time, their findings came as little surprise to people who contended with the violence of these sites in their daily lives, especially toxic air, water, and foodways.[20] The magnitude of campaigns powered by lived experiences of environmental racism and injustice demonstrated how predominantly white-led conservation movements to preserve majority-white neighborhoods from pollution obscured acute and chronic conditions of hazardous waste production and disposal that left communities of color and impoverished places exposed.[21] Despite decades of struggle, in the United States and elsewhere, these same communities and places continue to be the expected dumping grounds of hazards.[22] Meanwhile, the places where racially privileged people, especially white people, live remain the most protected from harm.

Administrative standards for environmental justice in the United States work to enact conditions in which "all people, regardless of income, race, color, national origin, Tribal affiliation, or disability [are] fully protected from disproportionate and adverse human health and environmental effects (including risks) and hazards."[23] Standards like this are contested and often set aside in the name of financial expediency.[24] Consider what almost happened when a shortage of readily available soil began driving up the costs of demolitions in Detroit. At the time, demolition contractors could fill excavated holes and grade over sites using only soils that met the standards for residential construction projects. One demolition administrator explained to me, "We want Detroiters to get dirt that's clean enough to be in a suburban yard." A state-appointed financial manager suggested reducing demolition costs by allowing demolition contractors to use earth drawn from highway construction projects—material that the state government would provide at no charge. Given that roadside soil is invariably laced with hydrocarbons, plastics, pesticides, salts, and other hazards laid down by year after year of routine traffic, relocating it to residential areas was typically not allowed due to known health risks. As demolition administrators explained in meetings with financial authorities, spreading highway soil following building removals would subject residents in majority-Black Detroit to a lower level of environmental protection than people in the majority-white suburbs. Ultimately, administrators did not approve highway soils for use.

Detroiters often asked me where the mixture of brown and black earth that contractors spread in place of demolished buildings came from. Was it safe? Should people worry? For their part, demolition agencies maintained that administrative oversight ensured removing empty buildings created lots where it was safe for Detroiters to grow food. And yet, as years passed, it became evident that administrative offices did not have sufficient staff to track down soil sources noted on thousands of individual load tickets. After Detroiters documented certain contractors filling basement cavities with construction waste before layering on topsoil and grass seed, municipal staff began to scrutinize their work more carefully. When probing into the ground revealed buried debris, administrators ordered soil-quality analyses for every site where the contractors in question had worked. For one contractor, soil tests on 200 recently completed demolitions found 87 with concentrations of hazardous materials like lead, arsenic, asbestos, and PCBs that exceeded regulatory standards for industrial emissions.[25] For those 87 sites, administrators brought in new contractors to dig a rectangular cavity across the surface of each lot and fill it with soil that had been screened for contaminants. Whenever situations like this happened, administrators insisted that fining or suspending contractors for not following specified procedures would prevent similar acts going forward.[26] It did not.[27]

Nevertheless, for immediate neighbors, the removal and replacement of contaminated earth from demolition sites was a meaningful, small-scale environmental justice victory. Consider Marta, a southwest Detroiter in her sixties who filmed contractors dumping bricks, drywall, and other debris into the depression created by the removal of an apartment building near her home. Marta had sent the clip to demolition agencies and state regulators but did not anticipate a response. Those same offices had proven unable to prevent firms from storing uncovered, unpermitted piles of hazardous waste in other parts of her neighborhood. As Marta put it to me wryly, "They've been dumping stuff on us for centuries. Why would this be different?"[28] And yet, when a team of excavator operators and laborers began to dig up the site of the demolished apartment building, it suggested that a different response was possible. Marta and I watched as the crew excavated a six-foot-deep hole across the lot surface. Workers funneled excavated earth into white plastic sacks, each one containing around thirty cubic feet, before stacking them on a flatbed truck to await transportation to their next destination. A week or so later, Marta texted me, "THEY PUT IN NEW DIRT!" Earlier that day, an employee from the municipal demolition office had knocked on Marta's door to thank her for her video and drop off a copy of the laboratory testing report for the newly delivered soil. It showed a *U* for "undetected" next to hundreds of possible contaminants.

Contaminated soils unearthed from Marta's block remained nearby. Flatbeds stacked with sacks of soil drove for a little over nine miles before arriving at a row of warehouses. There, workers unloaded the plastic sacks for processing at a facility whose corporate owners promised to process hazardous materials for long-term storage. As at similar facilities in Detroit and elsewhere, its neighbors were mostly Black and impoverished.[29] Corporate documents suggested it was possible for their facility to safely remove PCBs, lead, and other toxins from sediments so that the soil could be returned for use in road construction. And yet, those same documents showed discharges of arsenic and mercury, among other hazards into the air, water, and soil in neighborhoods where residents contended with health problems associated with exposure to these materials.[30] Despite ongoing campaigns against the operation of hazardous waste storage and processing facilities in Detroit, they continue to receive state approval to expand on the grounds that they are necessary to protect the city's populace from environmental harm. Corporate spokespeople successfully argued that expansions were essential to handle the steady stream of toxicants flowing in from production lines and pre-demolition asbestos-abatement sites.[31] So, even as Marta and her neighbors were excited by the removal of hazardous materials from their blocks, the stakes of that action required compounding environmental burdens in another corner of the city.

Industrial toxicants like PCBs and asbestos cannot be eliminated. Once brought into the world, they can only be moved around. Even in the absence of state and national environmental regulations, demolition contractors could abide by local requirements that they draw from approved soil sources and refrain from dumping debris into excavated cavities. Whenever Detroiters like Marta celebrated contaminated soils being replaced with cleaner ground, the replacements were the result of demolition administrators enforcing contractual requirements—sometimes but not always in response to pressure from city residents. Nevertheless, even as administrators could call in workers to dig up hazardous ground from one Detroit neighborhood, the requisite destination for bags of hazardous soils was a waste storage and processing infrastructure that was the source of health concerns for Detroiters in another neighborhood. The concentration of hazardous waste facilities in Detroit, especially in some of the most impoverished neighborhoods of a majority-Black city reflects circumstances that are nearly identical to the leaky PCB landfill that North Carolina regulators built in Warren County more than fifty years ago. To this end, moves to scoop up hazardous materials in the wake of building removals trouble the notion that making people "fully protected" from contamination can be accomplished by removing hazards from their immediate environment. Alleviating inequitable distributions of environmental hazards demands putting those hazards somewhere. It bears repeating that elsewhere is always somewhere.

ACCOMMODATING HAZARDS

For the most part, hazardous soils remained exactly where they were in Detroit. In 2015, an estimated 8.8 percent of children in Detroit experienced symptoms of lead poisoning. To put this in context, international outrage flared that same year when it surfaced that at least 5 percent of children in Flint, Michigan, were lead poisoned after state officials demanded cost-saving changes to the municipal water system.[32] Lead is a naturally occurring element that serves no physiological purpose, and no concentration of lead is known to be safe in human bodies.[33] As lead molecules build up in human blood and tissue, they interfere with cell replication, with consequences including fatigue, pain, memory loss, and organ failure. These concerns are heightened in children since lead poisoning alters cognitive and developmental trajectories, with ramifications across the life course. In Flint and other cities, lead leached into municipal water supplies from pipes and fittings, touching off subterranean efforts to locate and replace corroded service lines. In Detroit, however, municipal health workers linked elevated levels of lead in residents' blood to demolitions that pulverized lead-painted walls.[34] Even when contractors diligently followed requirements to soak buildings with fire hoses to minimize heavy metal emissions during removal, swirls of lead dust settled into soils around four hundred feet from their points of origin.[35] Subsequent efforts to address sedimented lead relied on people living in those neighborhoods implementing soil amendment practices that could accommodate but never eliminate lead below their feet.

Leaded soils exemplify how toxicities are coproduced through overlapping natural and human forces. Alongside ten other heavy metals, lead occurs naturally at low levels in soils around the present-day state of Michigan. It forms part of a peculiar geologic background in an expected range of 0.5 to 38.9 parts per million (ppm). But lead also precipitates from human-created materials that are deposited into the ground in much higher concentrations. Leaded paint flaking off the outside of a building, for example, can produce concentrations of several hundred ppm or more. Industrial waste incinerators are regularly surrounded by sediments with concentrations of more than 2,000 ppm. Given the collision of geologic background, industrial facilities, and demolished lead-painted walls, soil samples submitted by Detroit gardeners commonly tested positive for lead.[36] For results between 40 and 320 ppm, environmental scientists suggested people could safely grow food if they planted in raised beds and containers rather than in the ground.[37] One in five samples exceeded that range, and gardeners were encouraged to avoid those sites entirely. The twenty lots closest to Aubrey and Jay's house contained suspensions of lead between 98 and 390 ppm. Significant variation between sites that were so close together marked how the presence of lead in Detroit's soil was expected but the specifics of its concentration could be a surprise.[38] Magnitudes of lead reflected the peculiar circumstances of individual lots, especially paints used on surrounding buildings, the prevailing winds during demolition, and whether workers had tilled new soil into the earth or spread it on top.

Aubrey and Jay's encounters with lead-contaminated soil as they worked to establish a subsistence garden were emblematic of the ways Detroiters navigated such terrains. The pair were particularly concerned by suggestions that they should avoid bringing shoes and clothing inside after working on lead-contaminated earth and should discourage their two children from playing on it entirely. Thankfully, routine tests conducted as part of early childhood medical visits showed neither of their children were lead poisoned. Still, pamphlets delivered with soil-testing results and from medical providers warned that playing in leaded soils or tracking them into the house was a common vector for lead poisoning. Aubrey made several calls to the Detroit Land Bank Authority and various municipal offices to request the replacement of contaminated soil. Clicking through recent invoices, a DLBA representative found that contractors for recent demolitions had submitted analytic reports showing the soils they trucked in were clean. As the administrative staffer explained, the agency could order replacements only with proof contractors had deliberately dumped toxic earth. Because that evidence did not exist, Aubrey and Jay were left with a choice between leaving the contaminated soil in place or paying a firm to handle this work on their own. At an estimated cost of $7,500 for a single lot, removal and replacement was financially out of reach for most Detroiters, including Jay and Aubrey. Despite knowledge of sedimented hazards on their blocks, they learned no administrative actions would be forthcoming to address them.

On social media, Jay spotted a workshop on how to safely grow food despite contaminated soil, offered by an organization established to support Detroit's household and community gardeners. With a handful of other Detroiters, we gathered one afternoon under a high tunnel, nestled on a corner of a community farm on the near east side. An early spring rain peppered the top of the plastic tunnel as we looked out upon a block covered with parallel earthen mounds. Each mound was just under a foot high, two feet wide, and a hundred feet long, with the spaces between filled by woodchips. People huddled close as Gayle, a Black Detroiter in her fifties and one of the farm's most experienced members, explained how those rows allowed people living in the surrounding blocks to cultivate thousands of pounds of produce on soils that were laced with significant concentrations of lead and arsenic, among other contaminants. Gayle described how some years before, she and some neighbors had gotten their start with a single lot acquired from a municipal office following a demolition. Soil testing conducted by the organization that sponsored the workshop had shown lead concentrations exceeding 300 ppm. To create a buffer, the neighbors had followed an established practice of covering the existing ground with cardboard before adding rows of clean soil and compost.[39] Gayle distributed a how-to guide that included locations where Detroiters could source lead-free cardboard, soil, compost, and woodchips at low to no cost.

A month or so later, I spent a weekend working alongside Jay, Aubrey, and their roommates to build a set of mounded garden beds on one of the lots adjacent to their home. It was one where a building had been leveled in 2012, and laboratory analyses indicated the presence of lead, barium, and asbestos. Following Gayle's instructions, Jay had picked up stacks of produce packing boxes out of a grocery store recycling container. A roommate had procured a load of no-cost woodchips from a pile public works employees had created by shredding downed trees. Aubrey had ordered piles of a compost-rich growing mix from an agriculture supply house that delivered to city residents for a reduced price. After flattening a double layer of cardboard over the lot, we shoveled three mounds of soil into place, separating them with woodchips. The mounds ran the length of the lot and would soon be overflowing with beans, tomatoes, squash, and cucumbers. Jay and Aubrey's children, who were one and four years old at the time, spent the weekend at Aubrey's grandmother's house a mile away. As Aubrey explained it to me, given that so many people would be busy preparing the garden site, it would have been difficult to impossible for them to keep the children from digging around in the soil for themselves. As an added precaution, the entire household removed shoes and work clothes before entering their house to avoid tracking hazardous sediments inside.

The raised bed garden next to Aubrey and Jay's house resembles thousands of others across Detroit. Whether in freestanding mounds or surrounded by wood, brick, or stone, raised beds floated pockets of cleaner soil where people could grow food safely atop dangerous earth. During the first harvest season, Jay and I were plucking pole beans when he expressed frustration with this setup. He reiterated his previous imagination of trading out the contaminated soils around his home with what he presumed would be cleaner earth from wealthy, overwhelmingly white suburbs. Doing so would end the need for constant vigilance and concern about what might happen when dirt inevitably was carried away on shoes, tools, gloves, and hands. In Jay's words, "I don't want my kids to be afraid of the ground, you know? I want them to know it's safe. Like why do kids in Detroit have to deal with that when not everybody does?" On several occasions, I observed Aubrey and Jay leaping across garden beds when they spotted one of their offspring or other young children pulling up a stray corner of cardboard, prepared to push into the soil with their bare hands. Years later, the garden remained strong, powered by annual layers of compost and woodchips. But when Jay tested the soil beneath a still-decomposing layer of cardboard, the concentrations of lead and other hazardous materials were almost unchanged.

Gardens like the ones cultivated by Gayle and her neighbors or Aubrey and Jay's household quite literally sustain people. But they do not eliminate the uneven conditions of sedimented hazards that underlie them. When it comes to contaminated soils, cleaner earth piled atop layers of cardboard is a harm reduction strategy. It creates buffers atop the known, ongoing presence of sedimented hazards and prevents them from seeping into food or tagging along in residual dirt. In so doing, the kinds of strategies that Gayle modeled for others prevent conditions like lead poisoning, especially among children who are most likely to experience longer-term health issues from early-life exposures to toxicities. Aubrey and Jay illustrate the ways that Detroit's gardeners took up harm reduction strategies after learning of contaminated soils. Jay was not alone in relating to these strategies as necessary, if far from ideal. Like Jay, many Detroiters I encountered desired a more permanent, comprehensive means of removing elevated levels of lead from their surroundings, alongside arsenic, asbestos, barium, vinyl chloride, and other hazards that popped up on soil-testing reports from time to time. Sedimented hazards, as they understood, did not exist everywhere. They were specifically and unevenly concentrated, with sometimes granular variations from one lot to the next. In the absence of a systematic plan enacted by staff in a municipal office, state agency, or the land bank, Detroiters were left to their own devices to accommodate varying degrees of contamination that formed the material wakes of building removals.

SEDIMENTED PRIVILEGE

Jay could not shake the desire to grow plants directly in the ground without fear of imparting contaminants into the food his household grew or the people who ate it. For most of my time in Detroit, Jay worked installing stone countertops. This meant that, depending on the day, he was driving his small pickup truck to jobsites anywhere within a fifty-to-sixty-mile radius of his home. From time to time, Jay and his coworkers heaved granite, marble, and quartz slabs into place for kitchen and bathroom renovations in Detroit's middle-income enclaves and gentrifying city center. For the most part, however, the addresses where Jay worked were in suburbs where clients were significantly wealthier than the average city resident and often, though not always, white. Jay would tell me about recent jobsites while we worked in his household's garden. Many were routine orders where do-it-yourselfers were swapping out existing countertops with new ones. Occasionally they involved opulent new builds with stone slabs spanning multiple kitchen islands or covering walls from floor to ceiling. Sitting back in a lawn chair, Jay noted how smooth roads, verdant lawns, and expansive parks around his worksites contrasted with the potholes, scraggly grass, and disinvestment from civic infrastructure around his home.[40] It seemed commonsensical that the soil beneath these tidy, suburban aesthetics would be cleaner than that in Detroit. But Jay lacked evidence to back up this claim.

Laboratory analyses of soil contents provided a method for Jay to test his hypothesis. He suggested, "I think we should test every lot in the city. Just so the people know what's in the environment." He and Aubrey received one no-cost soil assessment each year from an organization that provided these assessments to city residents. Running additional samples cost around $30 apiece, something that made Jay's interest in a regional perspective on sediments prohibitively expensive. This changed after another neighborhood gardener boosted a social media post from a team of environmental scientists at an out-of-state university into Jay's timeline. The scientists were undertaking a nationwide study of "urban soils"—which to them meant any patch of ground within a metropolitan statistical area—and were seeking volunteers to send samples of the ground around their homes.[41]

People who signed up received testing instructions, a set of gloves and specimen bags, and a prepaid mailer. A month or so later, researchers would share a copy of their analytic report with the person who submitted the sample. Jay phoned a study coordinator, explained how his job took him all over Detroit's metropolitan sprawl, and asked if there was a maximum number of samples he could submit. The researcher agreed for Jay to submit as many as he could, so long as they were drawn from places he had permission to sample or from public lands, like parks and traffic medians.

Over the course of a few months, Jay used a small plastic shovel and sampling bags to package up earth from sixty-seven locations. They included a few from his household's gardens and ones from the backyards of houses where relatives lived in downriver suburbs. Those latter locations were traversed by the same industrial corridors that radiated outward from Detroit. For example, the backyard of the house where Jay's mother lived in Lincoln Park—a suburban town that abuts Detroit's southwestern corner—contained the highest lead concentrations of any samples Jay submitted. Testing reports also signaled significant concentrations of PCBs and hydrocarbons, among other hazardous materials. Like most of Detroit's suburban municipalities, when developers first built dwellings in Lincoln Park during the twentieth century, they designed them as fortified bastions of a particular kind of white, middle-class life.[42] Just like the parts of Detroit they border, dwellings in many of the city's adjacent suburbs were built within walking distance of plants producing steel, automobiles, and oil, and other industries. Proximity ensured that suburban residents, especially white men, had priority access to the highest-waged work in these facilities. Since the late-twentieth-century, those municipalities have shifted from being exclusively white, middle-class locations to being increasingly home to Black, Middle Eastern, and Latine residents. While some of the industrial facilities that once spilled from Southwest Detroit into adjacent suburbs have closed, many remain operational. As a result, when people like Jay's family made their homes in Detroit's inner-ring suburbs, they inherited a century of combined emissions from refineries, blast furnaces, and factories that had settled into the earth.

For Jay, one of the most surprising analytic reports came from a soil sample he collected from a public playground in one of the Grosse Pointes—a chain of predominantly white, eastside suburbs where the typical household earned almost $200,000 each year. The analytic results emailed to Jay stated that the sample contained traces of 4,4-dichlorodiphenyltrichloroethane, a pesticide that you might know as DDT. While the concentration did not meet state reporting thresholds, the report recommended caution, especially for children who might inhale or consume the earth. This analytic report, as well as a few others, pushed against Jay's initial assumption that the sedimentary conditions in wealthy, majority-white places were necessarily free from hazards. Indeed, the lush green aesthetic that Jay initially took as an indicator of environmental safety is almost always made possible by chemical violence that removes weeds and insects from the scene.[43] That violence lingers. DDT was removed from use in the United States in 1972 and incrementally decomposes. And yet, molecular chains of DDT remain present in soil decades after it was last used.

More than half the samples Jay submitted for analysis yielded laboratory reports with the phrase "Did not meet thresholds for concern" printed next to dozens of possible hazards. This means the bags of earth Jay had mailed to university researchers were free not only from human-produced PCBs and hydrocarbons but also from elements like lead, barium, and mercury that are part of the naturally occurring background of soils in the region. Such absences are indicative of building practices that substitute existing soil with soil previously screened for possible contaminants. People who made use of newly built dwellings, parks, and facilities could do so without concern for negative side effects from their encounters with the ground. When marked on a map, most of the neutral samples formed a collar near the perimeter of Detroit's metropolitan region. They came from municipalities with names like Plymouth, Northville, Birmingham, and Harrison Township. Without exception, all these places were ones in which the median household income was four or more times that of the typical Detroit household. Without exception, all these places were ones in which upward of 90 percent of residents identified as white. To this end, the shovelfuls of earth Jay scooped up from across Detroit's metropolitan region did not reflect a simple binary between majority-Black and impoverished locations having contaminated soils and majority-white, wealthy ones being free from contaminants. They nevertheless confirmed his expectation that areas with relatively nontoxic ground would be overwhelmingly wealthy and white.

Jay encouraged other Detroiters to submit samples from their yards and gardens to university researchers for no-cost analysis. One of his recruits was a white couple in their thirties who were relocating to Northwest Detroit from Ann Arbor.

As Jay told it, on his visit to their home to make a template for new kitchen counters, he overheard the pair planning a backyard vegetable garden. To his surprise, they had never considered that there might be any number of hazardous materials in the ground where they were planning to grow food. As anthropologist Melissa Checker learned from conversations with environmental justice activists in New York, it is often the case that racially and economically privileged transplants are unaware of harmful conditions that are all too familiar to their neighbors.[44] For example, Black and Latine organizers who were longtime Brooklynites worried about the well-being of typically white and wealthy people who flocked to renovated waterfront apartments seemingly without concern for nearby facilities that processed radioactive materials. When Jay returned to the same Northwest Detroit home to install finished countertops some three months later, he found seedlings planted in two-foot-tall garden beds arranged in the backyard. His clients thanked him profusely for raising their attention to the prospect of contaminated soils. Despite the healthy appearance of bright green grass, the ground below contained concentrations of lead, vinyl chloride, and other hazards.

With sixty-seven sampling locations, Jay complicated a simplistic binary which might have assumed that, as a majority-Black, poorer city, Detroit's soils would necessarily be more hazardous than those in surrounding suburbs. Testing reports Jay received from university researchers gave evidence to the ways neither Detroit's ground nor that of its surrounding suburbs formed a homogenous block. Sometimes, the earth dug up within the city limits did not contain significant cause for concern. Likewise, the embodied privileges of wealth and racial identity concentrated among suburban residents did not always buffer against the history and presence of emissions that spew from industrial facilities and exhaust spray. Manicured turf and other aesthetics are calling cards of decisions that exclusive, lily-white suburbs have made to cover their surroundings with durably toxic chains of chemical pesticides. Despite contamination across places coded "city" and "suburb," the only samples Jay took that returned testing reports without signs of any hazards whatsoever, including naturally occurring elements, were mostly ones he had picked up from public parks in suburban municipalities in which residents were almost exclusively wealthy and white. The samples that Jay collected gave a complex view of the interplay between whiteness, wealth, and interactions with contaminated soils. Specifically, he found evidence of the ways socially constructed identities and locations did not register as a generalized aggregate of protection from or exposure to hazardous soil. On the contrary, samples reflected the somewhat uneven way in which privilege and protection are literally sedimented.

RAINING BARIUM IN THE SUBURBS

On an afternoon when I joined Aubrey to help her prepare the garden for spring plantings, she had printouts of soil-testing reports spread out across the table in the spotlessly cleaned kitchen. Aubrey joked that she had found the perfect places to plant early season potatoes. The soils were rich in organic matter, had no discernable presence of contamination, and slightly acidic in ways that would provide an optimal growing environment. One key difficulty was that the spots were in outer-ring suburbs, the closest of which was some twenty miles from Aubrey and Jay's home. The layers of cardboard, compost, and mulch that Aubrey, Jay, and their roommates had built up over the surface of their gardens had created a protective buffer and kept lead, asbestos, and other hazards several inches below. For this reason, the household did not have reservations about planting corn, tomatoes, and beans in their garden. But produce like potatoes and carrots that grew directly in the ground remained off limits. Instead, Aubrey planned to sow them in large plastic bins filled with earth certified as nonhazardous by a garden center. As we finished drilling drainage holes in the bottom of the bins, I asked Aubrey how she felt about the additional cost of growing potatoes in uncontaminated soil. "I mean, there's only one other option," she noted, recalling Jay's suggestion about swapping out the ground entirely. "We can go rain that barium dirt in the suburbs."

Over the years, making it rain barium in the suburbs became a refrain in Aubrey and Jay's household, as well as among others who tended household garden plots in their neighborhood. It commonly emerged whenever someone completed the additional steps needed to safely grow food despite toxic ground, especially the annual routines of spreading yet another protective layer of cardboard and compost over a lead-contaminated lot or preparing containers to grow root vegetables. The trouble was not that people did not know where they could procure cleaner fill. Jay's contributions to soil sampling research had made that clear. Making this vision a reality seemed logistically impossible, however. By Jay's calculations, swapping the upper two feet of earth on a single lot would take require filling the bed of his pickup nearly one hundred times in both directions. Given work and care obligations, that would likely take several months, even if neighbors could chip in to help. For these reasons, quips about making it rain barium in the suburbs remained a redistributive imaginary in which a handful of Detroiters talked about the prospect of dredging up hazards from their neighborhood and raining them down in majority-white suburbs.

The conditions created by the pandemic respiratory illness sweeping the globe presented an unexpected possibility. In early 2020, Jay and Aubrey, alongside tens of millions of working people in the United States, summarily lost their jobs. Though she could no longer do hair and nails inside the beauty shop where she normally worked, Aubrey took clients in their backyard to make sure they could cover rent. But Jay was left entirely without the prospect of paid construction work during the first weeks of the pandemic. One afternoon, I answered a video call from Aubrey. She flipped the camera to show soil and grass cascading from the bed of their truck and into a trench. Panning around, I could see a space I recognized as part of their neighborhood garden site, but with a cavity a couple feet deep spreading across part of the surface. Jay, clad in a bandana and neon-yellow safety vest, was using a broom to push the mass forward and over the edge into a trench. In the background, I could see two other people, also in bandanas and safety vests, using shovels to scoop the upturned lot into large plastic bins. Once Jay had broomed out the truck bed, people began dumping bins over the sides to fill it with earth once again. After a few minutes, the group tied a blue tarp over the bed and drove away.

In subsequent conversations, I learned that twenty people had worked for three days to replace the ground on two lots. Earlier soil testing had identified concentrations of lead in those sites, as well as asbestos and other toxicants. The team drew replacement earth from various locations that previous sampling showed as having safe growing conditions. They included a large pile of soil excavated to build a home in the far reaches of the metropolitan region. In a significant surprise, the developer who had hired Jay's company to install countertops in the addition even suggested Jay could scatter garden remnants across the dozens of woody acres surrounding the house. Like me, Aubrey, Jay, and their neighbors could only guess why a white suburbanite would make this suggestion about soils laced with hazards. Some suspected the developer doubted the piles of brownish soil were truly dangerous. Others suggested that he did not think the sedimented hazards would affect him.[45] Regardless of the reason, the neighbors' work successfully removed and replaced the upper layers of two previously contaminated lots. By the time Jay and many of his neighbors were called back to work, they had sectioned the rectangles of relatively clean soil into smaller plots to be shared among households that contributed to exchanging the soil. The plots offered locations for cultivating carrots, radishes, sweet potatoes, and other roots directly in the ground without fear of drawing up lead and other hazards.

The landscapes that Aubrey, Jay, and their neighbors created were rare. In the decade I spent talking with Detroiters about their attempts to cultivate gardens on lots emptied by demolitions, I commonly encountered people who imagined swapping out contaminated soil with cleaner fill. Jay and Aubrey are among the few people I met who pulled it off.[46] More often, Detroit's gardeners followed the same practices that Aubrey, Jay, and their neighbors employed in other gardens. They built raised beds, planted in containers, or stacked up alternating layers of cardboard and compost to insulate themselves and their food supplies from soils laden with hazardous materials like lead and petrochemicals. Such routines mitigated harms, but the existence of chemical residues just below the surface remained a cause for concern. In contrast, exchanging the upper two feet of soil from two lots removed those residues from Detroiters' lives. Unlike conventional environmental remediation practices, which would have shifted those hazards into storage and processing facilities in other majority-Black, Latine, and poor neighborhoods, Aubrey and Jay worked to distribute leaded soils into other possible locations. Rather than allowing contaminated earth to compound among the same people who had borne it for some time, they set their sights on places where people were already relatively protected from harm.

During a video call some months after the soil exchange, I spoke with Aubrey as she pulled a crop of fall beets from one of the squares of uncontaminated earth. At a corner of the frame, I could see her youngest child—four at the time—drop a dirt-encrusted beet into a basket before moving one of her now dirt-encrusted fingers to her mouth. Whereas I had previously seen Aubrey and Jay vault over raised beds to prevent children—theirs and others—from consuming garden dirt, Aubrey appeared entirely unconcerned. Golden-hour light illuminated Aubrey's face as she strode back to her house carrying her phone, child, and a basket of beets. I asked how it sat with her that creating nontoxic conditions for growing beets had required shifting hazards into places in the suburbs where other people might come across them. Aubrey was quiet as she maneuvered to get into her house. Once our conversation resumed, she held up one of the flyers that demolition teams distributed to warn surrounding residents about the possibility that dust created by building removals could contain aerosolized lead. As Aubrey put it, "We didn't empty out all those houses. The suburbs did. Why should we have to deal with it on our own? Isn't it fair for folks in the suburbs to deal with just a little bit?" Indeed, the contaminants Jay, Aubrey, and their neighbors exchanged with suburban soils were routinely allowed to remain in the ground around Detroiters' homes.

Aubrey did not feign innocence about the possible downstream consequences of transferring contaminated soils into suburban land as a condition of creating a few hundred square feet of relatively clean earth for people to grow food on her block. On the contrary, for her, more broadly distributing the sedimented hazards created by demolitions was part of the point. Recall the central objective of Jay's words when he initially imagined it raining barium in the suburbs, "I'd really like to be able to take this dirt and give it to the people who made it." Like Jay, Aubrey offers a historical reading of precisely how the process of demolishing empty buildings made it possible for materials like lead to sediment from painted walls and components into her neighborhood's soil. Yet those buildings did not empty themselves. Racist processes of suburbanization and disinvestment incrementally shifted people from Detroit to elsewhere, especially its suburbs. Whether as a speculative or a practical project, Jay and Aubrey's practices of making it rain barium in the suburbs involved a double movement. One part entailed moving contaminants produced through demolitions away from themselves and their neighbors, Detroiters who are Black, Latine, and working class. The other part entailed moving those same hazards toward wealthier, white suburbanites who otherwise enjoyed protection from environmental burdens.

EQUITABLE DISTRIBUTIONS

In the wake of the pandemic, I found myself in a place where Jay's soil sampling had identified concentrations of various petrochemicals and other hazardous substances. The site was a park—a flat, grass- and tree-filled expanse abutting one of the large six-lane thoroughfares that cut through most of Detroit and its surrounding region. Sitting on one of the benches that lined an asphalt perimeter path around a small pond, I watched a few handfuls of people walking and jogging. Besides us, the park was empty. After a while, I returned to the car and drove the hour to Aubrey and Jay's Detroit home. On their block, I joined people who were walking up and down garden rows to harvest zucchini, cucumbers, and some of the season's first tomatoes. Unlike in the suburban park, where contaminated soils blended seamlessly into the surrounding landscape, I could note the spectrum of possibly harmful conditions as I approached. Makeshift fences built out of salvaged wood pallets walled off lots where interactions with concentrated contaminants like lead could result in acute injuries. Mounded raised beds indicated where people had capped over hazards. In two lots, signs pointed to sweet potatoes growing directly in the ground. Unremarked toxicities in a suburban park contrasted with the active work of providing safer growing conditions in Detroit. That work pointed to small-scale ways neighbors maneuvered to redirect systems that would otherwise inscribe racism through durable environmental conditions.

When people submitted samples of earth to testing programs designed to help Detroiters learn the degree to which gardening soils were safe, the reports they received gave evidence of the patchwork of conditions in which the chemical makeup of the ground could vary significantly from one lot to the next. Decades of running through buildings with heavy machinery transformed certain components, especially lead-painted walls, into hazardous dust that settled into the surrounding ground. Sometimes, the earth that contractors trucked in to fill in the cavities left by excavated basements and foundations were themselves laced with various PCBs, petrochemicals, and industrial toxicants. In a context where nearby residents often looked to the grassy lots produced by demolitions as places of collective enjoyment or locations to grow food, the prospect of their being laden with hazardous materials cast those uses into doubt. By casting a further net and submitting samples from across Detroit's metropolitan region, Jay attempted to locate safer growing conditions. In so doing, he contended with sedimentations in which Black, Latine, and poor people almost always shoulder greater burdens of contamination than people who are wealthy and white. At the same time, demographic privileges of whiteness, income, and suburban administrative boundaries did not always guarantee a nontoxic environment. Like the burdens of contamination, such sampling articulates privilege as a material condition.

The speculative—and later, actualized—intervention of making it rain barium in the suburbs suggests that the sometimes-toxic aftermaths of demolitions should not be Detroiters' alone to bear. Jay, Aubrey, and their neighbors were not alone in imagining this prospect, but they were among the few I met who brought it into being. Let's return once more to Jay's imagination in its entirety: "They take down the buildings and we get a bunch of toxic dirt. I'd really like to be able to take this dirt and give it to the people who made it. Maybe trade it out with those folks living out in Livonia or Birmingham. Wouldn't that be some shit? Make it rain barium in the suburbs!" It is telling that their imagined route of returning contaminated sediments "to the people who made it" does not see it rained down upon demolition laborers and excavator operators but instead upon "the suburbs." Given the ways that demolitions were the outcome of long-running processes of suburbanization and disinvestment that created empty buildings in Detroit, Jay and others imagined distributing contaminated soils to locations that had benefited from those processes. In so doing, they proposed exchanging contaminated soil from a predominantly Black, Latine, and poor location with clean ground from a predominantly white, wealthy one to even out the status quo. With no-cost analyses, trucks, and plastic bins, they made small-scale moves to level the expectation that wealthy, white places should be most protected from harm.

In a moment when uneven distributions of contamination enact structural injustice across regions and continents alike, Jay and Aubrey are not alone in considering what it would take to transform such conditions. Consider the intervention feminist historian of technoscience M. Murphy imagines in a downtown Toronto skyline filled with the offices of financial services firms. As Murphy puts it, "Finance capital leaks PCBs." By this they mean how, historically and at present, record profits accruing in banks and investment funds are dependent on extractive petrochemical economies—wells, pipelines, refineries, and so on—that exact a toll on the same people, land, air, and water that have been burdened by industrial contaminants for some time. To call attention to the ways this distribution of burdens and incremental gains operates as an infrastructure of settler-colonial violence, Murphy imagines pumping PCB-soaked materials into Toronto's office towers. They give this advice to capital's beneficiaries:

> Breathe in. With each inhalation, the extensive relations of finance capital are pulled into your lungs, passing through membranes, attaching to receptors, rearranging metabolism, altering gene expression. Breathe out. With each exhalation, you are reconnecting to the greater fulsomeness of our relations. Breathe in, feel the fragility of white privileged life for the few around you. Breathe out.[47]

Such directions bring to the fore how experiences of wealth and racial privilege are materially constructed through systems that deposit harms elsewhere. Evening out those inequities begins with connecting the dots and bringing systemic relationships into account.

Proposals to route PCBs through Toronto's skyline or contaminated soils into Detroit's suburbs clarify how stemming the violence of racial capitalism requires fundamentally changing material conditions of privilege. In the context of longstanding movements to contest environmental racism, commitments to ensure "all people, regardless of income, race, color, national origin, Tribal affiliation, or disability [are] fully protected from disproportionate and adverse human health and environmental effects (including risks) and hazards" are vital.[48] But these commitments do not enact transformative change. Consider how soil testing could arm Detroiters with knowledge that certain lots were contaminated, but more often than not, soils laden with lead, mercury, nitrobenzene, and other hazards remained exactly where they were. Rather than full protection, gardeners were encouraged to pile up cardboard, compost, and mulch in hopes of preventing toxicities from entering their food supply. Even when evidence compelled contractors to excavate hazardous debris, those toxic burdens never traveled very far. Once scooped up and trucked out, they were channeled into hazardous waste processing and storage facilities in another part of the city. This meant that the stakes of removing the chemical violence of hazardous soils from majority-Black, Latine, and poor neighborhoods in Detroit involved dropping them into infrastructural systems that leaked chemical violence into majority-Black, Latine, and poor neighborhoods. In the provocation of making it rain barium in the suburbs, Jay and Aubrey provide a lesson in how evening out structural inequities entails reconfiguring material conditions so that privileged places shoulder their fair share of the load.

CONCLUSION

TOWARD REPAIR

With all of this said, what's the point? The point is that racism and intersecting inequities endure because they are built into the landscapes of dwellings, neighborhoods, worksites, and metropolitan regions. Some of us largely experience these landscapes as the source of privileges and benefits we may take for granted. Some primarily encounter systems of burdens, barriers, and constraints. Detroiters identified the endurance of structural racism through the transformation of empty buildings into grass-covered lots, including as neighbors, administrators, and workers. It has been in conversation with them that I have come to understand how destruction does not necessarily wipe the slate clean. Consider how Detroiters navigated building removal as the source of heightened scrutiny, unstable housing, precarious work, hazardous air, and contaminated soil. All the while, tearing down buildings was a source of reliable profits for demolition contractors and excavator operators, who were typically, though not exclusively, white suburbanites. Such stark, racially differentiated outcomes trouble hopes that it is possible to demolish our way out of racist systems tuned to enact white supremacy through antiblackness. Explicitly racist institutions, decisions, and policies may disappear, but the inequitable distributions of power, resources, benefits, and harms remain durable—so durable that they are reproduced even when excavators level everything in sight. But this does not have to be. Even as Detroiters navigated a racist status quo, they surfaced what it might take to produce different outcomes—that is, to make moves toward repair.

The research for this book was supposed to conclude in summer 2020. For a project that began to take shape in 2010, a decade seemed long enough. Instead of meeting up with interlocutors in backyard gatherings, meeting rooms, and other venues, I spent those months more than seven hundred miles away, staring at screens and talking with Detroiters on the phone as we struggled to come to grips with shared losses. One of the video streams we watched together was of hearses leading lines of cars as they snaked around Belle Isle over the course of a late summer day. Fifteen funeral processions slowly made a several-mile loop across the island of parkland in the Detroit River—one procession for each one hundred city residents who died after testing positive for COVID-19 during those early months of the pandemic. Municipal staff organized the memorial using photos submitted by surviving relations of departed city residents. City employees printed the images on large signs and installed them at regular intervals along the procession route. Cool breezes, swimming beaches, and large pavilions made Belle Isle a popular hangout any summer, especially that first pandemic summer. But during the days of the funeral processions, thousands filled the island to capacity to memorialize people who were no longer there. Masked volunteers reminded visitors to please remain distanced if they stepped out of their vehicles to sit with an image.

People also carried names and images from the Belle Isle memorial in protest marches organized by a collective of city youth who called themselves Detroit Will Breathe. Legal observers and journalists counted hundreds, sometimes thousands of participants in near daily marches that moved from neighborhood to neighborhood across the city for more than a year. Detroit Will Breathe's marches first took shape alongside a global uprising at police killings of people of color, especially Black people—George Floyd, Breonna Taylor, Aiyana Jones, Adam Toledo, and so many others. But as people carried images of Detroiters who had died after contracting COVID-19 alongside those of people from Detroit and elsewhere who had been killed by police, they situated ending police violence within a broad platform for racial justice. Detroit Will Breathe organizers livestreamed public forums in which city residents articulated this platform. Some demands reflected those issued by parallel movements in other cities, especially demilitarizing Detroit's police and ending the use of facial recognition surveillance systems. But participants also came to agreements that pushed for further changes. Specifically, they requested that state actors uphold Indigenous treaty rights, end evictions and foreclosures, guarantee basic income, establish formal sanctuary policies, improve support for survivors of interpersonal violence, and curb industries from polluting communities of color. These demands built on generations of coalition-based organizing in Detroit that has yoked racial, environmental, and economic justice.

Like state entities across the continent, a constellation of police forces attempted to quash Detroit Will Breathe's protests by firing rubber bullets and tear gas into groups of marchers before arresting them for alleged violations of pandemic-related stay-at-home orders. The one-hundredth night of marches coincided with a judicial order preventing police from arresting protestors. That evening, I watched a former neighbor's livestream as she slowly drove down one of the city's wide, radial boulevards in the gathering dusk. Around her, people dancing to techno pumping from mobile speakers gave local specificity to chants of "No justice, no peace! Fuck these racist-ass police!" and "We need federal aid, not federal raids!" For much of the time, the livestream I watched was framed by three signs attached to another car. The signs read:

THE WHOLE SYSTEM IS RACIST

DEMOLISH WHITE SUPREMACY RACISM + CAPITALISM

RACISM HAS NO PLACE HERE

I have seen signs like this at racial justice mobilizations in Detroit and elsewhere, long before 2020 and since. Perhaps you have too. On the ground, people know that the constituent inequities of racial capitalism are systemic and structural. Tearing everything down before building something else from the ground up seems to be the only workable path toward a just world—or even a less unjust one.

By way of the causes, processes, and consequences of demolitions in Detroit, this book has offered a grounded account of how tearing things down is not a sure path to structural change. Demolitions maintained racist distributions of precarity and injury that were already deeply familiar to many Detroiters, including but not limited to Black residents. When demolitions produced wealth and stability, they tended to flow to white people who were already wealthy. Such racist outcomes were not the grand design of racist people. Indeed, to the extent that removing empty buildings was anyone's grand design, it was administrators who expected deploying wrecking crews would create a city in which Black Detroiters could thrive. This is how structural racism endures—with the best of intentions and despite hopes to the contrary. It happens through the confluence of systems that route hazardous conditions to places that already bear their burdens in ways that make it possible for benefits and privileges to continue flowing for those of us who already have them. As a result, demolitions compounded inequities through neighborhoods, institutions, and worksites. This happened through concepts people used, the machineries they operated, the air they inhaled, and the ground beneath their feet. Overall, demolitions showed how racist systems do not have a simple shutdown mechanism. Excavators may topple empty buildings that were the material products of white supremacy, but they leave the structures of racial capitalism that produced those buildings to begin with relatively undisturbed.

Accounting for the durability of structural racism can make us question whether injustices of the past will forever become the stuff of the present and future. Demolitions certainly confirm that systems are racist, and even rendering existing landscapes into dust is insufficient to strip them of that settlement. But this loop is not guaranteed. Removing empty buildings unleashed a mess of legal concepts, heavy machinery, structural components, atmospheres, and earth that tends to reinforce racial whiteness as the gateway to well-being at the expense of everyone else. But Detroiters also intervened in that mess to make moves toward something else. Residents worked administrative systems to connect property speculators to the production of empty buildings. They refused invitations to collateralize dwellings as financial instruments in order to maintain them as homes for extended kin. Sometimes, people made it rain barium in the suburbs. Though temporary and partial when set against the scale of the problem, such occurrences make clear that structural racism may be durable but it is not completely intractable. Demolition alone will not be enough to shift the burdens of structural violence. Doing so will take building up new systems from within the conditions of an unjust present: systems that return stolen land and people, systems that make sure everyone has a house to call home, systems that ensure the burdens of toxicity and precarity are equitably shared. Detroiters show us how horizons of reparative projects can be constructed from materials and tools that people already have at hand.

RACIST SYSTEMS ENDURE

While this book has approached the endurance of structural racism and intersecting inequities by way of empty buildings and demolitions in Detroit, durable inequities are not merely a Detroit problem. White supremacy is constitutive of the United States.[1] Systems of racial capital operate across global contexts.[2] In the United States and elsewhere, efforts to restrict evidence-based understanding of systemic inequities like racism often hinge on the suggestion that systematically racist conditions may have existed in the past but are no longer relevant. Detroit offers an emblematic case of why pretending that racism, including but not limited to white supremacy, ended in the past will not keep it there. Demolitions show how the status quo of racism endures through projects that removed empty buildings from Detroiters' sightlines but along the way focused surveillance on their neighborhoods, maintained the precarity of their homes, and made it possible for contamination to settle around them. No single person, company, organization or government office can be blamed for racially unequal outcomes that accrued on and flowed outward from demolition sites. But that does not mean we cannot account for who benefits from the endurance of racism as a structural condition. The movements of excavators, concepts, buildings, and people make evident how racism endures through material transformations, especially as racially uneven distributions of resources are structured into landscapes.

In a moment when legislatures, university regents, and school boards across the United States are making increasing attempts to ban research and teaching about systems of privilege and oppression, especially racism and white supremacy, it is worth maintaining focus on how those systems work. Executive orders and legislation promise to punish educators who teach evidence-based lessons about enslavement, colonization, Jim Crow, environmental injustice, segregation, land dispossession, and more.[3] In forbidding formal learning and knowledge about racism, these actions strive to make it increasingly difficult to point out injustice.[4] But striking racism, antiblackness, white supremacy, disparities and other so-called divisive concepts from funding calls and educational curricula will not work as intended. Bans on research and discussion about structural inequity and injustice proceed from the privileged assumption that people encounter structural inequities only in classrooms or books. My interlocutors show us otherwise. To be sure, some of the Detroiters I came to know learned to name structural racism in schools. But many learned to name it far from the classroom. People did so in discussions among neighbors about the conditions that produced empty buildings on their blocks, as well as while sitting in the routine traffic that moved from one side of Detroit's city limits to another. Because the trouble with racism in general and white supremacy in particular is that they are not merely academic concepts or historical conditions. They are ever-present realities. Refusing to recognize them will not make their material conditions disappear.

Elite efforts to sweep racism and related inequities into a black box are nothing new. When political theorist Charles Hamilton and Black liberation organizer Kwame Ture defined institutional racism in the wake of twentieth-century civil rights uprisings in the United States, they did so in purposeful contrast with individual racism.[5] The pair noted how the same white liberals who expressed outrage at individual racism, including white mobs attacking Black people moving into all-white neighborhoods, were typically unconcerned with formal policies and informal practices through which white people could access housing, employment, and services on better terms than anyone else. What Hamilton, Ture, and others identify as the "white power structure" of the United States could exist only through the concentration of environmental harms, lesser pay for equal work, and disinvestment in the places where Black, Brown, and Indigenous people live.[6] The result is landscapes of privilege and oppression in which racism "is less overt, far more subtle, less identifiable in terms of the *specific* individuals committing the acts. But it is no less destructive of human life."[7] It should come as no surprise that Hamilton and Ture's definition of "institutional racism" was the basis for subsequent definitions of structural violence[8]—that is, violence that can be tracked through disparate material conditions and life chances. Those structures route privileges to some and burdens to others, even though no person or policy explicitly says this must be so.

The results of demolishing thousands upon thousands of empty buildings in Detroit ask us to grapple with how material structures of privilege and oppression can remain relatively unchanged even as the conditions in which they are embedded seem to disappear. Residents, planners, and policymakers alike hoped leveling structures emptied out by racist disinvestment would be the process through which their city could heal from that disinvestment. At first pass, grassy lots opened by the removal of empty buildings certainly looked to make good on this potential. But razing empty buildings did not disrupt Detroiters' lived experiences of unstable housing, patchy employment prospects, and environmental hazards. If anything, it compounded them. Following demolitions, Detroit's city limits continue to be lines on the map marking where a majority-Black, high-poverty metropolis meets up with a region that is on average significantly wealthier and majority-white. It would be convenient if responsibility for this endurance could be pinned on discrete human actors who intentionally set out to ensure inequities were sustained from the past into the present and possibly the future. But structural racism endures even in the absence of ideologically racist people. It endures through systems built to maximize profits for some at the expense of others. The very conditions that produced empty buildings also drove the production of legal concepts, algorithms, regional labor regimes, heavy machinery, and regulations that made demolitions possible. Ultimately, the apparatus that made empty buildings disappear reinforced the very power relations it seemed to disrupt.

Those of us who benefit from these power relations, including but not limited to those of racial capitalism tuned through white supremacy, cannot absolve ourselves of complicity by noting that we did not create them or that we do not individually support them. That is not how systems work. Detroit's empty buildings map racial whiteness as the bridge between the profits of settler coloniality with those of suburbanization and industrial abandonment. Refusing or even contesting racist ideologies does not preclude suburban metropolitan Detroiters from benefiting from white supremacy. We inherited those benefits by virtue of our positions within a region where profits extracted from what is now Detroit have routinely served to bolster privilege elsewhere. The causes, procedures, and aftermaths of demolitions in Detroit distill how this dynamic tumbles forward. As someone who has spent a significant portion of his life in Detroit and its broader region, demolition is a process that underscores how the clean air, physically stable dwellings, benign soils, and secure employment I took for granted were made possible by toxic atmospheres, dispossession, contaminated ground, and economic precarity elsewhere. Racially differentiated experiences and life chances are reproduced through systems that hold people in unequal relationships, even if those of us privileged within those systems might wish otherwise.

There is a broader lesson at stake here. At the turn of the twenty-first century, critical scholar of racism and coloniality Michel-Rolph Trouillot observed an outpouring of apologies from Euroamerican individuals, corporate leaders, and heads of state for racist projects that took place centuries before they were born. Individually and collectively, they issued statements apologizing for organizational involvement in enslavement, the transatlantic trade, colonization, and genocide. Rhetorically, such apologies for racism suggested it was a past problem rather than an ongoing reality. In Trouillot's words, "historical responsibility cannot hark back to an original sin that the collective-individual supposedly committed. Rather, it needs to take into account the structures of privilege unleashed by a history of power and domination and to evaluate the current losses induced by the reproduction of these structures."[9] Presidents, boards of directors, and CEOs may not necessarily be interested in completing this accounting. But people attending to their lived material realities do find ways of getting their arms around the problem. From the sidelines of empty buildings and demolition sites, Detroiters accounted for histories of privilege and domination and evaluated losses induced by the reproduction of these structures. People did so by excavating how things like the concept of blight, the air in their lungs, and the instability of their homes connected lived experiences to structural conditions. With such connections, they provide guides to tracking the ways racism endures, even when dominant narratives may suggest the systems that produce it have been powered off.

As excavators rip through foundations and rooflines, they cast into relief how all of us are hooked into racist systems—albeit in highly unequal ways. For people engaged around the intersections of racial and economic justice, including but not limited to scholars of racial capitalism, the mutual reinforcement of racism and capital accumulation have been clear for some time.[10] This includes contemporary labor and property systems established through the conjoined dispossession of Black people and Indigenous lands for the benefit of European settlers and their descendants.[11] Likewise, for scholars and activists engaged around the intersections of racial and environmental justice, it has long been clear that racism articulates where people are protected from harms and who is exposed to them.[12] This includes majority-white, low-income places in the United States being less likely to be saddled with contamination than majority-Black, high-income locations.[13] Alongside others,[14] this book contributes to charting the expansively material conditions that engrain racial capitalism through white supremacy as features of our world. It shows how racism is not simply a matter of disparate economic or environmental or political conditions. It is all of them. Racism and intersecting inequities endure as those conditions compound and reinforce each other through the material construction of our shared landscapes, including neighborhoods, workplaces, and cities.

SOME PRACTICAL CONSIDERATIONS

At this point, it is worth asking what might be done to stop the endurance of structural racism and address the cumulative harms associated with it. After all, this is what many people, including Detroit residents and demolition administrators, imagined that building removals would do for their city. Federal policymakers often pointed to Detroit's demolition program, the most extensive in the country, as a model for other municipalities struggling with empty buildings produced by population loss and deindustrialization. For example, at a reception during a conference for government, nonprofit, and community advocacy workers from across the continent, I found myself standing with a staffer from a federal office that funded demolitions in cities around the United States. He had been to Detroit recently and was certain that the tens of thousands of federally funded demolitions were "really moving the needle for environmental and economic justice." I interjected that I was not so sure, describing how demolitions created new instances where Detroiters confronted barriers to economic and environmental dignity. The staffer smiled and nodded as I spoke before responding, "You're being academic and not practical. You seem to think there's some magic wand we could wave and make people not racist so the world would be better. This is the problem with academics. You're all theoretical and not practical." He then excused himself to join another table.

I have replayed this interaction in my mind in the years since it happened. It contrasted with breakout discussions at that very conference among people working in Detroit, Baltimore, Flint, New Orleans, Chicago, and other places leveling empty buildings. In those discussions, administrators discussed things like how demolitions produced lead and asbestos hazards or the ways working people struggled with spiking rents after empty buildings came down in their neighborhoods. But suggesting academic research is not practical also reflects how academic efforts to understand how the world works can appear disconnected from the nitty-gritty of changing it.[15] It is certainly true that research of the sort I have had the privilege of time and space to undertake has not been encumbered by obligations to demonstrate immediate results to funders, supervisors, and members of the public. So, to be clear, I am not against a wand for warding off racist sentiments. But such a wand would not end racism for all time. Demolitions show that systematically racist distributions of resources and life chances do not require racist people. Ending racist ideologies and commitments to white supremacy is important. It is as urgent as ever. And yet, if those ideologies and commitments disappeared tomorrow, we would still be left with the same racialized arrangements of poverty, wealth, contamination, and opportunity that exist today. Racism is built into our world; if left unchanged, that world will continue to reproduce it. This is a practical matter.

The notion that cities can demolish their ways to environmental and economic justice suggests there is a straightforward fix for racism. And yet, hundreds of thousands of demolitions in Detroit show how excavators can bulldoze empty buildings without dislodging the racist political economic relations that created them. Those relations include the lines on the map that section Detroit into some 400,000 parcels and define the municipality against its surrounding region. When Detroiters pored over municipal land records to learn what entities nominally owned empty buildings in their neighborhoods, they encountered chains of title transfers in which "the beginning" was the French occupation of Waawiiyaataanong to make Detroit. These same records situate how recurring waves of antiblack dispossession have burnished a settler colonial property system. Excavators remove buildings from the landscape while still reproducing their constitutive logics. These logics stretch far beyond Detroit. They reflect the world-historical context of antiblackness that historian of Black life Saidiya Hartman diagnoses as one in which "Black lives are still imperiled and devalued by a racial calculus and political arithmetic that were entrenched centuries ago [and] skewed life chances, limited access to health and education, premature death, incarceration, and impoverishment." [16] There is no quick technical fix for the violence of racism, though it is sometimes expedient for political leaders to suggest differently.[17] Even moving the needle on environmental and economic justice demands fundamentally changing the racial calculus and political arithmetic that shape our world.

Rather than simply issuing apologies or tearing things down, changing the baseline conditions of structural racism demands building up more restorative possibilities. It takes repair. Philosopher of justice and the Black radical tradition Olúfẹ́mi O. Táíwò lays out a moral imperative for reparations for colonization, enslavement, and their afterlives.[18] Given long-standing commitments to reparations as the common ground of abolition and anticolonial organizing, Táíwò is far from alone in providing a political and economic case for reparations as a means of evening out inequities created by stealing land and displacing people.[19] But Táíwò's case is also instructive for the ways he identifies how movements for reparations are not simply demands to tear down the material infrastructures of privilege and oppression. They imagine reworking material conditions to make it possible for all people to thrive. "What is done is done. History has already built the pipes through which advantages and disadvantages flow," Táíwò writes. "This sets which pipelines will have to be redirected, expanded, or destroyed if we want things to flow differently tomorrow or the next day."[20] Sometimes, the pipes of advantages and disadvantages are actual pipes that send potable water into some dwellings and injury into others. But pipes can also be work practices and regulatory protocols in which the most marginalized people confront hazards and precarities so that the most privileged remain the most protected. Whether the pipes of inequitable systems are actual or figurative, destruction is only one of many possible moves needed to make things flow differently.

Reparative projects can happen in highly local ways. This book includes a few examples of how Detroiters worked to blunt the edges of racist systems. They include city residents who maintained their homes as something other than a fungible unit of debt capital. Banking terms that encoded antiblack outcomes by excluding people living around empty buildings from access to home mortgages and renovation loans meant that Detroiters had become accustomed to shoring up unstable dwellings piecemeal. While leveling empty buildings removed structural barriers to home finance, refusing to transform their dwellings into financial instruments made it possible for Detroiters to maintain dwellings as places for extended relations to live. Likewise, soil-quality analyses showing lead, asbestos, and other hazards lurking beneath layers of grass, belie hopes that demolitions would secure fresh starts free from conditions of racism and disinvestment. When Detroiters replaced contaminated soil from their neighborhood with nontoxic earth drawn from the far-flung edges of the metropolitan region, they attempted to move hazards into places that were previously protected. Because sedimented contaminants had to go somewhere, they surfaced important considerations about the stakes of carving out more livable prospects amidst fallouts of white supremacy and racial capitalism that are both unevenly distributed and ongoing. Instead of equal protection, Detroiters who made it rain barium in the suburbs asked what it might look like for structurally privileged places to shoulder their fair shares of the load.

It is true that the examples provided in this book of how Detroiters worked to deflect racist structural violence are relatively ad hoc and small-scale compared to the magnitude of the problem. As historian of race and policy in the United States Tom Sugrue observes, "Grassroots change starts from below but cannot stop there. . . . That requires acknowledging that locally oriented, community-control activism and do-it-yourself urbanism are microlevel solutions to macrolevel problems."[21] To this end, it is worth noting how Detroiters have led regional and national coalitions on the frontlines of organizing for macrolevel solutions to the macrolevel problems of structural racism.[22] This includes advocating for federal and state policies that would have expanded access to affordable housing, dignified work, and healthy environments. It also includes spearheading local ordinances that would have ended predatory evictions through tax foreclosure and stopped water shutoffs that deprived Detroiters of access to safe drinking water. At each turn, elected officials rejected organizers' proposals with the suggestion that they could never find the funds needed to enact them.[23] Such rejections came at the same time as federal, municipal, and state entities were channeling tens of millions of public dollars into demolitions every year—to the tune of nearly $750 million dollars in public funds between 2010 and 2024 alone. Put simply, the seeming absence of structural solutions to the problems of structural racism does not reflect an absence of imagination or resources. It reflects a failure to direct institutional resources toward grassroots priorities.

Excavators certainly provided meaningful relief to Detroiters who were tired of contending with empty buildings on their blocks. But those same people were often attuned to how demolitions did not alter the ways racism remained structured into the fabric of their city. In practical, material ways, demolitions reinforce racist systems in which capital accrues as some places thrive at the expense of others. They show how, on its own, tearing things down can reconfigure what the conditions of injustice look like. But destruction alone does not facilitate repair for structural racism. Alone, demolitions have the effect of melting down statues of enslavers without making good on the debts owed to the descendants of enslaved people. They resonate with municipalities painting Black Lives Matter on the street in front of City Hall while permitting heavy industries to pollute majority-Black neighborhoods. Or universities that implement institutional land acknowledgments while resisting Indigenous nations' requests to return their lands. Make no mistake, melting down statues of enslavers, renaming streets that commemorate them, and acknowledging the land do work to displace racist norms embedded in public space. They are important interventions in that respect. But, like the rush of excitement that people described when watching an empty building collapse into a cloud of dust, feelings of progress can obscure how some changes do not make systems flow in a significantly different way. Destruction alone does not build different systems. In so many ways, it does not even come close.

TOWARD REPAIR

The systemic engines of structural racism can endure through the destruction of their material remains—but ending structural racism is possible. I cannot offer you a step-by-step guide to doing this—a punch list for a just and equitable world, such as it might be. But I hope I can leave you with the certainty that people can work not only to imagine such a world, but also to build it. As I write this, Detroiters are actively engaged in a formal reparations initiative to "address historical discrimination against the Black community in Detroit."[24] This initiative is an effort to carve out meaningful repair in the ongoing midst of racism. Over more than a year of monthly public meetings, Detroiters stepped up to microphones to speak about their lived experiences of antiblackness, including being denied housing in during periods of legal segregation, of being demolished from their homes through urban renewal, of police surveillance of their neighborhoods, and of the difficulties of finding employment after interacting with the carceral state. People spoke about the ways recent tides of predatory foreclosures and evictions had transformed dense majority-Black neighborhoods into street after street of empty houses. And yet, optimistic though some contributors were, many noted that any program that stopped at the city limits would be insufficient. They noted how struggles for reparations for antiblack discrimination in Detroit were aligned with struggles to end white supremacy elsewhere in their region, on their continent, and in the world.

Detroit's reparations initiative emerged from decades of organizing. Proponents connected local efforts to global movements for racial justice.[25] This includes proposals to compensate people harmed by antiblack policies in the United States. For example, in 2019, Evanston, Illinois, began a program to provide housing grants to current and former Black residents to compensate for antiblack segregation, housing discrimination, and eviction through twentieth-century urban renewal programs. In 2023, a statewide reparations task force in California proposed cash transfers to Black residents as compensation for the overlapping conditions of housing discrimination, excessive policing, mass incarceration, and environmental racism. Drawing on an actuarial calculus of stolen wages, wealth, and life expectancy, the final report suggested Black Californians and their descendants could be due more than $1.2 million apiece, though state actors have balked at this figure, as well as narrower proposals. Proposals for reparations transfers like those made in Evanston and California frame repair as a market transaction in which racism is an outstanding debt to be repaid.[26] Translating suffering into dollar values does not produce justice, but it can shuffle resources to people so they can get by in the meantime.[27] To this end, when proposals for reparations funds stall out, they make apparent how the barrier to reparations is not a lack of evidence or a refusal to put a cash price on misery. Reparations, like the constructive work of repair in general, are forestalled by an absence of political will.

Audiences at reparations initiative meetings in Detroit applauded when people detailed Evanston's housing grant system. They applauded louder when someone described the more expansive proposal developed in California. People took to the microphone to speak about how cash transfers could ensure they remained in the city where they were born despite rising rents, tax bills, and utility costs. But people who identified themselves as Black Detroiters also spoke up to note how building a city in which they and their relations could thrive would take so much more than simply one-time payments. In a moment when Black residents were acutely struggling to afford housing, food, energy, and water, people made proposals to provide those necessities to all Black Detroiters who needed them. Others raised well-documented connections between the beltlines of heavy industry crisscrossing Detroit and the elevated rates of illnesses like asthma among Black residents. They suggested that the municipality shutter those industries entirely. More than once, Black Detroiters spoke up to note how antiblackness was not the only form of racism that shaped life in their city. They insisted that any reparations programs established to support Black Detroiters and their descendants should be only one part of a more expansive platform of racial justice. Specifically, people requested the municipality take actions to uphold Indigenous sovereignties and use reparations to Black Detroiters as a stepping stone to building a city that sheltered Black and non-Black Detroiters of color from the structural burdens of racism.

Detroiters who spoke up at meetings of their local reparations task force seemed acutely aware of the ways that, even on the scale of a single city, meaningful repair for racism will take so much more than paying debts owed to Black people and communities. Again, such payments could be meaningful in helping people make ends meet. But alone they are not enough.[28] We inhabit a political economic system of racial capitalism. This system is one in which the access some of us have to stable housing, reliable resources, relatively healthy environments, and other benefits exists in relation to—that is to say, because of—oppression experienced elsewhere. Even if the systems that extract profit through racist configurations of precarity and contamination ended tomorrow, the cumulative effects of existing operations would still be there. Moreover, as I have listened to Black Detroiters insist time and again, the cutting effects of unstable housing, economic disinvestment, and environmental injustice did not affect Black Detroiters alone. Non-Black Detroiters of color and impoverished white Detroiters contended with being on the short end of systems that propped up whiteness as wealth and well-being. Their experiences of these systems were not identical to their Black neighbors and coworkers, but they were connected. From the scale of a single city, it is evident how reparations payments that cushion against the ongoing grind of antiblackness are one harm-mitigation step among many necessary to shift the material conditions of white supremacy toward a more equitable status quo.

Meaningful repair is a horizon. Tearing down monuments to white supremacy will not be enough to reach it. But listening to Detroiters who engaged with empty-building demolitions as neighbors, workers, and observers points to strategies and tactics that might. Crucially, the work of intervening in racist systems begins by understanding how those systems came to be as they are. This work happens wherever and whenever people narrate and question the unequal conditions under which they live their lives. The people named in this book helped me parse the granular realities of white supremacy and racial capitalism in Detroit around kitchen tables, on front porches, at backyard kickbacks, and on lunch breaks. From those locations, they made clear that ending structural racism at the scale of a single city, to say nothing of a continent or the world, will require working with every tool at our disposal. Petitions, hearings, regulations, and protests are only some of the tools on hand for this task. Sometimes, those tools succeed in shifting the status quo to something meaningfully more just. Sometimes, they do not achieve their desired ends. When procedural tools fail, recall what a handful of Detroiters did to address the racially unequal fallout of contaminated earth produced by demolitions. With shovels and pickups, they trucked sediments filled with lead and other hazards out to the suburbs and returned with cleaner ground. In material ways, they made a racist system work otherwise.

NOTES

Introduction

1. People whose knowledge and experiences animate this book are presented with pseudonyms and other specifics we agreed on.

2. Here are some clips of this if you want to watch for yourself, though I cannot promise they will be accessible forever. "Detroit Resident Celebrates Demolition of Vacant Homes in Her Neighborhood," WDIV Detroit, November 10, 2021 (https://youtu.be/RCvHabYka10?si=RH-yDyY1Tm9dDa_T, accessed April 24, 2025); "Watch Detroit demolish 10,000 houses in 2½ years," City of Detroit, July 21, 2016 (https://youtu.be/WvdfFsr2QfA?si=p1FC8QX4kcd1KkZq, accessed April 24, 2025).

3. Helpful histories of Detroit's present include Kinney 2016; Mays 2022; Sugrue 2005; Thomas 2013. For statistical specifics, see Massey and Denton 1998; Menendian, Gailes, and Gambhir 2021.

4. Marisa Solomon (2019) makes clear how aspirations of urban renewal enact a "racialized temporality of betterment," which in the United States is predicated on the physical displacement of Black people (see also Caverly 2022; Fennell 2015; Thomas 2013). Emblematic cases of demolition as a means of displacing people can also be found in Palestine (Azoulay 2013; Halper 2021) and Vietnam (Harms 2016).

5. For examples of this, see Kvik et al. 2022; Regan and Myers 2020; Torrejón, Paredes, and Skidmore 2023.

6. Andrew Highsmith's twentieth- and twenty-first-century history of urban renewal, *Demolition Means Progress* (2015), takes its name from the slogan of a demolition contractor

based in Flint, Michigan. Highsmith and others show how the idea that demolition unlocks the possibility of radical change is not limited to Detroit or the United States (Hackworth 2016; Slyomovics 2024).

7. Rodriguez 2021; Fennell 2015.

8. It was only after the suburbanization of production that factories moved offshore (Sugrue 2005, 127–30).

9. Atuahene 2025.

10. Robinson 2020, 26.

11. Writing on white supremacist hierarchies of value as sociomaterial engines of racial capitalism is expansive. W. E. B. Du Bois's (1935) articulation of this in *Black Reconstruction* is a common foundation for this work, including Robinson's *Black Marxism* (2020). Observing how white supremacy endured through the post-emancipation project of reconstruction, Du Bois writes, "The political success of the doctrine of racial separation, which overthrew Reconstruction by uniting the planter and the poor white, was far exceeded by its astonishing economic results. . . . It must be remembered that the white group of laborers, while they received a low wage, were compensated in part by a sort of public and psychological wage. They were given public deference and titles of courtesy because they were white. They were admitted freely with all classes of white people to public functions, public parks, and the best schools. The police were drawn from their ranks, and the courts, dependent upon their votes, treated them with such leniency as to encourage lawlessness" (1935, 688). Alongside *Black Marxism*, Charles Hamilton and Kwame Ture's *Black Power* (1992) distinguishes how antiblack hierarchies become structural conditions. Black feminist interventions are key to situating how racism operates beyond seemingly straightforward distinctions of race, including but not limited to Patricia Hill Collins's (2000) formulation of matrices of power and domination and Cheryl Harris's (1993, 2022) identification of the "racial alchemy" underlying whiteness as a property relation. David Roediger's *Wages of Whiteness* (2020) helpfully traces how the "public and psychological wage" of white masculinity Du Bois identified in the nineteenth century became the material basis of twentieth- and twenty-first-century political economies in the United States.

12. Bhandar and Toscano 2015; Koshy et al. 2022; Nichols 2020.

13. la paperson (2017) provides a critical initial orientation to the power relations of this note and the two preceding it. For greater explication, see Harris 2022; and Johnson and Lubin 2017.

14. There is expansive work on this. To get started, see McKittrick 2013; Inwood, Brand, and Quinn 2021; Solomon 2019, 2022; and Voyles 2015.

15. Ruth Wilson Gilmore (2009, 86) credits this turn of phrase to Amiri Baraka.

16. Lipsitz 2011, 28–32.

17. By way of St. Louis and its surrounds, Walter Johnson (2021) shows how the United States has been structured—materially and symbolically—through the overlapping "spoils" of white supremacy and colonization. For more on the persistent structures of white supremacy underlying shifting particularities of racial whiteness in the United States' settler colonial context, see Kelley 2017a; Speed 2020; and Halvorson and Reno 2022.

18. My understanding of racism as a structure that operates in global contexts, of which

the conjuncture of white supremacy and settler coloniality observed in the contemporary United States is only one example, is indebted to Charles Mills's (1997) examination of the racial contract. Mills, of course, is not alone in this project. Jemima Pierre's (2012) examination of racial formations in Ghana is critical for identifying how "structured as it is within a worldwide hierarchy of race, Whiteness is global and local in scope and impact" (84). Key sources to consider include Byrd et al. 2018; Chari 2024; Hall 2021; and Harris 1993.

19. Mills 1997, 11.

20. Mills 1997, 11, emphases original.

21. Gilmore 2007, 28. Elsewhere, Gilmore (2002) provides more textured definition: "Racism is a practice of abstraction, a death-dealing displacement of difference into hierarchies that organize relations within and between the planet's sovereign political territories. Racism functions as a limiting force that pushes disproportionate costs of participating in an increasingly monetized and profit-driven world onto those who, due to the frictions of political distance, cannot reach the variable levers of power that might relieve them of those costs" (16). Gilmore's work is worth learning from in its entirety.

22. This is important. Racial categories are a product of racism, not the other way around. Arguments to the contrary enact what Karen Fields and Barbara Fields (2014) describe as "racecraft" that obscures the endurance of racism.

23. Edward Lynch, Ashley Williams Clark, Anika Goss, Shari Williams, and Sema Abulhab, 2021, "The State of Economic Equity in Detroit," Detroit Future City, 80–83, https://detroitfuturecity.com/wp-content/uploads/2021/05/The-State-of-Economic-Equity-in-Detroit.pdf.

24. Rector 2022; see also Jenkins 2022.

25. Rector 2022.

26. Jain 2006.

27. Benjamin 2016, 148. See also Braun 2014.

28. Feminist examinations of technoscience provide essential guides to seeing how this happens, since they foreground how systems are distributions of power relations. Scholars like M. Murphy (2017); Safiya Noble (2018); and Lundy Braun (2014) provide helpful touchstones here. Susan Leigh Starr's (1990) contributions should not be overlooked.

29. This is what Hecht (2023) means when she describes Mills's racial contract as "technopolitical." That is, as a contract enforced deliberately and not through technological systems. For more on technopolitics, see von Schnitzler 2016; Winner 1980.

30. Hecht 2023, 12.

31. For an explanation of how such ideologies motivate discriminatory housing systems, see Lipsitz 2024, 2011. For a broader critique, see Bonilla-Silva 2013.

32. Clyde Woods's (1998, 2017) close attention to New Orleans to understand how built environments are key vectors for white supremacist uneven development is foundational to efforts to surface these dynamics elsewhere. See also Brown 2022; Pulido 2015, 2016; Lewis 2022.

33. Johan Galtung (1969) introduced the concept of "structural violence" as a means of contrasting with "direct violence." As he put it, "In both cases, individuals may be killed or mutilated, hit or hurt [and] manipulated. . . . But whereas in the [case of direct violence,]

these consequences can be traced back to concrete persons and actors, in the [case of structural violence,] this is no longer meaningful. There may be no person who directly harms another person in the structure. The violence is built into the structure and shows up as unequal power relations and consequently as unequal life chances" (170–71). Thom Davies (2019) and Akhil Gupta (2012), among others, have given ethnographic substance to Galtung's framework.

34. Detroit provides emblematic cases of how this system was constructed (Freund 2007).

35. Jenkins 2022; Jenkins and Leroy 2021.

36. Taylor 2019.

37. Lipsitz 2024; Perry, Stephens, and Dogoghoe 2024.

38. For examples of this beyond the ones I offer in the pages to come, see Cox 2015; and Stovall 2020.

39. Kurashige 2017; Surkin and Georgakas 2012.

40. Rector 2022; Safransky 2023.

41. Gramsci [1971] 1992, 324.

42. Freund 2007; Kinney 2016.

43. Safransky 2023.

44. Safransky 2023, 191.

45. See also Caverly 2023.

46. Safransky details this at length, as does Claire Herbert (2021).

47. This is the urban frontier as Neil Smith (1996) conceives of it. Marisa Solomon (2019) and Rebecca Kinney (2016) both productively expand on Smith's framework in relation to building removals.

48. Fennel 2015.

49. Finkelstein 2019; Harms 2016.

50. Burawoy 2009.

51. Joe Dumit (2014), building on Donna Haraway (1988).

52. In total, I regularly spoke with twenty-six laborers, four excavator operators, two waste haulers, and five demolition firm owners.

53. Günel and Watanabe 2024.

54. For a critique, see De León 2018.

55. As James and Boggs (1974) write, "ordinary working people in factories, mines, fields, and offices, are rebelling every day in ways of their own invention. Sometimes their struggles are on a small personal scale. [. . .] Always the aim is to regain control over their own conditions of life and their relations with one another" (5). Similarly, with respect to racism and interlocking systems of oppression, Avery Gordon (2008) writes, "ordinary people ascertain these evidentiary things not also, but more often than professional seers" (195). For more on the ways people embody structural analyses, consult Agard-Jones 2013.

56. Marx 1973, 749–50. Joseph Schumpeter (1950) builds on Marx to suggest that capital demands a process of "creative destruction [that] incessantly revolutionizes the economic structure from within, incessantly destroying the old one" (82–83).

57. For George Galster (2012) Metropolitan Detroit's "combined easily buildable topography, unfettered development rules, fragmented local government, and frightened popu-

lace have constructed a continuous disassembly line stretching out from the urban core to the suburban fringe" (237).

58. Whether or not Marx would have recognized this is a question beyond my capacity to definitively answer. But historical materialism can always be "slightly stretched" (Fanon 1965, 40) to go beyond Marx's understanding.

59. Sugrue 2005.

60. Importantly, this is not to suggest that Black, Brown, and poor communities have been "left behind" by capital. On the contrary, racist disinvestment that produces empty buildings is itself the site for extracting capital. See Bledsoe and Wright 2019; Caverly 2022.

61. Gilmore and Lambert 2018. Elsewhere, Gilmore builds on Audre Lorde's (1984) warning that "the master's tools will never dismantle the master's house (110–13). For Gilmore (1993), "If the master loses control of the means of production, he is no longer the master. . . . The house must be dismantled so that we can recycle the materials to institutions of our own design, usable by all to produce new and liberating work" (70). I draw significant inspiration from this insight. The central questions are not whether or not to oppose oppressive systems—a binary choice of yes or no on whether the house must be dismantled. Instead, the central questions are ones like who bears the burdens of this process? For whose liberation? And toward what possible futures?

62. Mays 2022; Thompson 2017.

63. Sharpe 2016, 8. For the braided operations of enslavement and empire in Detroit, see Miles 2017 and Mays 2022. For elsewhere, see Koshy et al. 2022; paperson 2017.

64. Táíwò 2022.

65. Franke 2019; Scott 2018.

66. Táíwò 2022, 123. When it comes to repair, Michel-Rolph Trouillot's (2000) caution against conflating apologies with material change is critical. So is Jovan Scott Lewis's (2022) grounded account of how Black people and communities in Tulsa convey demands for repair through organizing for reparations and self-determination.

67. Simpson 2018, 84–85.

68. Stuelke 2021, 10.

Chapter 1

1. Ahmann 2022, emphasis original. See also Stoetzer 2022; Voyles 2015.

2. Caverly 2023; Safransky 2023; Kinney 2016.

3. Like the names of most people in this book, 2615 Bezner Avenue is also a pseudonym. Although a street with this name existed in Detroit in the early twentieth century, that road no longer exists. Exit Strategy May 5 LLC is also a pseudonym. My interlocutors sometimes requested that I obscure where they lived to avoid unwanted scrutiny.

4. Kurashige 2017; Sugrue 2005; Thomas 2013.

5. Houses and dwellings are good to think with because they are structural in multiple senses of the term (Harris 2013; Mueggler 2001). For more on this, consider how Mary Pattillo (2008) builds a history of Black middle-class life in Chicago from a single address or Elizabeth Grosz's (1995) methodological orientation to built environments as spatiotemporal archives of embodied experiences.

6. Buildings are made of land—trees, earth, plastics, water, and so on. In Detroit at present, they are also situated within technologies of settler colonial land relations that claim land as private property. Such land relations are the mutually reinforcing substrate of white supremacy, antiblackness, and Indigenous genocide. Cheryl Harris and Jodi Byrd's conversations around Black-Indigenous solidarity in the face of "whiteness as property" are particularly clarifying (Harris 2019; Byrd 2019). For more, see Bhandar 2018; and Moreton-Robinson 2015.

7. Mays 2022.

8. Harris 1993, 1761.

9. The most intensive discussions happened on Bedrock Detroit's Facebook feed, beginning with an initial post attributed to the company's founder on July 23, 2017.

10. Caverly 2022; Story 2019.

11. Keith Owens, July 24, 2017, "This May Be How You See Detroit, Bedrock, but Detroit Doesn't See Detroit That Way," *Michigan Chronicle*, https://michiganchronicle.com/this-may-be-how-you-see-detroit-bedrock-but-detroit-doesnt-see-detroit-that-way/.

12. Bedrock Detroit, July 23, 2017. This statement was also attributed to the company's founder.

13. Kinney 2016, 153.

14. For examples, see Ahmann 2024; Caverly 2022; and Finkelstein 2019.

15. Kim Kinder (2016) shows how Detroiters moved to preserve buildings for later use, even when public institutions did not. For more on these efforts, see Herbert 2021.

16. Freund 2007.

17. Sugrue 2005, 128–29. Detroit's Black workers' movements resisted these changes (Surkin and Georgakas 2012).

18. Aimee Cox (2015) and Maya Stovall (2020) detail how the Great Migration continues to meaningfully ripple in Black Detroiters' lives in the early twenty-first century. Individually and collectively, people construct home around places where relations lived before relocating to the city.

19. Since 2020, Detroit has been the second largest majority-Black city.

20. Surkin and Georgakas 2012; Thompson 2001.

21. Rector 2022; Ward 2016.

22. Detroit's Black political leaders were forced to contend with debts built up by white predecessors, including financial obligations for the ongoing maintenance of a regional water and sewerage infrastructure built to support suburban growth (Kurashige 2017; Montgomery 2020). Clyde Woods (2017) refers to this as "trap economics" in the case of New Orleans.

23. Bartlett 2017; Kinder 2016.

24. The census category of "race" is a technology of what Karen Fields and Barbara Fields (2014) describe as "racecraft." It makes race appear as a precursor to racism rather than as a product of it. Consider how census enumerations recode Arab Detroiters as "white" to make them fit within "ethnoracial grids" (Shryock 2008).

25. Woods (2023, 78) identifies this from the Lower Mississippi Delta, especially how regional political economic hierarchies and regional racial hierarchies become spatially embedded in mutually reinforcing ways. See also Woods 2017.

26. From their experiences in Detroit, Grace Lee Boggs and James Boggs (2011) argued that cities in the Americas were a key foothold for building Black political power. In their words, "The city is the base we must organize as the factories were organized in the 1930s. We must struggle to control, to govern the cities, as workers struggled to control and govern the factories" (167).

27. Patricia Hill Collins's (2000) formulation of the "matrix of domination" is foundational to understanding the ways race and racism interlock with other systems of power.

28. Kyla Schuller (2021) historicizes how this move—a refusal to see how racism shapes lived and structural realities—is constitutive of white feminism.

29. Douglas Massey and Nancy Denton (1998) used twentieth-century Detroit as emblematic of antiblack segregation in the twentieth century. In the 2020s, Detroit is the most segregated city in the United States and fourth most segregated metropolitan region (Othering and Belonging Institute, 2020, "Most-to-Least Segregated Cities and Metro Regions," https://belonging.berkeley.edu/most-least-segregated-cities-in-2020).

30. Boyle 2005; Freund 2007.

31. Karen Miller (2015) suggests that Detroit is emblematic of how northern cities imitated southern patterns of Jim Crow segregation in everything but name.

32. Jodi Byrd (2019) flags this with her insistence that African-descended people in American settler colonies are "arrivants," not settlers—naming how the violence of the Middle Passage and its afterlives are categorically distinct from the structures of white privilege into which European people were incorporated. Robin D. G. Kelley (2017b) provides a related but distinct critique of certain formulations of settler colonial studies that elide the resonant ways racism enabled colonial political economies in Africa, Asia, Europe, and the Americas (see also Lowe 2015).

33. Bavery 2020.

34. This is one of Cedric Robinson's points of departure in *Black Marxism* (2020).

35. Baldwin 1985, 22.

36. John Hartigan's (1999) ethnography of whiteness in Detroit during the late twentieth century provides a grounded, local account of the structures of whiteness that Walter Johnson (2021), David Roediger (2020) and others build on W. E. B. Du Bois (1935) to describe from other contexts.

37. Halvorson and Reno 2022, 161.

38. Over time, any building will break down. But whereas maintaining the common façade of an apartment building can conceal knowledge of empty units from outsiders, when single-family homes lose their occupants, they also tend to lose the people who would identify emerging maintenance issues. For more on Detroiters narrating dispossession and population loss through the material conditions of detached dwellings, see Caverly 2021; Yezbick 2020.

39. Even academic analyses of the city sometimes gloss over how the proportion of detached dwellings in Detroit's building stock (67%) is higher than notoriously car-centric Los Angeles (42%) (Galster 2012).

40. Harris 2013; Hayden 2003.

41. Kim Kinder (2016) calls this "defensive architecture."

42. Burton 1922, 40–55; see also Miles 2017.

43. Burton 1922, 88–89.

44. Political theorist of property Robert Nichols's observation of property creation as a core infrastructure of settler colonization is helpful for contextualizing this process. In his words, settler colonizers "did not simply steal a stable, empirical object called 'land' from Indigenous peoples. Rather, as they transferred control over the land, they also recoded its meaning, rendering it a relatively abstract legal entity. So, unlike ordinary cases of theft, dispossession created an object in the very act of appropriating it: making and taking were fused" (2020, 145). Titles claiming parts of the river bank into Campau family property are the oldest held in the Wayne County Registry of Deeds, and the process of issuing a deed to Jacques Campau (also spelled Campaux and Campeau) is credited with standardizing French settler-colonial claims across the region (Telesphore St. Pierre, 1895, *Histoire des Canadiens du Michigan et du Comté d'Essex d'Ontario*, Bibliothèque et Archives Nationales du Québec, 121–23). See also Acte de concession à Jacques Campaux (Campeau), habitant du fort Pontchartrain, 10 juillet 1734, Bibliothèque et Archives Nationales du Québec.

45. Mays (2022, 28) reworks Richard White's (1991) framing of Detroit as the center of a "middle ground" of negotiated agreements between Indigenous and settler sovereignties by marking the ways settlers tilted the ground to serve settler interests.

46. Acts expropriating Wendat, Ojibwe, Bodwewademi, and Odawa lands for the purposes of a growing American settler colony include the 1795 Greenville Treaty and 1807 Detroit Treaty.

47. Silas Farmer, 1884, *The History of Detroit and Michigan: or, The Metropolis Illustrated*, Burton Historical Collection, Detroit Public Library; Alexander Henry, 1809, *Travels and Adventures in Canada and the Indian Territories between 1760 and 1776*, University of Michigan Libraries.

48. Land Claims in the Michigan Territory, Communicated to Congress, *American State Papers III*, https://hdl.loc.gov/loc.law/amlaw.lwsp, 305–400.

49. Report Concerning the Second Concessions Under the Act of May 11, 1820, *American State Papers V*, https://hdl.loc.gov/loc.law/amlaw.lwsp, 98–139.

50. Miles 2017.

51. Littlejohn 2018.

52. Detroit's first white supremacist riot occurred in 1833, when white Detroiters burned down forty buildings belonging to Black Detroiters following the escape of Rutha and Thornton Blackburn, two freedpeople, to Canada. Afterward, white elites enacted local ordinances requiring Black people to carry lanterns at night so they could be visible to police (Martelle 2012, 36–38).

53. Burton 1922, 197; Joseph Campau is also credited as Detroit's first "slumlord" (Detroit Historical Society 2023).

54. George Bates, 1877, "The By-Gones of Detroit," *Detroit Free Press*, November 4, 3.

55. The Campau family controlled infrastructural chokepoints that funneled goods and people between Chicago and the Atlantic. For Chicago's importance within the western push of American settler colonization, see Cronon 1991.

56. Family disagreements became matters of public record in local circuit court filings,

many of which are incorporated within *Hope v. Detroit Trust 266 N.W. 326 (Mich 1936)*, in which the presiding judge writes, "The lands of the Campau family have been a fruitful source of litigation."

57. Miller 2015; Sugrue 2005.

58. Edward Lynch, 2022, "Understanding the Rental Landscape," Detroit Future City, https://detroitfuturecity.com/wp-content/uploads/2022/08/FINAL-Understanding-the-Rental-Landscape.pdf.

59. Akers et al. 2019. See also Caverly 2021.

60. Akers and Seymour 2018; Atuahene and Hodge 2018; Atuahene and Berry 2018.

61. Eisenberg et al. 2020.

62. Tom Perkins, May 4, 2016, "Are Real Estate Investors from Oakland County to Hong Kong Driving Detroit's Blight?" *Metro Times*, https://www.metrotimes.com/news/are-real-estate-investors-from-oakland-county-to-hong-kong-driving-detroits-blight-2441828; Alex Alsup, September 7, 2022, "Bids on Detroit," *The Chargeback*, https://detroit.substack.com/p/bids-on-detroit.

63. In a paradigmatic case, Gwendolyn Warren and other participants in the Detroit Geographical Expedition and Institute (DGEI) began tracing rental payments to illustrate the "direction of money transfers in Metropolitan Detroit." For more on DGEI, see Warren, Katz, and Heynen 2019.

64. In 2023, 75 percent of the 3.7 million people counted in Detroit's suburbs as part of the US census were white identified. Eleven percent of suburbanites who identified as Black and 5 percent who identified as Asian represented the next largest racialized demographics.

65. Violet Ikonomova, December 18, 2019, "Dearborn Property Maintenance Worker Has Blighted Detroit Buildings—and County Lets Him Buy More," *Deadline Detroit*, https://deadlinedetroit.com/articles/23964/dearborn_building_inspector_has_blighted_detroit_properties_and_county_lets_him_buy_more.

66. Allie Gross, August 17, 2018, "Detroit Real Estate Game Creates Chaos in Neighborhoods," *Detroit Free Press*, 1A, 10A–12A.

67. Taylor (2019, 30) demonstrates the predatory ways federal policies did not merely slant precarious and unsafe housing conditions toward Black Americans, but they did so in ways that made it possible for white people to profit directly and indirectly from this process.

68. Work on this is vast. Alongside Taylor (2019), George Lipsitz (2024) and Safiya Noble (2018) are particularly clarifying.

69. Josh Akers (2013) notes that this neoliberal sentiment was central to the bipartisan enactment of tax foreclosure policy, which was supported by Detroit's political elites.

70. For an illustration of this, consider Sarah Alvarez, October 12, 2017, "Owe Taxes? That's OK. Wayne County Will Still Sell You Foreclosed Homes," Michigan Public Radio, https://www.michiganpublic.org/families-community/2017-10-12/owe-taxes-thats-ok-wayne-county-will-still-sell-you-foreclosed-homes.

71. W. E. B. Du Bois 1920, 30.

72. What Du Bois ([1935] 2007) named the "public and psychological" wages of whiteness

are fundamentally material (Roediger 2020). Those conversations are robust and ongoing, especially around colonial racial capitalism in its contemporary and historical guises (Koshy et al. 2022). Cheryl Harris's (1993, 2022) identification of "whiteness as property" is an elaboration on Du Bois's intervention.

Chapter 2

1. Photos taken by city surveyors were preserved in the special collections of the Detroit Public Library. They were not opened for public view until 2017. Emily Kutil curated a physical and digital installation of these images, "Black Bottom Street View," https://www.blackbottomstreetview.com.

2. Principally, this is Public Act 344 (MCL 125.72), first enacted by the Michigan state legislature in 1945, with amendments as recently as 2013.

3. MCL 127.72, Section 2. This authorization has remained consistent across almost ten revisions of the legal text.

4. Sean Mallin (2016) summarizes these common threads in his examination of how such statutes came to matter in shaping relationships between neighbors, advocacy organizations, and municipal governance in post-Katrina New Orleans. For him, "People connect blighted properties to wider questions about urban citizenship and belonging, reflecting on property not as a natural or inevitable thing, but as a social and material problem" (8).

5. Jennifer Light (2014) considers this at length in the US context. Social reformer Mabel Walker's *Urban Blight and Slums* (1938) offers a representative identification of a "blighted area" as "one which has deteriorated from an economic standpoint" (6–7). While the categorization of such locations as "blight" might have emerged in the US context, they are resonant with conceptual and legal differentiations between what Frantz Fanon (1963) describes as the "settlers' town" and the "town belonging to the colonized people" (38–39). See also Wright 1991.

6. Colin Gordon (2004) contends the "elusive definition of blight" is its constitutive feature, and "courts have granted local interests almost *carte blanche* in their creative search for 'blighted' areas eligible for federal funds or local tax breaks" (305–6). Flexible categories hold immense power. As St. Clair Drake and Horace Cayton ([1962] 2015) note in their foundational ethnography of Black life in Chicago, "Over half of Black Metropolis lies in that area which the city planners and real-estate interests have designated as 'blighted.' . . . Housing already there is allowed to deteriorate and is then torn down" (206).

7. Callon (1986) coined this phrase to identify people, organizations, and other actors who "define and coordinate" (211) collective understandings of environmental conditions. For Callon, "The result is a situation in which certain entities control others. Understanding what sociologists generally call power relations means describing the way in which actors are defined, associated, and simultaneously obliged to remain faithful in their alliances" (224). For instances of obligatory passage points as an analytic for municipal governance, especially in the context of institutions that are necessary but not sufficient to address problems of structural inequity, see Amin 2013; Rydin 2013.

8. Producing images is always a question of power relations. Photography reifies racial categories as inherent to bodies (Browne 2015). Territorial images captured by cameras,

drones, and other apparatuses have also proven essential to racist securitization (Azoulay 2017; Goodfriend 2021). Blight provides an empirical case of how imaging racially subjected places is always already imaging racially subjected people and vice versa.

9. James Scott's (1999) *Seeing Like a State*, which suggests governing programs fail because they do not consider hyper-local conditions, is a persuasive analytic for critiquing modernist visions. And yet, as Mariana Valverde (2011) argues, Scott's identification of the "state" obscures how the actors involved in municipal governance—public employees, city residents, and others—are constantly immersed in hyper-local conditions. I follow Valverde in seeing municipal governance as a helpful vantage on just how local conditions come to matter, as well as how deep reckoning with such conditions does not necessarily ensure outcomes match planful intents (see also Hull 2022).

10. Municipal staff tasked with this decision described a tension between their desire to "advocate a program of site selection solely on the basis of deterioration" and "the fact that the Housing Commission, by city policy, does not have the power to open up new areas for [occupancy by Black people]." They ultimately chose to begin in majority-Black neighborhoods to avoid integrating majority-white neighborhoods. "Racial Considerations in Urban Renewal," City Plan Commission 1947: Box 8, "Master Plan Technical Report," Burton Historical Collection.

11. Browne 2015, 16.

12. Much of this cohered in the gray literature of the Vacant Property Research Network, a collaboration between university researchers and government practitioners (https://vacantpropertyresearch.com/). See also Mallach 2018.

13. Such alleged "tipping points" obscure structural conditions that separate people from buildings. See Akers 2017; Hackworth 2019; Yezbick 2020.

14. MCL 125.72, Public Act 344 of 1945, "Blighted Area Rehabilitation."

15. Light 2014; Photographer Jacob Riis's (1996) accounts of tenements in New York's lower east side during the late nineteenth century are an example of such efforts to locate blight in the lifeworlds of racially marginalized people to elicit sympathy from wealthy white viewers. People emplaced as subjects of "shantytown blight" (Blair 2018, 18) also spoke back to these conditions on their own terms.

16. Herscher 2015, 40.

17. "Housing Plans Are Mapped Out," December 9, 1910, *Detroit Free Press*, 8. The pamphlet was read at a meeting of the Ohio State Board of Health (Oscar Hasencamp, 1912, "Better Housing for Our Industrial Classes," *Ohio's Health* 2 (1–2): 26–37, University of Michigan Libraries).

18. Ford Motor Company, 1915, *Helpful Hints and Advice to Employees to Help Them Grasp the Opportunities Which Are Presented to Them by the Ford Profit-Sharing Plan*, 7, Ohio State University Libraries.

19. John W. Smith, "The Menace of the City Slum," October 11, 1939. "Your Government," WWJ Radio, Detroit, Mayor's Papers, 1939, Box 6, "Blight," Burton Historical Collection; files from condemnation proceedings, including images and plot maps of buildings ordered demolished, remain in the Detroit Public Library, Corporation Counsel, Real Estate Division, Boxes 18–23, Burton Historical Collection.

20. June Manning Thomas (2013) summarizes how "racial discrimination in code enforcement was documented; Black renters could not depend on the city either to enforce the code or to prevent landlords from evicting them once they complained about violations. This led to a protracted war by civil rights organizations against 'slum landlords' " (89).

21. If blight seems like a forerunner to repeatedly disproven "broken windows" theories that served to justify the targeted policing of communities of color in the United States, that is because it is (Ansfield 2020). But the racist ramifications of circular arguments that construct allegedly deficient people as products of allegedly deficient built environments extend beyond the particular context of the US (Ghertner 2015; Yezbick 2020).

22. Thomas 2013; Drake [1962] 2015.

23. "Map War on Blight, City Urged," July 8, 1962, *Detroit Free Press*, A3.

24. Facing a growing number of complaints from city residents about empty buildings, beginning in 1964, Detroit's municipal government organized citywide surveys to categorize buildings on a seven-point scale from "Sound" to "Extreme Dilapidation" (Mayor's Committee for Community Renewal, 1964, Blight Rating Test, Wayne State University Purdy-Kresge Library). Lacking sufficient staff, city planning and building departments contracted this and other efforts to understand the landscape to private firms (Market Opinion Research Company, 1964, Vacancy Study for Mayor's Committee for Community Renewal, Wayne State University Purdy-Kresge Library).

25. Dewar and Thomas 2012.

26. David Weiss and Derek vanPelt, March 25, 1976, "What Can Be Done About Detroit's Abandoned Buildings?" *The Sun*, Bentley Historical Library.

27. Hall [1997] 2021, 362.

28. Yezbick 2020.

29. Mayor's Papers, 1939, Box 6, "Blight," Burton Historical Collection; Corporation Counsel, Real Estate Division, Boxes 18–23, Burton Historical Collection.

30. Officially, Detroit has a 138.73-square-mile land area. Some round up (I do). Others round down.

31. Patricia Montemurri, Zachare Bell, and Roger Chesley, July 9, 1989, "15,215 Buildings Stand Empty. Fast Growing Cancer Leaves Few City Neighborhoods Unscathed," *Detroit Free Press*, 1A, 9A–11A.

32. "Demolition Chief: 'I Think This Program Will Do It,' " July 9, 1989, *Detroit Free Press*, 11A.

33. W. Kim Heron, August 29, 1984, "Candidate Costa Leads an Illegal Demolition," *Detroit Free Press*, 3A; Anne Kim, July 9, 1989, "House-Busters Say They Feel No Regrets, May Wreck Again," *Detroit Free Press*, 3A; Mike Williams, July 3, 1989, "Neighbors Keep Up Demolition," *Detroit Free Press*, 3A.

34. The decades of cuts to Detroit's municipal budget leading up to wholesale elimination of certain services in 2013–2014 bankruptcy proceedings are a "not-so-special case" (Peck and Whiteside 2016) of how white flight and capital disinvestment deprive people of the support they need for a dignified life in the United States.

35. Detroit became known for so-called do-it-yourself urbanism as residents made do

with budget cuts that eliminated many core public services from the municipal government between the 1970s and 2010s (Kinder 2016). While outsiders celebrated Detroiters' DIY provisioning, residents often chafed at the need to fill gaps created by austerity and disinvestment (Bartlett 2017).

36. "Program for Replanning and Rehabilitation of Blighted Areas," Mayor's Papers 1940: Box 1, "Blight," Burton Historical Collection; "Racial Considerations in Urban Renewal," City Plan Commission 1947: Box 8 "Master Plan Technical Report," Burton Historical Collection.

37. Notably, the Field Relocation Office established to ensure displaced people were rehoused could not account for every person's whereabouts after they were forced out. Thomas 2013, 55–81.

38. boyd and Crawford 2012; Wang 2013.

39. Thick data has been persuasive in efforts to construct cities that facilitate the desires of residents (Hong et al. 2023). But thick data is not necessarily emancipatory. The creation of "postcolonial thick data" around life expectancy and health in Bangladesh (Murphy 2017, 59), for instance, "built extensive social science infrastructures that aspired to stimulate the 'acceptance' of contraception" (61).

40. Murray 2015.

41. I looked for these instances—really looked—finding only a single case between 2014 and 2020. In it, Daniel Murray was living in his lifelong home without utilities. He was not home when workers came to test for asbestos, nor when a demolition team knocked down the house. With assistance from an eviction defense collective, Murray sued the Detroit Land Bank Authority for damages (Jennifer Dixon, June 18, 2017, "Detroiter Sues, Says His Lifelong Home Demolished in Ambush-Style Eviction," *Detroit Free Press*, A1, A4).

42. Detroit's mayor and demolition officials made this a routine talking point. (Christine Ferretti and Beth LeBlanc, May 30, 2019, "Mayor Duggan Pledges Blight-Free Detroit Neighborhoods by 2024," *Detroit News*, https://www.detroitnews.com/story/news/local/detroit-city/2019/05/30/mayor-mike-duggan-seeks-200-million-bond-blight-demolition/1285027001/).

43. Alex Alsup, October 1, 2024, "Zooming in on Detroit's Sweat Equity," *The Chargeback*, https://detroit.substack.com/p/zooming-in-on-detroits-sweat-equity.

44. Violet Ikonomova, November 14, 2018, "Despite Demolition Efforts, Blight Spreads Undetected Throughout Detroit's Neighborhoods," *Detroit Metro Times*, https://www.metrotimes.com/news/despite-demolition-effort-blight-spreads-undetected-throughout-detroits-neighborhoods-17692371; Violet Ikonomova, October 13, 2019, "'Easy Politics': Why Duggan's $420M Plan to Wipe Out Blight Could Fall Short," *Deadline Detroit*, https://www.deadlinedetroit.com/articles/23465/easy_politics_why_duggan_s_420m_plan_to_wipe_out_blight_may_fall_short.

45. Detroiters have organized extensively against police surveillance (Petty 2020).

46. "What About Personal Privacy?," 2019, *Detroit Street View*, https://detroitmi.gov/departments/department-innovation-and-technology/detroit-street-view.

47. Computer vision and associated technologies are predicated on and reproduce an "anti-Black box" (Benjamin 2019, 34–36). Scholarly examinations of racism and intersecting

inequities embedded in computer imaging are extensive. For instance, Browne 2015; Jefferson 2020.

48. Broussard 2023.

49. Browne 2015; Petty 2020; Zuboff 2019.

50. Consider the entanglements between the infrastructures of Google Street View and those of settler occupation that anthropologist of surveillance Sophia Goodfriend (2021) documents in Palestine. Far from a transparent perspective, people who click through Google Street View representations produced from roadways in occupied territories receive a censored view scrubbed of military bases, checkpoints, and compounds that enact the state of Israel as a settler colonial project.

51. Kayleigh Lickliter, 2024, "Insider Detroit's War on Abandoned Cars," NextCity, August 28, https://nextcity.org/features/inside-detroits-war-on-abandoned-cars.

52. Gailloux 2022; Harris 2013.

53. Sznel 2020; cf. Valverde 2011.

54. Ghertner 2015; Herscher 2015; Solomon 2022.

55. Crawford 2020; Sznel 2020.

56. Valverde 2011.

57. Mattern 2021, 72, emphases original.

58. 69 percent of Detroit households met this threshold compared to 41 percent of households statewide (United Way of Southeast Michigan, 2021, *2021 Asset Limited, Income Constrained, Employed Report*, https://unitedforalice.org/state-overview/Michigan).

Chapter 3

1. In 2022, the median Detroit household took in around $36,500, and more than one in three Detroit households lived below the federal poverty line. For decades, Detroit has been among the most impoverished large cities in the United States (Erika Barker, Liang Hu, Hasan Alaswaf, Owen Fleming, and Sarah Klammer, 2023, "Detroit Economic Indicators Report," City of Detroit, https://detroitmi.gov/sites/detroitmi.localhost/files/2024-04/Q2%202023%20Economic%20Indicators%20Report.pdf).

2. For community and university researchers alike, the goal of this project was to identify possibilities for stabilizing Detroit's existing housing stock for the benefit of existing residents (Ryan Ruggiero, Josh Rivera, and Patrick Cooney, 2020, "A Decent Home: The Status of Home Repair in Detroit," University of Michigan Poverty Solutions, https://poverty.umich.edu/files/2020/10/The-Status-of-Home-Repair-in-Detroit-October-2020.pdf; Alexa Eisenberg, Connor Wakayama, and Patrick Cooney, 2021, "Reinforcing Low-Income Homeownership Through Home Repair: Evaluation of the Make It Home Program," University of Michigan Poverty Solutions, https://poverty.umich.edu/files/2021/02/PovertySolutions-Make-It-Home-Repair-Program-Feb2021-final.pdf).

3. Urban Institute, 2017, "The Detroit Housing Market: Challenges and Innovations for a Path Forward," https://www.urban.org/sites/default/files/publication/88656/detroit_path_forward_0.pdf; Joel Kurth and Mike Wilkinson, March 30, 2017, "That Detroit Rarity: A Home Mortgage," *Bridge Magazine*, https://www.bridgemi.com/urban-affairs/detroit-rarity-home-mortgage; Kendall Nash, 2023, "Small-Dollar Mortgages," Detroit Future

City, https://detroitfuturecity.com/wp-content/uploads/2023/10/BWDC_Final_2023_10_16.pdf.

4. Alan Mallach (2018) summarizes many of those cases.

5. Onuoha (2017) builds "algorithmic violence" in explicit dialogue with Johan Galtung's structural violence. Other key works on the computational dimensions of structural violence include Benjamin 2019; Eubanks 2019; Noble 2018. Sara Safransky (2020) articulates these connections in Detroit.

6. As Brian Jordan Jefferson (2022) observes, racist distributions of value that reflect and reproduce colonial racial capitalist ends "might not be mere surface effects but rather are operational logics written into the very source code" of algorithmic systems, even if unintentionally (233).

7. Keeanga-Yamahtta Taylor (2019) describes how, following the civil rights act, deliberate antiblack exclusion been complemented by "predatory inclusion." See also: Brown 2024 for a discussion of how housing systems in the United States have always been racialized.

8. Noelle Stout (2019) shows how this was compounded by the "predatory bureaucracy" of market-driven recovery instruments that kept banks whole as people lost their homes.

9. Put simply, racism, especially antiblackness, is constitutive of debt instruments (Taylor 2019; Bledsoe and Wright 2019).

10. Pasquale 2016, 41.

11. For examples of how the prospect of home finance was imbricated in arguments for demolition funding, see Anna Clark, December 7, 2015, "The Threat to Detroit's Rebound Isn't Crime or the Economy, It's the Mortgage Industry," NextCity, https://nextcity.org/features/detroit-bankruptcy-revival-crime-economy-mortgage-loans-redlining; Christine MacDonald and Joel Kurth, June 3, 2015, "Foreclosures Fuel Detroit Blight, Cost City $500 Million," *Detroit News*, June 3, https://www.detroitnews.com/story/news/special-reports/2015/06/03/detroit-foreclosures-risky-mortgages-cost-taxpayers/27236605/; Erick Trickey, May 18, 2017, "Detroit's DIY Cure for Urban Blight," *Politico Magazine*, https://www.politico.com/magazine/story/2017/05/18/how-detroit-is-beating-its-blight-215160/.

12. For examples of this work, see Torrejón, Paredes, and Skidmore 2023; Dynamo Metrics, 2015, "Estimating Home Equity Impacts from Rapid Targeted Residential Demolition in Detroit, MI," Dynamo Metrics, https://web.archive.org/web/20170712165323/http://www.demolitionimpact.org/#thereport.

13. As Tess Lea (2021) puts it, "bureaucracies are peopled." This is to say that their decisions and operations are made by people, even if they may appear opaque. As a person within Detroit's demolition bureaucracy, Sam was immensely generous in helping me learn the administrative processes of building removal. You may notice how I am not locating Sam or their identities. This is because Sam asked me not to.

14. As a public authority, the land bank was publicly funded but independent of the municipal government. Gail Radford (2013) historicizes how public authorities in the United States "fracture the capacity of the public sector" (14) while also making it possible to address highly local issues related to housing, territory, and infrastructure.

15. Other statistical analyses showed that even as demolitions occurred across the city's census blocks, they were more likely to occur on blocks with slightly higher percentage of

white residents on average than the city as a whole (Jay et al. 2019). Such analyses utilize different methods and spatial units than Sam's team. Measurement strategies matter. I choose to trust that Sam and their colleagues were not being deceptive.

16. Margaret Hu (2017) describes this as "algorithmic Jim Crow." In contrast to decisions explicitly based on racial categories (e.g. of people, of neighborhoods, of cities), algorithmic systems make decisions based on pools of data that can make it impossible to know from the outside why certain outcomes happen rather than others. See also Benjamin 2019.

17. Madden et al. 2017, 86.

18. Eubanks 2019; Broussard, 2018, 156.

19. Campbell et al. 2020, 217–19.

20. Safransky 2020, 16.

21. Brown 2024; Harris 2013.

22. Sara Safransky describes this as a process of "municipal redlining." See also Kinder 2016; Peck 2014.

23. Jason Hackworth (2019) suggests that demolition became the sum total of state-level urban policy in the American Rust Belt following arguments that stable financial conditions would take hold once cities had removed enough empty buildings.

24. Campbell et al. 2020, 217–19. See also Safransky 2020.

25. Such "algorithmic auditing" is key to surfacing instances where computational metrics, intentionally or not, encode inequities. For more, see Costanza-Chock, Raji, and Buolamwini 2022.

26. This has been relatively consistent over the past five decades, with the rate of homeownership in Detroit peaking at 60 percent in 1970.

27. Detroiters' reliance on cash purchases contrasts with the rest of the United States, including similarly sized cities (Anna Clark, December 7, 2015, "The Threat to Detroit's Rebound Isn't Crime or the Economy, It's the Mortgage Industry," NextCity, https://nextcity.org/features/detroit-bankruptcy-revival-crime-economy-mortgage-loans-redlining).

28. Reflecting the symbolic and material importance of homeownership, supporters for increasing Detroiters' ownership of their home came from organizations that sometimes found themselves in opposition to each other's initiatives. For example, eviction defense groups and municipal administrators who typically frustrated each other shared the same goal of increasing homeownership opportunities for Detroiters.

29. Freund 2007, 115.

30. New Detroit, 2020, "Racial Equity Highlights," https://www.newdetroit.org/racial-equity-highlights/.

31. Edward Lynch, Vinita Wagh, and Ashley Williams Clark, 2023, "Black Homebuyer Demand," Detroit Future City, https://detroitfuturecity.com/data_reports/black-homebuyer-demand/.

32. In many cases, people lost their homes despite completing lengthy applications for state assistance. Noelle Stout (2019) describes how this was common across the United States.

33. Eisenberg, Alexa, and Kate Brantley, 2023, "The Crisis Is Not Temporary: Evictions

After Emergency Rental Assistance in Detroit," University of Michigan Poverty Solutions, https://sites.fordschool.umich.edu/poverty2021/files/2023/06/CERA-report-may-2023.pdf.

34. Akers et al. 2019.

35. Quizar 2024, 817.

36. Simone 2004. See also Stack 2008.

37. Toyia Watts, a Black Detroiter in her late sixties, helpfully explained her experience of home repair as "you give people hope and we wait and we wait and we wait." Quoted in Nushrat Rahman, February 1, 2024, "Home Repair Fund: Need for Fixes Could Range from $5B to $20B in Detroit," *Detroit Free Press*.

38. Herbert 2021, 3–4.

39. Aaron Mondry, November 10, 2021, "Detroit Home Repair Program Proves Helpful—for the Few Who Qualify," Outlier Media, https://outliermedia.org/detroit-home-repair-program-proves-helpful-for-the-few-who-qualify/; Nushrat Rahman, February 1, 2024, "Home Repair Fund: Need for Fixes Could Range from $5B to $20B in Detroit," *Detroit Free Press*, A4, A12.

40. They highlighted calculations of demolitions and home-repair loan programs contributing to a $1 billion increase in Black Detroiters' wealth between 2019 and 2021. See also Mayor's Office, 2024, "Roadmap to Recovery: Rebuilding Black Wealth," City of Detroit, https://playbook.detroitmi.gov/articles/rebuilding-black-wealth.

41. Benjamin 2019, 422. See also Eubanks 2019; Jefferson 2022; Noble 2018.

42. Zhang 2023.

43. This is the "constructive view" of reparations for which Olúfẹ́mi Táíwò (2022) argues. See also So et al. 2022.

44. Zhang 2023, 4.

Chapter 4

1. For overviews, see Brodkin 2014; Roediger and Esch 2012. Also helpful is Joshua Reno's (2015) ethnography of a Michigan landfill, which addresses the intersections of gender and race, especially whiteness and masculinity with respect to waste work in this context.

2. Insights from Stuart Hall, Chas Critcher, Tony Jefferson, John Clarke, and Brian Roberts (1978) are worth reflecting on at length. In their words, "The structures through which black labour is reproduced, we argued, are not just coloured by race; they work by means of race. . . . Race enters into the way black labour, male and female, is distributed as economic agents on the level of economic practice - and the class struggles which result from it. . . . This gives the matter of race and racism a theoretical as well as a practical centrality to all the relations and practices which affect black labour. The constitution of this class fraction as a class, and the class relations which inscribe it, function as race relations. The two are in separable. Race is the modality in which class is lived. It is also the medium in which class relations are experienced" (394). This observation is foundational to what is now discussed as intersectionality. See Collins 2000, 221–38.

3. In Karen Brodkin's (2014) phrasing, gendered experiences are always "corporeal embodiments" of the relationship between racism and political economy.

4. Du Bois (1935) 2007. See also Hartman 1997; Roediger 2020.

5. Du Bois (1935) 2007, 5.

6. Freshour 2017; Torkelson 2021.

7. As feminist scholars of technoscience have shown, racialized, feminized work is foundational to the calculated worth of "life" itself (Murphy 2017), as well as to the routinized accumulation of capital (Atanasoski and Vora 2019; Torkelson 2021).

8. Reflecting on the ways Ford's factories transformed entire polities, Antonio Gramsci ([1971] 1992) remarked that Ford had undertaken "the biggest collective effort to date to create, with unprecedented speed, and with a consciousness of purpose unmatched in history, a new type of worker and a new type of man." While Detroit may have been Ford's origin, as Greg Grandin (2010) shows, he cultivated the industrial empire of "a new world, a new heaven, and a new earth" (42) on a global scale.

9. Ford was an early pioneer at plant suburbanization. In the 1910s, to avoid Detroit's municipal taxation and regulatory regimes, he shifted operations out of the city into Highland Park and Dearborn. The Highland Park plant has been shuttered since the 1970s, but pickup trucks are still produced at the River Rouge facility in Dearborn.

10. Christine Walley's (2013) account of southeast Chicago is particularly instructive; see also Allison 2012.

11. Even the most developed Fordist-Keynesian systems were predicated on the exclusionary allocation of benefits, especially along the intersections of race, gender, and class (Roediger and Esch 2012; Sugrue 2005).

12. Grandin 2010.

13. Denby 1989, 131. Henry Ford and other major industrial employers in Detroit enforced segregation regimes on and off the line. See also Esch 2018.

14. Insecure work arrangements are normative in the United States, though they do not have to be (Doussard 2013; Purser 2019).

15. This model is the basis of state policy and collective imagination in the United States and elsewhere.

16. In practice, Fordist regimes do not operate with such stability. Nevertheless, by comparison to increasingly flexible work arrangements, Fordist stability is retrospectively notable (Muehlebach and Shoshan 2012; Walley 2013).

17. As Marc Doussard puts it in his examination of this disjuncture, cyclical labor "draws our attention because it dramatizes a series of surprisingly widespread threats to the experience of work as it has long been understood" (2013, viii). And yet, precarity is not new in the Global North, just somewhat more generally distributed (Millar 2017).

18. Distilling feminist analyses of social reproduction, Laura Briggs (2018) reminds us how such labors are essential to everything else.

19. Again, Briggs's (2018) examination of social reproduction is essential. In it, she historicizes how the intersections of racism and sexism permeate what counts as "work" and "labor."

20. Consider the linkages of "global whiteness" that Tiffany Willoughby-Herard (2015) tracks between South Africa and the United States by way of the Carnegie Corporation, pushing against the assumption that whiteness was more secure in one location or the

other. Across them, propping up the connections of wealth with whiteness in general and white masculinity in particular demanded constant work by industrial and state actors.

21. Tsing 2015, 2.

22. Muehlebach 2012; White 2012.

23. As Ruth Wilson Gilmore reminds us, all capitalism is racial capitalism, no matter its Fordist or post-Fordist guises. People who fell outside the triangulation of European-descended masculinity were only ever contingent beneficiaries of Fordist social contracts, often in ways that created greater deprivation than what is experienced by the majority-white ranks of professional class employment in the twenty-first century Global North; see also Millar 2017.

24. Reno 2015.

25. Presentation slides cited statistics from public agencies to enumerate the move from an estimated 759,000 people employed in Detroit (349,000 in manufacturing) in 1950 to 202,000 people employed (20,000 in manufacturing) in 2010 (McDonald 2014). This shift was not evenly distributed. Thomas Sugrue (2005) identifies how, by 1960, "bustling plants were abandoned and boarded up as companies moved production outside the city or went out of business. . . . 19.7 percent black auto workers were unemployed, compared to only 5.8 percent of whites. Discrimination and deindustrialization proved to be a lethal combination for blacks. Seniority protected some black workers from permanent layoffs, but it disproportionately benefited white workers" (144).

26. In several instances, firm owners were themselves excavator operators.

27. Reno 2015, 199.

28. Fredericks 2018; Millar 2018.

29. As Elana Resnick (2021) shows, the racialized and gendered embodied labors of managing waste are embedded in local contexts. In the United States, that context is one in which waste management is masculine labor with men of color routed into the most precarious assignments (Solomon 2019).

30. In 2012, a man from Ohio purchased a building in a densely inhabited east side neighborhood known for large mansions that had been built for Detroit's white industrial elite during the late nineteenth and early twentieth centuries. Shortly after the purchase, workers began disassembling the house and packing the pieces to construct a lakefront home in Ohio. Although neighbors intervened to block the disassembly, the case is indicative of how pieces of Detroit's buildings were known to be valuable. So does a piece from a satirical paper that suggests Detroit paid off its municipal debts by selling empty buildings for scrap (*The Onion*, April 5, 2006, "Detroit Sold for Scrap," https://theonion.com/detroit-sold-for-scrap-1819568384/).

31. Emergency demolitions for structures that could imminently collapse, typically following a building fire, occurred year-round.

32. Claire Herbert (2021) discusses scrapping as one of the broader techniques of "appropriation" that Detroiters used to make space for themselves in their city, including a typology of scrapping in which Detroiters differentiated between materials available for appropriation and materials to be left (91–92, 107–13)

33. During the late nineteenth century, workers in Detroit's brickyards turned out over

60,000,000 bricks per year, rising to more than 200 million bricks a year in the early twentieth century to keep pace with new construction ("West Detroit Is Making 200,000,000 Bricks a Year in Radius of One Mile," February 16, 1914, *Detroit Free Press*, 6).

34. Josh Lepawsky and Chris McNabb's (2010) geography of electronic wastes is a useful guide to this process.

35. Solomon 2019.

36. It is also the sort of place where a local antiques seller purposefully auctioned a Klan robe on the national holiday honoring Martin Luther King Jr.

37. To see what one of these programs entailed, see "Access for All," United Way of Southeastern Michigan, https://youtu.be/B2ZcplO62D4?si=JO_cjGlFhtQadrum.

38. At recruitment fairs in Detroit, unions who organized carpenters, plumbers, electricians, and other skilled trades often made a point of how their training facilities were in Detroit or its inner suburbs.

39. With respect to building trades unions, Lawrence Mishel (2017) summarizes, "Informal hiring and training structure perpetuated exclusionary 'whites-only' hiring and training practices. Competing for scarce jobs in the industry exacerbated whites-only racism (for decades throughout the 20th century, white ethnic groups also faced discrimination). Some building trades unions, such as the Sheet Metal Workers International Association, had 'Caucasian only' clauses in their constitutions through the mid-twentieth century, until forced by federal, state, and city regulators to remove them" (5). See also Thompson 2001.

40. To be clear, there is nothing inherently gendered about any technology or work. That claim is the product of sociohistorical relationships (Oldenziel 1999).

41. Since the early 2000s, municipal contracting guidelines have prioritized demolition firms based in Detroit and those that employ city residents. It is notable that the two largest demolition firms operating in Detroit between 2010 and 2020 were Detroit based. However, they were also owned by white suburbanites.

42. Kat Stafford, June 15, 2018, "Detroit's Demolition Program Under Fire for Lack of Diversity," *Detroit Free Press*, A4, A14.

43. Joe Guillen, October 23, 2016, "Why Did Feds Suspend Detroit's Demolition Program?" *Detroit Free Press*, 1A, 5A.

44. Small contractors had voiced this difficulty since at least the 1980s, especially through the Inner City Black Wreckers Association. See also Kat Stafford, June 15, 2018, "Detroit's Demolition Program Under Fire for Lack of Diversity," *Detroit Free Press*, A4, A14.

45. A laid-off Chrysler plant worker told Kate Dudley (1997), "When they start tearing [the plant] down, I'm going to go get a brick. I would just keep it. My kids know mama spent fifteen years of her life [in the plant] working, and to tell my future grandkids about it. You know, tell them that it was a place where we worked and that when they tore the building down, Grandma went and got herself a brick. For all that I put in there, I figure at least I deserve a brick" (173).

46. Hackworth 2019; Metzl 2019.

47. Jefferson Cowie and Joseph Heathcott (2003) discuss how centering "smokestack nostalgia" for industrial projects can obscure inequities that undergirded those same projects. See also Strangleman 2013.

Chapter 5

1. Depending on the job and employer, these respirators were sometimes full face-piece, supplied-air respirators and more typically P100 cartridge respirators. You are probably familiar with disposable N95 respirators, so designated because they meet US National Institute of Occupational Safety and Health metrics for filtering out at least 95 percent of airborne particles. P100 respirators meet NIOSH testing metrics for filtering out at least 99.97 percent of airborne particles. If a disposable N95 respirator is a "high filtration" mask, a P100 is even higher. Supplied air and filter cartridge respirators are fit to a person's face and reusable. For more on asbestos respirators, see OSHA, January 4, 2024, Standard Interpretation Letter on Respirators for Asbestos Class 1 Work, Responding to Future Environment Designs.

2. In recent years, environmental regulators employed by the State of Michigan have been housed in a variety of departments. In 2009, they existed in the Department of Natural Resources and Environment (DNRE). In 2010, an executive reorganization created the stand-alone Department of Environmental Quality (DEQ). In 2019, that department was renamed the Department of Environment, Great Lakes, and Energy (EGLE). Reflecting the status quo of most of my fieldwork, as well as popular use even after the name change, I refer to this division as DEQ.

3. This regulatory provision is part of the asbestos National Emissions Standards for Hazardous Air Pollutants (NESHAP), rev. 2004, 40 Code of Federal Regulations (CFR), part 61, subpart M.

4. Municipal administrators sidestepped asbestos abatement following austerity-driven requirements to stretch demolition budgets further (Steve Neavling, April 6, 2010, "Detroit Demolition Plan Comes to Grinding Halt. No Asbestos Testing Violates Law," *Detroit Free Press*, 1A, 6A).

5. EPA, July 15, 1993, Asbestos Applicability Letter, Responding to Missouri Air Pollution Control Program, Control Number A930028: "Although some cities may only demolish one building at a time, or several buildings scattered throughout the city, over the course of the year, a city may demolish a significant number of buildings. In an extreme case, more than 1,000 abandoned homes were demolished in one month. Typically, these houses are in run-down or poor neighborhoods, and the question of environmental equity arises. The asbestos NESHAP clearly allows for individual homeowners to renovate or demolish their own homes without being subject to the NESHAP. However, it was not EPA's intent to allow for the mass demolition or continuing demolition of vacant or dilapidated houses without such demolitions being subject to the requirements of the NESHAP. The responsible parties (including cities) must inspect for asbestos, and if none is found, the only requirement is to notify EPA or its delegated agency of the demolition."

6. Detroit Demolition Program information page, "Protecting Our Neighbors and the Environment," https://detroitmi.gov/departments/construction-and-demolition-department/protecting-our-neighbors-and-environment.

7. Quoted in Christine Feretti, September 8, 2014, "Detroit Raises Safety in Residential Razings, Empowers Neighbors to Report Contractors," *Detroit News*, https://www.detroitnews.com/story/news/local/wayne-county/2014/09/08/detroit-raises-safety-in-residential-razings-empowers-neighbors-to-report-contractors/15264883/.

8. Jennifer Dixon, May 21, 2017, "After Asbestos Frustrations, a Crackdown on Detroit Demolitions," *Detroit Free Press*, A1, A12; Sarah Rahal, July 14, 2022, "Detroit Temporarily Bans Three Abatement Companies Involved in Demolitions," *Detroit News*, https://www.detroitnews.com/story/news/local/detroit-city/2022/07/14/detroit-bans-3-abatement-enviornmental-companies-involved-demolitions/10058148002/.

9. Bullard and Wright (2012) articulate what people who live in the vicinity of refineries, factories, waste transfer centers, and other hazardous installations know well—within the operating protocols of polluting industries in the United States, communities of color, especially Black and Indigenous communities, have been less protected from environmental burdens when compared to majority-white places. This is a robust area of scholarship and activism that connects the "slow violence" (Nixon 2011) of chemical valley (Davies 2019) and extractive wastelands (Voyles 2015) in North America to the reproduction of racial capitalism as an intercontinental environmental force (Anthias and Asher 2024; Hecht 2023).

10. In 2016, after finding the DLBA was paying contractors who demolished buildings without completing abatements and noting that this was likely spreading asbestos-laden dust through Detroit's neighborhoods, the DEQ staff ended their "enforcement discretion" and obtained a consent judgment against the land bank's demolition program that levied fines and other consequences. *Michigan Department of Environmental Quality v. City of Detroit, City of Detroit Building Authority, and Detroit Land Bank Authority*, Ingham County Circuit Court, File No. 18-862-CE; DEQ and DLBA staff email discussions reviewed under FOIA.

11. Practically as much as legally, having state agents' eyes literally on worksites is crucial to enacting regulatory standards. Consider the following example. A contractor demolished a building known to contain asbestos without ever filing paperwork to show it had been removed. The contractor also filed paperwork noting the structure was interred at a standard landfill, rather than one rated to contain asbestos wastes. State regulators noticed this, issued a violation notice to the contractor for failure to abate asbestos prior to demolition, and attempted to levy fines. Attorneys for the contractor ultimately had the violation and fines suspended by arguing that because regulators had not personally seen the demolition, they could not prove it had produced a dust cloud. DEQ AQD SRN File: U821610182 (16835 Prairie Street, Detroit), reviewed under FOIA.

12. Detroit Health Department, 2017, "Lead and Demolition Report," City of Detroit, https://www.bridgemi.com/sites/default/files/task_force_recommendations.pdf; Detroit Health Department, 2020, "Proximate Demolition Activity and Elevated Blood Lead Levels Among Children in Detroit, 2014–2018," City of Detroit, https://detroitmi.gov/sites/detroitmi.localhost/files/2020-05/Demo%20Lead%20Report%20to%20post.pdf.

13. This distinction evinces a regulatory system in which protection is enacted only in response to demonstrations of harm (e.g., poisoned people and landscapes) rather than based on precautionary principles. Plastics pollution researcher Max Liboiron (2021) discusses the racist, colonial logics of this system in detail, as well as how precautionary principles alone are not a surefire means of equitable protection.

14. Eilis O'Neill, February 21, 2017, "Are We Doing All We Can to Prevent Lead Poisoning?" *The Nation*, https://www.thenation.com/article/archive/are-we-doing-all-we-can-to-prevent-lead-poisoning/.

15. Bullard and Wright 2012; Zimring 2016.

16. Helpful places to orient toward these demands include Melissa Checker's (2005; 2020) examinations of environmental racism in Augusta, Georgia, and environmental gentrification in New York City, Chloe Ahmann's (2024) ethnography of late industrial Baltimore, and Lindsey Dillon and Julie Sze's (2016) exploration of the intersections of pollution and police violence.

17. Murphy 2006, 64–65.

18. Asbestos is, to borrow Annemarie Mol's (2002) phrase, something that has been made to "hang together" through classification.

19. Paul Brodeur's (1968) historicizes how this moniker enabled industrial actors to continue production despite evidence of occupational and environmental violence from asbestos. His piece was typically cited in asbestos-worker trainings I attended. So was a 2005 exchange in which a real estate developer, who would later become US president, defended the use of asbestos-containing materials in his buildings by calling it "magic" (US Senate Homeland Security and Governmental Affairs Subcommittee, July 22, 2005).

20. Brodeur 1980.

21. Jessica van Horssen's (2016) environmental history of Asbestos, Quebec, a town next to one of the world's largest asbestos mines, offers useful illustrations of this. For other contexts, see Johnston and McIvor 2004; Rose 2024.

22. Seidman and Selikoff's (1990) review of consequences of asbestos exposure on worker health was included in packets provided to abatement workers in trainings. So was the US OSHA standard (1926.1101) for asbestos exposure, which details mortality rates.

23. Many trainees' course fees were paid by state employment funds, including funds earmarked for people with recent interactions with the criminal legal system. Others were paid by programs designed to transition people receiving state benefits to paid employment. Such programs carry their own forms of capture and enclosure that resonate with carceral logics (Purser and Hennigan 2018). I paid my fees using research funds.

24. When announcing the program, one official proclaimed, "We really do have a miracle mineral on our hands."

25. Taken together, asbestos exposure claims are one of the longest running and most costly set of tort claims in US history (Carroll et al. 2005). Despite the large payouts, it is important to remember that financial compensation is rarely equivalent to justice (Jain 2006).

26. US Dept. of Interior, Bureau of Mines with Johns-Manville Inc., 1922, *The Story of Asbestos*, 31 min. (To view, see https://archive.org/details/0929StoryOfAsbestos.)

27. Sven Lindqvist (1979) reflects on "silvery fibres" of asbestos recovered from lungs of deceased cement workers, to argue for a worker-centric study of the history of capitalism, "because the results of history are still with us" (28). See also Rose 2024.

28. Rose 2024.

29. There is a deep literature on this in science and technology studies. Among others, Gabrielle Hecht's (2012, 2018) examinations of nuclear empires, Kim Fortun's (2001) on industrial disasters, and Max Liboiron's (2021) critique of the coloniality of pollution, are helpful places to orient toward it.

30. Feminist scholars of technoscience Angeliki Balayannis and Emma Garnett (2020) helpfully frame the production of industrial life as one of "chemical kinship," in which being related can be constructive or destructive depending on when, how, and who is placed at the center of those lineages. They build from M Murphy's (2013) framing of these relations between capital, materials, peoples, and places as "chemical infrastructures."

31. This definition originated in US OSHA regulations and became integrated in US EPA regulations. From OSHA 1926.1101(b), "*Critical barrier* means one or more layers of plastic sealed over all openings into a work area or any other similarly placed physical barrier sufficient to prevent airborne asbestos in a work area from migrating to an adjacent area."

32. For more, see US OSHA 1926.1101 and the EPA Asbestos NESHAP (40 CFR Part 61). Subpart 145 specifically attends to demolitions.

33. Lindqvist 1979; Rose 2024; van Horssen 2016.

34. Plastics researchers Rebecca Altman (2021) and Max Liboiron (2021) show how the weight of this violence is unevenly shouldered in industrial bodies, places, and infrastructures.

35. Asbestos and plastics were developed under what Kim Fortun (2015) calls "high industrialism," or systems of extraction, production, consumption, and disposal that some assumed could last forever. And yet, they clearly will not. Increasingly, Fortun argues, we inhabit a period of "late industrialism" characterized by the prolonged collapse of industrial projects into new trajectories of exhaustion and toxicity. In their own ways, Chloe Ahmann (2024) and Alison Kenner (2018) have elaborated on Fortun's insights.

36. I have written on this in the context of Detroiters constructing subsistence gardens on land laced with industrial toxicants and nominally owned by real estate investors (Caverly 2023).

37. Parenthetically, Roberts (2017) observes how people who live within harmful circumstances, "in fact, don't need anthropologists, STS scholars, or even Marx to explain how objects are made of relations" (596).

38. Materials from the abatement of the 1,200-square-foot structure filled a massive, truck-mounted container. On average, the plastic necessary to complete an abatement would fill a 30- to 40-cubic-yard dumpster.

39. Austerity did an even better job at limiting inspections altogether. Owing to limited staff following decades of limited budgets, MiOSHA and DEQ inspectors struggled with the volume of demolitions occurring . Jennifer Dixon, May 1, 2016, "EPA, DEQ Tougher on Asbestos Than Worker Safety Agency," *Detroit Free Press*, A9.

40. For Sofia (2000), containers are "a structurally necessary but frequently unacknowledgeable condition of becoming" (188). In a twist on STS scholar Annemarie Mol's (2002) dictum "To be is to be related," "to be" is also, it seems, "to be contained." In a similar vein, environmental anthropologist Victoria Nguyen (2020) details how Beijing inhabitants find collective sustenance as they contain themselves within face masks and air conditioning systems that keep out toxic atmospheres.

41. Jobsite humor offers a mode of critiquing workplace hierarchies. In male-dominated fields this often comes across as questioning the masculine fitness of another to work in particular ways (Ekers 2013; Ramirez 2011).

42. Dorothy Roberts's (1997) *Killing the Black Body* is a foundational examination of this ideology. If you have not read it, you should.

43. This remains so even in the third decade of the twenty-first century (Amutah et al. 2021; Pollock 2021).

44. Monitoring workers' health can be integral to facilitating health protections. For instance, beginning in 1967, the entire membership of the International Association of Heat and Frost Insulators and Asbestos Workers—17,800 men in the US and Canada—was enrolled in prospective health surveillance. Evidence of their common breathing difficulties and cancer diagnoses became the basis for regulatory action. And yet, these same efforts also perpetuated racialized (and sexed/gendered) typologies of breathing. See Braun 2014.

45. Braun's excavation of the spirometer (2014) comes alongside similar arguments made by other STS scholars critiquing the reproduction of racism through ostensibly race-neutral characterizations of biophysical capacities (Pollock 2021; Roberts 1997).

46. In 2020, the American Thoracic Society removed certain racialized breathing standards. However, "race correction" remains the standard for spirometers, the most widely used measure of pulmonary functioning (Madhusoodanan 2021).

47. "Spirometry Testing in Occupational Health Programs," United States Occupational Safety and Health Administration, Department of Labor, 3637-03 2013.

48. Inspectors told me that this is often the first question people asked them about their work.

49. Spirometry analyses document metrics like forced expiratory volume (FEV, the volume of a person exhales in a period), forced vital capacity (FVC, the total volume of air a person can blow out), and peak expiratory flow (PEF, the maximum speed at which a person exhales). Biophysical characteristics like height and age doubtless affect lung size and how a person breathes. Arguments that these metrics are sexed and raced are dubious at best.

50. The geographies of environmental racism are often airborne (Pulido 2017; Ybarra 2021). This reality drives literary scholar Christina Sharpe's (2016) argument that the wake of enslavement is a sustained "atmosphere of antiblackness" (112) in which the formerly enslaved and their descendants continue to be denied free breath.

51. In 1987, the United Church of Christ's report *Toxic Wastes and Race* coined the term "environmental racism" to describe the disproportionate siting of hazardous waste facilities in communities of color, especially majority-Black communities, in the US. A 2007 follow-up found "the conclusions are very much the same as they were in 1987" (Bullard et al. 2007, xi).

52. Joshua Reno (2016), among other discard studies scholars, shows just how this is an impossible promise.

53. The complete interview is not available on the internet, but part of it was spliced into a health promotion spot, "Asbestos for Workers," distributed by the San Diego County Air Pollution Control District (https://youtu.be/M-OY6IoVgWo).

54. Environmental-justice scholars Julie Sze and Lindsey Dillon (2016) explain, "We interpret the phrase 'I can't breathe' as condensing the histories of persistent patterns of

police violence, both which have denied breath and healthy breathing spaces to low-income communities of color. In this sense, the inability to breathe can be understood of both a metaphor and a material reality of racism, which constrains not just life choices and opportunities, but the environmental conditions of life itself" (7).

55. Feminist scholar Traci Brynne Voyles (2015) describes this process as one of "wastelanding" that differentially pervades bodies, landscapes, and their relations.

56. Here, I am thinking of the legions of mostly fair-skinned people who took to the streets of the United States in mid 2020 and afterward demanding an end to public health protections. Repeatedly, these people framed requirements that they wear masks or receive vaccinations in the interests of collective care as tantamount to police brutality.

57. Environmental justice scholar David Pellow (2021) suggests environmental injustice is a form of criminalization. By way of Detroit's local jail, I (2022) have shown how the antiblackness of environmental racism and mass incarceration are entailed within the material infrastructures of incarceration.

58. As la paperson (2017) writes in their discussion of the coloniality of environmental violence, "To be subject to anti-Indian technologies does not require you to be an Indigenous person." Far from an absolution of violence, this standpoint is an insistence on reckoning with how racism is enacted through systems, not identities.

59. A person breathing slowly could inhale around 150,000 asbestos fibers over this period. The constitutive problem with permissible limits is that they allow harm to occur under the guise of protection (Krupar 2013; Liboiron 2021).

60. Lindqvist 1979, 30.

61. Melissa Checker (2007) details how the regulatory optic of identifying singular hazards from singular sources obscures the multi-source experiences of toxicity in the air, water, soil, and people around industrial sites.

62. While I can't say where the contractor's clip came from, I can offer this viral video, "Detroit House Demolition," in which a demolition excavator produces similar circumstances: https://youtu.be/2VjiQocDgdo.

63. Ahmann and Kenner 2020, 424.

64. For some time, social scientists have predicted that the risk of global threats would come to overshadow existing forms of embodied inequity, especially racism, sexism, and class hierarchy. Despite the solidarity implied by clarion calls to shared vulnerability, such calls mask how protections of wealth and geography, as well as racialized, sexed, and gendered privilege endure even when their holders believe they melt away (Fennell 2016; cf. Tsing 2015).

65. I will not amplify their work here, but it is not difficult to find on your own. The people associated with it occupy prestigious positions in research centers, government offices, and universities.

66. Victoria Team and Lenore Manderson (2020) are two of many scholars and advocates to address "how COVID-19 reveals structures of vulnerability."

67. Heynen and Ybarra 2021.

68. Bullard 1990; Fortun 2014.

69. Regulatory protections attempt to care at the scale of population and territory.

Murphy (2017) shows how, from the jump, the biopolitical frameworks for such protections trend toward "racist and economized distributions of value" (140), even if they could work otherwise.

70. Liboiron (2017, 519) draws helpful inspiration on this front from anthropologist Charles Hale's (2006) reflections on the contradictions of resistance-based strategies for social change.

Chapter 6

1. Reports of such findings created by government agencies are records that surfaced in publicly accessible archives. This includes records from Detroit's municipal government. For example, Detroit Construction and Demolition Department, 2022, "Fill Material Sampling and Analytical Report," City of Detroit, https://detroitmi.gov/sites/detroitmi.localhost/files/2022-06/Soil%20Sample%20Report%20-%20HHF%20sites.pdf; Detroit Office of the Inspector General, 2021, "Demolition Backfill Issues," City of Detroit, https://detroitmi.gov/sites/detroitmi.localhost/files/2021-03/19-0012-INV Final Report.pdf. It also includes findings generated by federal agencies that funded demolitions in Detroit. For example, Special Inspector General for the Troubled Asset Relief Program (SIGTARP), 2020, "Progress in Protecting Against Asbestos Exposure, Contaminated Soil, and Illegal Dumping in the TARP-Funded Demolition Program in Detroit," US Treasury Department, https://www.oversight.gov/reports/audit/progress-protecting-against-asbestos-exposure-contaminated-soil-and-illegal-dumping.

2. For more on this, see Caverly 2023.

3. The physiological consequences of consuming lead—fatigue, neurological difficulties, and death in severe cases—have been clear for some time (Warren 2000). Industries that profited from lead knew of these consequences (Markowitz and Rosner 2013). And yet, amidst the fallout, it is important to bear in mind, as Catherine Fennell (2016) does in her examination of leaded water in Flint, Michigan, that despite broad usage of lead paints and pipes, as well as sustained state-enabled corporate obfuscation, risk of lead contamination is not equal. It is deeply channeled, compounding racist, classed experiences of disinvestment. In Fennell's words, suggesting " 'We are all Flint' isn't just hogwash: it's whitewash."

4. For connections between lead and demolition, see Ayayna Rubio, 2015, "Lead Exposure and HHF Demolition Activity in Detroit," Data Driven Detroit, https://datadrivendetroit.org/files/INT/InternReport_Ayana.pdf; Detroit Health Department, 2020, "Proximate Demolition Activity and Elevated Blood Lead Levels Among Children in Detroit, 2014–2018," City of Detroit, https://detroitmi.gov/sites/detroitmi.localhost/files/2020-05/Demo%20Lead%20Report%20to%20post.pdf. For an understanding of industrial lead sources, see Howard, Dubay and Daniels 2013.

5. Monica White (2018) situates Detroiters' home gardens within the trajectory of Black freedom struggles. At the same time, however, Alesia Montgomery (2020) demonstrates how these very gardens also become alibis for organized abandonment.

6. Caverly 2023.

7. Lyons (2020, 176) complicates sedimented archives as fields of care alongside small-scale farmers, rural communities, and state soil scientists that enacted them to different

ends. In so doing, Lyons presses on the ways people are unevenly organized within systems of industrial capitalism and empire that produce hazardous soils that require specific kinds of care (cf. Puig de la Bellacasa 2021).

8. Richter and Yaalon 2012, 766.

9. Soils are sociotechnical processes. Efforts to understand their contents, especially in contexts where people grow food in close relation to industrial toxicants, are harm-reduction practices that engage with the impossibility of completely mitigating human-created harms (Caverly 2023; McClintock 2015).

10. Asking how elsewheres come to be is a process of engaging with the ways environmental racism is constitutive of racial capitalism. For more on this, consider these starting points to the field of discard studies: Pulido 2015; Liboiron 2021; Solomon 2022.

11. Joshua Reno's (2016) ethnography of a southeastern Michigan landfill provides a vantage on one of these locations. As Reno and others make clear, sanitary landfills are predicated on a technocratic sleight of hand that renders waste out of sight to the most privileged while making it a constant occupation of others. See also Zhang 2024.

12. Besides asbestos removal, no federal environmental regulations apply during demolitions. The best practices required in Detroit's publicly funded demolitions resulted in lead dust spreading 100–200 yards. Typically, lead settled between two and eight centimeters into the ground (Partial Deconstruction Pilot Project, 2016, *Final Report*, https://www.deconstructionproject.com/).

13. Voyles (2015, 10) provides a key entry into how the spatial and racist politics of environmental injustice are constitutive of symbolic and material inequities. Murphy (2006; 2013; 2017a) notes how these inequities are an inheritance of the narrow ways industrial chemicals are rendered within corporate and regulatory technoscience. See also Bensaude-Vincent and Stengers 1996.

14. Eileen McGurty (2007) provides a historical account of Warren County as the epicenter of environmental-justice struggles, though PCB dumping occurred across the United States and was almost always shunted into Black and impoverished places (Spears 2014). Importantly, as Tianna Bruno (2024) notes, people in Warren County refused to be defined by the deadly realities of environmental injustice and waged a decades-long struggle until the landfill was decommissioned.

15. McGurty 2007; Spears 2014.

16. Fred McNeese, September 14, 1982, "Enraged Residents of the Community of Afton Vowed Tuesday to Form a Human Barricade to Block State Trucks from Dumping PCB-Contaminated Dirt at a Landfill near Their Homes," UPI Wire Service Archive.

17. Bruno 2024; McGurty 2007.

18. The United Church of Christ's (UCC; 1987) *Toxic Wastes and Race* report emerged from collaborations with activists in Warren County. See also Bullard 1990.

19. By giving a name to "environmental racism," the UCC report connected struggles occurring across the country, especially across axes of race and class. See Checker 2005 and Sze 2020 for accounts of how activists and researchers have built on the legacy of *Toxic Wastes and Race* as part of local, national, and global movements for environmental justice.

20. Thom Davies (2019) identifies how the surprise that certain publics tend to have

about the ostensible "out of sight" character of what some call "slow violence" (Nixon 2011) reflects the structural privileges of those publics. Environmental burdens are fully in view to the people who experience them in intimate and intergenerational ways. Amplifying the insights of people who contend with antiblack burdens of petrochemical industries in South Louisiana, Davies argues that "slow violence does not persist due to a lack of arresting stories about pollution, but because those stories do not *count*" (411, emphasis original).

21. In the United States and elsewhere, conservation movements that began in earnest in the nineteenth century have invariably been predicated on dispossession and maintaining whiteness as property. This happened even when this was not their explicit intent (Hecht 2023; Taylor 2014)

22. As noted in the UCC's twenty-year follow-up to their initial report on environmental racism, "people of color make up the majority of those living in host neighborhoods within 3 kilometers (1.8 miles) of the nation's hazardous waste facilities. Racial and ethnic disparities are prevalent throughout the country" (Bullard et al. 2007, x).

23. This is text from Executive Order (EO) 14096, 2023, "Revitalizing Our Nation's Commitment to Environmental Justice for All."

24. Since the first federal environmental-justice standard was enacted in the United States in 1994, definitions of justice have been eliminated and restored depending on the commitments of Executive Office occupants. This includes EO 14096, 2023, which was eliminated by the subsequent executive. Even when standards have been in place, people have struggled against the proliferation of environmental racism in the United States. For an in-depth discussion of how, see Laura Pulido and colleagues' (2019) review. Max Liboiron (2021) also provides the crucial reminder that environmental standards often enact colonial capitalist projects. In Liboiron's words, "Pollution, scientific ways to know pollution, and actions to mitigate pollution are . . . essential parts of the interlocking logics (brain), mechanisms (hands and teeth), and structures (heart and bones) of colonialism that allow colonialism to produce and reproduce its effects" (15–16).

25. City of Detroit 2022.

26. EPA Region 5, 2013, "On the Road to Reuse: Demolition Bid Specification Development Tool," Environmental Protection Agency, https://www.epa.gov/sites/default/files/2013-09/documents/road-to-reuse-residential-demolition-bid-specification-201309.pdf; SIGTARP, 2020, "Progress in Protecting Against Asbestos Exposure, Contaminated Soil, and Illegal Dumping in the TARP-Funded Demolition Program in Detroit," US Treasury Department, https://www.oversight.gov/reports/audit/progress-protecting-against-asbestos-exposure-contaminated-soil-and-illegal-dumping.

27. Koscielniak 2020.

28. Josiah Rector (2022) demonstrates how Detroit is a long-standing center of environmental injustice and organizing to contest it.

29. Melody Zhang, August 2, 2019, "There's No Debating Environmental Racism in Detroit," *Sojourners*, https://sojo.net/articles/there-s-no-debating-environmental-racism-detroit; Steve Neavling, August 25, 2022, "Environmental Racism in Detroit Takes Center Stage at Congressional Hearing," *Detroit Metro Times*, https://www.metrotimes.com/news/environmental-racism-in-detroit-takes-center-stage-at-congressional-hearing-30913374.

30. Jena Brooker, June 15, 2023, "Did Hazardous Waste Facility's Unreported Errors Put Detroiters at Risk?" *Bridge Detroit*, https://www.bridgemi.com/michigan-environment-watch/did-hazardous-waste-facilitys-unreported-errors-put-detroiters-risk; Jena Brooker, July 21, 2023, "US Ecology South in Detroit Fined Just $2,000 for Dozens of Violations," *Bridge Detroit*, https://www.bridgemi.com/michigan-environment-watch/dozens-violations-just-2000-fines-detroit-hazardous-waste-site.

31. Brian Allnutt, September 11, 2020, "Did Michigan Violate Civil Rights Law with Its Permit to US Ecology?" *Planet Detroit*, https://planetdetroit.org/2020/09/did-michigan-violate-civil-rights-law-with-its-permit-to-us-ecology/.

32. Christine MacDonald, November 15, 2017, "Detroit Kids' Lead Poisoning Rates Higher Than Flint," *Detroit News*, https://www.detroitnews.com/story/news/local/detroit-city/2017/11/14/lead-poisoning-children-detroit/107683688/.

33. In the United States, diagnoses of lead poisoning are currently given to adults with greater than 10 micrograms of lead per deciliter of blood and children with greater than 3.5 µg/dl. The difference between these numbers and the level of lead known to be safe (zero) exemplifies how threshold regulations produce harm. For more on the violence of threshold theories of pollution, see Liboiron 2021, especially 57–60.

34. Detroit Health Department, 2017, "Lead and Demolition Report," City of Detroit, https://www.bridgemi.com/sites/default/files/task_force_recommendations.pdf.

35. Ayayna Rubio, 2015, "Lead Exposure and HHF Demolition Activity in Detroit," Data Driven Detroit, https://datadrivendetroit.org/files/INT/InternReport_Ayana.pdf; Partial Deconstruction Pilot Project, 2016, *Final Report*, https://www.deconstructionproject.com/.

36. Rukiya Colvin, August 13, 2021, "Getting the Lead Out of Detroit's Soil," *Planet Detroit*, https://planetdetroit.org/2021/08/getting-the-lead-out-of-detroits-soil/. See also Howard, DuBay, and Daniels 2013.

37. Threshold violence still applies (Liboiron 2021, 55–60).

38. This chapter builds with Jay, Aubrey, and their neighbors. I contend with this alongside different gardeners who worked toward somewhat different ends in Caverly 2023.

39. EPA Region 3, 2020, "Lead in Soil," Environmental Protection Agency, https://www.epa.gov/sites/default/files/2020-10/documents/lead-in-soil-aug2020.pdf.

40. Such a contrast between the central city and its suburbs is not simply an artifact of Jay's individual experience; it is a broadly held spatial imaginary in the United States (Robbins 2007).

41. Though this was billed as an exercise in "citizen science," and academic researchers provided Jay with analytic reports for the samples he submitted, they did not provide any further information. This is not to fault these scientists. As Aya Kimura and Abby Kinchy (2019) note, "Building mutually beneficial and trusting relationships between professional scientists and communities seeking environmental justice will require reforms at the level of institutions, including universities, funding agencies, and other scientific organizations" (145).

42. Freund 2007.

43. Paul Robbins's (2007) political ecology of lawns is helpful here.

44. Checker 2020, 16–18.

45. Faith in the "assimilative capacity" of environments to sop up contaminants will do that (Liboiron 2021, 60–62, especially note 78).

46. Others did so in different ways, including by siphoning off supplies of screened fill from construction sites (Caverly 2023).

47. Murphy 2017a, 501.

48. EO 14096, 2023, "Revitalizing Our Nation's Commitment to Environmental Justice for All."

Conclusion

1. In case this is the first time you have turned to the notes, here are places to get started. Byrd 2019; Halvorson and Reno 2022; Harris 2022; Johnson 2021; Nichols 2020.

2. Similar to the footnote above. Anthias and Asher 2024; Koshy et al. 2022; Resnick 2021.

3. Actions of this sort are not new. Recent presidential administrations have prioritized them, as have state legislatures. For example, see HB 5097 of 2021 as passed by the State of Michigan House of Representatives and SB 460 of 2021 as introduced in the State of Michigan Senate.

4. There is a pattern in the way bans on learning and research around structural injustice unfold. Proponents of legislation and executive orders banning discussion of white supremacy insist they are not trying to make racism invisible. They insist that civil rights statutes enacted by local, federal, and state governments have eliminated racist systems, so learning about those systems is obsolete. It is difficult to take this argument seriously, since the people trying to demolish formal knowledge of racism are often active participants in white supremacist organizations. Moreover, there is overwhelming evidence that formal legal equality has not ended environmental racism or wealth disparities or segregated housing—it has just made their causes more difficult to pinpoint. For more, see Lipsitz 2024.

5. Hamilton and Ture 1992, 20.

6. Hamilton and Ture 1992; see also Pulido 2015, 2016, 2017; Voyles 2015.

7. Hamilton and Ture 1992, 23–28.

8. Justice and peace studies scholar Johan Galtung (1969) is often credited with formulating how uneven access to resources makes systems of privilege and oppression seem "as natural as the air around us" (173). Galtung's framework of structural violence builds explicitly on Hamilton and Ture's description of racism, originally published two years earlier (187–88).

9. Trouillot 2000, 183.

10. Robinson 2020; Gilmore 2007; Jenkins and Leroy 2021.

11. Bhandar 2018; Harris 2022; Safransky 2023.

12. Hecht 2023; Liboiron 2021; Pulido 2015, 2016, 2017; Voyles 2015.

13. Rector 2022; Zimring 2016.

14. Many other people's work warrants your attention here. The writings of Vanessa Agard Jones, Ruha Benjamin, Lundy Braun, Tianna Bruno, Sharad Chari, Virginia Eubanks, Ruth Wilson Gilmore, Gabrielle Hecht, Walter Johnson, Jovan Scott Lewis, George

Lipsitz, M Murphy, Laura Pulido, Joshua Reno, Marisa Solomon, Keeanga-Yamahtta Taylor, and Traci Brynne Voyles are good places to get started.

15. I'm far from the first person to sit with this tension. As Marx wrote in an often-quoted message to Engels in 1845, "The philosophers have only interpreted the world, in various ways; the point, however, is to change it." Tess Lea's (2020) constructive critiques of settler policymaking in Australia are also worth keeping in mind here.

16. Hartman 2008, 6.

17. As Ruha Benjamin (2019) and others show, the fix can be just as racist as what it claims to address. See also Braun 2014; Noble 2018.

18. Táíwò 2022.

19. In particular, see Bruno et al. 2024; Franke 2019; Inwood, Brand, and Quinn 2021; Lewis 2022.

20. Táíwò 2022, 207.

21. Sugrue 2020, 220.

22. Perhaps this book sits on a shelf near others who show this, especially work by Kyle T. Mays, Sara Safransky, Josiah Rector, and Dan Georgakas.

23. The Detroit Equity Action Lab keeps tabs on these dynamics and how people organize for a more just city despite them.

24. Resolution to place reparations initiative on ballot, 2021, Detroit City Council. In 2021, 80 percent of voters endorsed the City Council proposal and created a municipal reparations committee. Over almost three years, the thirteen-member committee heard testimony from city residents. Based on this testimony, the committee is anticipated to deliver a formal municipal reparations proposal in 2025.

25. This is no accident. Detroit activists who helped shepherd the local initiative into being, including JoAnn Watson, were longtime participants in much broader discussions around reparations for enslavement and colonization (Conyers and Watson 2003).

26. Referencing Ta-Nehisi Coates's case for reparations (2014), one Detroiter put it this way in his public comment to Detroit's municipal reparations taskforce: "Reparations is not a handout. This is about a debt that is owed because of our ancestors being free labor that benefited the country."

27. This is the crux of Táíwò's argument for a "constructive view" of reparations as a future-oriented project rather than one of cash transfers that retains the same structure of racial capitalism. See also Lewis 2022; Taylor and Reed 2019.

28. Again, Táíwò, Keeanga-Yamahtta Taylor, JoAnn Watson, Jovan Scott Lewis, Katherine Franke, and others who have considered repair in detail are critical reading. Repair demands cultivating conditions that do not take existing systems for granted. Detroiters show some concrete ways in which it is possible to build horizons toward those conditions from the here and now. To do otherwise is to fall into the constraints of existing systems that foreclose other possible futures by locking in justice as only ever a pursuit of payment or punishment.

WORKS CITED

Agard-Jones, Vanessa. 2013. "Bodies in the System." *Small Axe* 17 (3): 182–92. https://doi.org/10.1215/07990537-2378991.

Ahmann, Chloe. 2022. "Vacancy: Introduction." *Anthropological Quarterly* 95 (2): 241–75.

———. 2024. *Futures After Progress.* University of Chicago Press.

Ahmann, Chloe, and Alison Kenner. 2020. "Breathing Late Industrialism." *Engaging Science, Technology, and Society* 6: 416–38. https://doi.org/10.17351/ests2020.673.

Akers, Joshua. 2013. "Making Markets: Think Tank Legislation and Private Property in Detroit." *Urban Geography* 34 (8): 1070–95. https://doi.org/10.1080/02723638.2013.814272.

———. 2017. "A New Urban Medicine Show: On the Limits of Blight Remediation." In *A New Urban Medicine Show: On the Limits of Blight Remediation*, edited by Brian Doucet, 95–116. Policy Press. https://doi.org/10.56687/9781447327899-008.

Akers, Joshua, and Eric Seymour. 2018. "Instrumental Exploitation: Predatory Property Relations at City's End." *Geoforum* 91:127–40. https://doi.org/10.1016/j.geoforum.2018.02.022.

Akers, Joshua, Eric Seymour, Diné Butler, and Wade Rathke. 2019. "Liquid Tenancy: "Post-Crisis" Economies of Displacement, Community Organizing, and New Forms of Resistance." *Radical Housing Journal* 1 (1): 9–28. https://doi.org/10.54825/JGJT2051.

Allison, Anne. 2012. "Ordinary Refugees: Social Precarity and Soul in 21st-Century Japan." *Anthropological Quarterly* 85 (2): 345–70. https://doi.org/10.1353/anq.2012.0027.

Altman, Rebecca. 2021. "Upriver." *Orion Magazine*, Summer. https://orionmagazine.org/article/upriver/.

Amin, Ash. 2013. "Telescopic Urbanism and the Poor." *City* 17 (4): 476–92. https://doi.org/10.1080/13604813.2013.812350.

Amutah, Christina, Kaliya Greenidge, Adjoa Mante, Michelle Munyikwa, Sanjna L. Surya, Eve Higginbotham, David S. Jones, et al. 2021. "Misrepresenting Race—The Role of Medical Schools in Propagating Physician Bias." *New England Journal of Medicine* 384 (9): 872–78. https://doi.org/10.1056/NEJMms2025768.

Ansfield, Bench. 2020. "The Broken Windows of the Bronx: Putting the Theory in Its Place." *American Quarterly* 72 (1): 103–27. https://doi.org/10.1353/aq.2020.0005.

Anthias, Penelope, and Kiran Asher. 2024. "Indigenous Natures and the Anthropocene: Racial Capitalism, Violent Materialities, and the Colonial Politics of Representation." *Antipode* online early view: 1–22. https://doi.org/10.1111/anti.13078.

Atanasoski, Neda, and Kalindi Vora. 2019. *Surrogate Humanity: Race, Robots, and the Politics of Technological Futures.* Duke University Press.

Atuahene, Bernadette. 2025. *Plundered: How Racist Policies Undermine Black Homeownership in America.* Little, Brown.

Atuahene, Bernadette, and Christopher Berry. 2018. "Taxed Out: Illegal Property Tax Assessments and the Epidemic of Tax Foreclosures in Detroit." *UC Irvine Law Review* 9 (4): 847–86.

Atuahene, Bernadette, and Timothy Hodge. 2018. "Stategraft." *Southern California Law Review* 91: 263–302.

Azoulay, Ariella. 2013. "When a Demolished House Becomes a Public Square." In *Imperial Debris: On Ruins and Ruination*, edited by Ann Laura Stoler, 194–224. Duke University Press.

———. 2017. "The Imperial Condition of Photography in Palestine: Archives, Looting, and the Figure of the Infiltrator." *Visual Anthropology Review* 33 (1): 5–17. https://doi.org/10.1111/var.12117.

Balayannis, Angeliki, and Emma Garnett. 2020. "Chemical Kinship: Interdisciplinary Experiments with Pollution." *Catalyst: Feminism, Theory, Technoscience* 6 (1): 1–10. https://doi.org/10.28968/cftt.v6i1.33524.

Baldwin, James. 1985. *The Price of the Ticket.* St. Martin's Press.

Bartlett, Jackson. 2017. "'Raise Money, Raise Hell, or Leave': Contesting DIY Urbanism in the Black Outer City." PhD diss., Northwestern University.

Bavery, Ashley Johnson. 2020. *Bootlegged Aliens: Immigration Politics on America's Northern Border.* University of Pennsylvania Press.

Benjamin, Ruha. 2016. "Catching Our Breath: Critical Race STS and the Carceral Imagination." *Engaging Science, Technology, and Society* 2: 145–56. https://doi.org/10.17351/ests2016.70.

———. 2019. *Race After Technology: Abolitionist Tools for the New Jim Code.* Polity.

Bensaude-Vincent, Bernadette, and Isabelle Stengers. 1996. *A History of Chemistry.* Translated by Deborah Kurmes Van Dam. Harvard University Press.

Bhandar, Brenna. 2018. *Colonial Lives of Property: Law, Land, and Racial Regimes of Ownership.* Duke University Press.

Bhandar, Brenna, and Alberto Toscano. 2015. "Race, Real Estate and Real Abstraction." *Radical Philosophy* 4: 8–17.

Blair, Sara. 2018. *How the Other Half Looks: The Lower East Side and the Afterlives of Images*. Princeton University Press.

Bledsoe, Adam, and Willie Jamaal Wright. 2019. "The Anti-Blackness of Global Capital." *Environment and Planning D: Society and Space* 37 (1): 8–26. https://doi.org/10.1177/0263775818805102.

Boggs, Grace Lee, and James Boggs. 2011. "The City Is Black Man's Land." In *Pages from a Black Radical's Notebook: A James Boggs Reader*, edited by Stephen M. Ward. Wayne State University Press.

Bonilla-Silva, Eduardo. 2013. *Racism without Racists: Color-Blind Racism and the Persistence of Racial Inequality in America*. Rowman & Littlefield.

boyd, danah, and Kate Crawford. 2012. "Critical Questions for Big Data." *Information, Communication & Society* 15 (5): 662–79. https://doi.org/10.1080/1369118X.2012.678878.

Boyle, Kevin. 2005. *Arc of Justice: A Saga of Race, Civil Rights, and Murder in the Jazz Age*. Holt.

Braun, Lundy. 2014. *Breathing Race into the Machine: The Surprising Career of the Spirometer from Plantation to Genetics*. University of Minnesota Press.

Briggs, Laura. 2018. *How All Politics Became Reproductive Politics: From Welfare Reform to Foreclosure to Trump*. University of California Press.

Brodeur, Paul. 1968. "The Magic Mineral." *The New Yorker*, October 12.

———. 1980. *The Asbestos Hazard*. New York Academy of Sciences.

Brodkin, Karen. 2014. "Work, Race, and Economic Citizenship." *Current Anthropology* 55 (S9): S116–25. https://doi.org/10.1086/676667.

Broussard, Meredith. 2018. *Artificial Unintelligence: How Computers Misunderstand the World*. MIT Press.

———. 2023. *More than a Glitch: Confronting Race, Gender, and Ability Bias in Tech*. MIT Press.

Brown, Adrienne. 2024. *The Residential Is Racial: A Perceptual History of Mass Homeownership*. Stanford University Press.

Brown, Lawrence. 2022. *The Black Butterfly: The Harmful Politics of Race and Space in America*. Johns Hopkins University Press.

Browne, Simone. 2015. *Dark Matters: On the Surveillance of Blackness*. Duke University Press.

Bruno, Tianna. 2024. "More than Just Dying: Black Life and Futurity in the Face of State-Sanctioned Environmental Racism." *Environment and Planning D: Society and Space* 42 (1): 73–90. https://doi.org/10.1177/02637758231218101.

Bruno, Tianna, Andrew Curley, Mabel Denzin Gergan, and Sara Smith. 2024. "The Work of Repair: Land, Relation, and Pedagogy." *Cultural Geographies* 31 (1): 5–19. https://doi.org/10.1177/14744740231203713.

Bullard, Robert D. 1990. *Dumping in Dixie: Race, Class, and Environmental Quality*. Westview Press.

Bullard, Robert D., and Beverly Wright. 2012. *The Wrong Complexion for Protection: How the Government Response to Disaster Endangers African American Communities*. New York: New York University Press.

Bullard, Robert, Paul Mohai, Robin Saha, and Beverly Wright. 2007. *Toxic Wastes and Race at Twenty: 1987–2007*. United Church of Christ.

Burawoy, Michael. 2009. *The Extended Case Method*. University of California Press.

Burton, Clarence Monroe. 1922. *The City of Detroit, Michigan, 1701–1922*. S. J. Clarke Publishing Company.

Byrd, Jodi A. 2019. "Weather with You: Settler Colonialism, Antiblackness, and the Grounded Relationalities of Resistance." *Critical Ethnic Studies* 5 (1–2): 207–14. https://doi.org/10.5749/jcritethnstud.5.1-2.0207.

Byrd, Jodi A., Alyosha Goldstein, Jodi Melamed, and Chandan Reddy. 2018. "Predatory Value: Economies of Dispossession and Disturbed Relationalities." *Social Text* 36 (2 (135)): 1–18. https://doi.org/10.1215/01642472-4362325.

Callon, Michel. 1986. "Some Elements of a Sociology of Translation Domestication of the Scallops and the Fishermen of St Brieux Bay." In *Power, Action, and Belief, A New Sociology of Knowledge?*, edited by John Law, 196–229. Routledge.

Campbell, Linda, Andrew Newman, Sara Safransky, and Timothy Stallmann. 2020. *A People's Atlas of Detroit*. Wayne State University Press.

Carroll, Stephen, Deborah Hensler, Jennifer Gross, and Elizabeth Sloss. 2005. *Asbestos Litigation*. RAND Corporation.

Caverly, Nicholas. 2021. "Sensing Others: Empty Buildings and Sensory Worlds in Detroit:" *Environment and Planning C: Politics and Space* 39 (6):1079–96. https://doi.org/10.1177/2399654419858368.

———. 2022. "Carceral Structures: Financialized Displacement and Captivity in Detroit." *Anthropological Quarterly* 95 (2): 333–61. https://doi.org/10.1353/anq.2022.0018.

———. 2023. "Bending Possession: How Detroiters Care for Land by Remediating Settler Property." *Antipode* Online Early View: 1–23. https://doi.org/10.1111/anti.12997.

Chari, Sharad. 2024. *Apartheid Remains*. Duke University Press.

Checker, Melissa. 2005. *Polluted Promises: Environmental Racism and the Search for Justice in a Southern Town*. NYU Press.

———. 2007. " 'But I Know It's True': Environmental Risk Assessment, Justice, and Anthropology." *Human Organization* 66 (2): 112–24.

———. 2020. *The Sustainability Myth: Environmental Gentrification and the Politics of Justice*. NYU Press.

Coates, Ta-Nehisi. 2014. "The Case for Reparations." *The Atlantic*, January 6.

Collins, Patricia Hill. 2000. *Black Feminist Thought: Knowledge, Consciousness, and the Politics of Empowerment*. Routledge.

Commission for Racial Justice. 1987. *Toxic Wastes and Race in the United States*. United Church of Christ.

Conyers, John, and JoAnn Watson. 2003. In *Should America Pay?: Slavery and the Raging Debate on Reparations*, edited by Raymond Winbush, 14–21. Harper Collins.

Costanza-Chock, Sasha, Inioluwa Deborah Raji, and Joy Buolamwini. 2022. "Who Audits the Auditors? Recommendations from a Field Scan of the Algorithmic Auditing Ecosystem." *Proceedings of the 2022 ACM Conference on Fairness, Accountability, and Transparency*, 1571–83. https://doi.org/10.1145/3531146.3533213.

Cowie, Jefferson, and Joseph Heathcott. 2003. "The Meanings of Deindustrialization." In *Beyond the Ruins: The Meanings of Deindustrialization*, edited by Jefferson Cowie and Joseph Heathcott. Cornell University Press.

Cox, Aimee. 2015. *Shapeshifters: Black Girls and the Choreography of Citizenship*. Duke University Press.

Crawford, Margaret. 2020. "Why Planners Need Anthropologists." In *Life Among Urban Planners: Practice, Professionalism, and Expertise in the Making of the City*, edited by Jennifer Mack and Michael Herzfeld, 42–60. University of Pennsylvania Press.

Cronon, William. 1991. *Nature's Metropolis: Chicago and the Great West*. W. W. Norton.

Davies, Thom. 2019. "Slow Violence and Toxic Geographies: 'Out of Sight' to Whom?" *Environment and Planning C: Politics and Space*, April. https://doi.org/10.1177/2399654419841063.

De León, Jason. 2018. "The Photoethnographic Eye: Visualizing the Honduran Migrant Experience in Mexico." In *Photography and Migration*, edited by Tanya Sheehan, 115–29. Routledge.

Denby, Charles. 1989. *Indignant Heart: A Black Worker's Journal*. Wayne State University Press.

Detroit Historical Society. 2023. "Joseph Campau." In *Encyclopedia of Detroit*. Detroit. https://detroithistorical.org/learn/encyclopedia-of-detroit/campau-joseph.

Dewar, Margaret, and June Manning Thomas, eds. 2012. *The City After Abandonment*. University of Pennsylvania Press.

Dillon, Lindsey, and Julie Sze. 2016. "Police Power and Particulate Matters: Environmental Justice and the Spatialities of In/Securities in US Cities." *English Language Notes* 54 (2): 13–23. https://doi.org/10.1215/00138282-54.2.13.

Doussard, Mark. 2013. *Degraded Work: The Struggle at the Bottom of the Labor Market*. University of Minnesota Press.

Drake, St. Clair and Horace Cayton. (1962) 2015. *Black Metropolis: A Study of Negro Life in a Northern City*. University of Chicago Press.

Du Bois, W. E. B. 1920. *Darkwater: Voices from Within the Veil*. Harcourt, Brace and Howe.

———. (1935). *Black Reconstruction in America*. Russell and Russell.

Dudley, Kathryn. 1997. *The End of the Line: Lost Jobs, New Lives in Postindustrial America*. University of Chicago Press.

Dumit, Joseph. 2014. "Writing the Implosion: Teaching the World One Thing at a Time." *Cultural Anthropology* 29 (2): 344–62. https://doi.org/10.14506/ca29.2.09.

Eisenberg, Alexa, Eric Seymour, Alex B. Hill, and Joshua Akers. 2020. "Toxic Structures: Speculation and Lead Exposure in Detroit's Single-Family Rental Market." *Health & Place* 64 (July), art. 102390. https://doi.org/10.1016/j.healthplace.2020.102390.

Ekers, Michael. 2013. " 'Pounding Dirt All Day': Labor, Sexuality and Gender in the British Columbia Reforestation Sector." *Gender, Place & Culture* 20 (7): 876–95. https://doi.org/10.1080/0966369X.2012.737768.

Esch, Elizabeth. 2018. *The Color Line and the Assembly Line: Managing Race in the Ford Empire*. University of California Press.

Eubanks, Virginia. 2019. *Automating Inequality: How High-Tech Tools Profile, Police, and Punish the Poor*. Picador.

Fanon, Frantz. 1965. *The Wretched of the Earth*. Grove Press.

Fennell, Catherine. 2015. *Last Project Standing: Civics and Sympathy in Post-Welfare Chicago*. University of Minnesota Press.

———. 2016. "Are We All Flint?" *LIMN*, no. 7: Public Infrastructures/Infrastructural Publics, 21–25.

Fields, Karen E., and Barbara Jeanne Fields. 2014. *Racecraft: The Soul of Inequality in American Life*. Verso.

Finkelstein, Maura. 2019. *The Archive of Loss: Lively Ruination in Mill Land Mumbai*. Duke University Press.

Fortun, Kim. 2001. *Advocacy After Bhopal: Environmentalism, Disaster, New Global Orders*. University of Chicago Press.

———. 2014. "From Latour to Late Industrialism." *HAU: Journal of Ethnographic Theory* 4 (1): 309–29. https://doi.org/10.14318/hau4.1.017.

———. 2015. "Ethnography in Late Industrialism." In *Writing Culture and the Life of Anthropology*, edited by Orin Starn, 120–36. Duke University Press.

Franke, Katherine. 2019. *Repair: Redeeming the Promise of Abolition*. Haymarket Books.

Fredericks, Rosalind. 2018. *Garbage Citizenship: Vital Infrastructures of Labor in Dakar, Senegal*. Duke University Press.

Freshour, Carrie. 2017. "'Ain't No Life for a Mother!' Racial Capitalism and the Crisis of Social Reproduction." *Society and Space, November 17*. https://www.societyandspace.org/articles/aint-no-life-for-a-mother-racial-capitalism-and-the-crisis-of-social-reproduction.

Freund, David. 2007. *Colored Property: State Policy and White Racial Politics in Suburban America*. University of Chicago Press.

Gailloux, Chantal. 2022. "The Post-Political Violence of Racial Property Regimes: Maintaining Gardens' Land Insecurity through Abstract Codes in East Harlem, NYC." *Antipode* 54 (4): 1086–111. https://doi.org/10.1111/anti.12837.

Galster, George. 2012. *Driving Detroit: The Quest for Respect in the Motor City*. University of Pennsylvania Press.

Galtung, Johan. 1969. "Violence, Peace, and Peace Research." *Journal of Peace Research* 6 (3): 167–91.

Ghertner, D. Asher. 2015. *Rule by Aesthetics: World-Class City Making in Delhi*. Oxford University Press.

Gilmore, Ruth Wilson. 1993. "Public Enemies and Private Intellectuals." *Race & Class* 35 (1): 69–78. https://doi.org/10.1177/030639689303500107.

———. 2002. "Fatal Couplings of Power and Difference: Notes on Racism and Geography." *The Professional Geographer* 54 (1): 15–24.

———. 2007. *Golden Gulag: Prisons, Surplus, Crisis, and Opposition in Globalizing California*. University of California Press.

———. 2009. "Race, Prisons and War: Scenes from the History of US Violence." *Socialist Register* 45 (March): 73–87.

Gilmore, Ruth Wilson, and Léopold Lambert. 2018. "Making Abolition Geography in California's Central Valley." *The Funambulist Magazine*, no. 21: 14–19.

Goodfriend, Sophia. 2021. "A Street View of Occupation: Getting Around Hebron on Google Maps." *Visual Anthropology Review* 37 (2): 225–45. https://doi.org/10.1111/var.12247.

Gordon, Avery. 2008. *Ghostly Matters: Haunting and the Sociological Imagination*. University of Minnesota Press.

Gordon, Colin. 2004. "Blighting the Way: Urban Renewal, Economic Development, and the Elusive Definition of Blight." Special Series: Developing Sustainable Urban Communities. *Fordham Urban Law Journal* 31 (2): 305–38.

Gramsci, Antonio. (1971) 1992. *Selections from the Prison Notebooks of Antonio Gramsci*. Edited by Quintin Hoare and Geoffrey Nowell Smith. International Publishers.

Grandin, Greg. 2010. *Fordlandia: The Rise and Fall of Henry Ford's Forgotten Jungle City*. Macmillan.

Grosz, Elizabeth. 1995. *Space, Time, and Perversion*. Routledge.

Günel, Gökçe, and Chika Watanabe. 2024. "Patchwork Ethnography." *American Ethnologist* 51 (1): 131–39. https://doi.org/10.1111/amet.13243.

Gupta, Akhil. 2012. *Red Tape: Bureaucracy, Structural Violence, and Poverty in India*. Duke University Press.

Hackworth, Jason. 2016. "Demolition as Urban Policy in the American Rust Belt." *Environment and Planning A: Economy and Space* 48 (11): 2201–22. https://doi.org/10.1177/0308518X16654914.

———. 2019. *Manufacturing Decline: How Racism and the Conservative Movement Crush the American Rust Belt*. Columbia University Press.

Hale, Charles R. 2006. "Activist Research v. Cultural Critique: Indigenous Land Rights and the Contradictions of Politically Engaged Anthropology." *Cultural Anthropology* 21 (1): 96–120. https://doi.org/10.1525/can.2006.21.1.96.

Hall, Stuart. (1997) 2021. "Race, the Floating Signifier: What More Is There to Say about 'Race'" In *Selected Writings on Race and Difference*, edited by Paul Gilroy and Ruth Wilson Gilmore. Duke University Press.

Hall, Stuart, Chas Critcher, Tony Jefferson, John Clarke, and Brian Roberts. 1978. *Policing the Crisis: Mugging, the State and Law and Order*. Macmillan.

Halper, Jeff. 2021. "Militarising Bulldozers: Demolition in Israel/Palestine as Settler-Colonial Policy." *Arena*, no. 6 (June), 32–36. https://doi.org/10.3316/informit.960045229268288.

Halvorson, Britt E., and Joshua O. Reno. 2022. *Imagining the Heartland: White Supremacy and the American Midwest*. University of California Press.

Hamilton, Charles V., and Kwame Ture. 1992. *Black Power: Politics of Liberation in America*, 2nd ed. Knopf Doubleday.

Haraway, Donna J. 1988. "Situated Knowledges: The Science Question in Feminism and the Privilege of Partial Perspective." *Feminist Studies* 14 (3): 575–99. https://doi.org/10.2307/3178066.

Harms, Erik. 2016. *Luxury and Rubble: Civility and Dispossession in the New Saigon*. University of California Press.

Harris, Cheryl. 1993. "Whiteness as Property." *Harvard Law Review* 106 (8): 1707–91.

———. 2019. "Of Blackness and Indigeneity: Comments on Jodi A. Byrd's 'Weather with You: Settler Colonialism, Antiblackness, and the Grounded Relationalities of Resistance.'" *Critical Ethnic Studies* 5 (1–2): 215–28. https://doi.org/10.5749/jcritethnstud.5.1-2.0215.

———. 2022. "The Racial Alchemy of Debt: Dispossession and Accumulation in Afterlives of Slavery." In *Colonial Racial Capitalism*, edited by Susan Koshy, Lisa Marie Cacho, Jodi Byrd, and Brian Jordan Jefferson. Duke University Press.

Harris, Dianne Suzette. 2013. *Little White Houses: How the Postwar Home Constructed Race in America.* University of Minnesota Press.

Hartigan, John, Jr. 1999. *Racial Situations: Class Predicaments of Whiteness in Detroit.* Princeton University Press.

Hartman, Saidiya V. 1997. *Scenes of Subjection: Terror, Slavery, and Self-Making in Nineteenth-Century America.* Oxford University Press.

———. 2008. *Lose Your Mother: A Journey Along the Atlantic Slave Route.* Farrar, Straus and Giroux.

Hayden, Dolores. 2003. *Building Suburbia: Green Fields and Urban Growth, 1820–2000, a History of Seven American Landscapes.* Pantheon.

Hecht, Gabrielle. 2012. *Being Nuclear: Africans and the Global Uranium Trade.* MIT Press.

———. 2018. "Interscalar Vehicles for an African Anthropocene: On Waste, Temporality, and Violence." *Cultural Anthropology* 33 (1): 109–41.

———. 2023. *Residual Governance: How South Africa Foretells Planetary Futures.* Duke University Press.

Herbert, Claire W. 2021. *A Detroit Story: Urban Decline and the Rise of Property Informality.* University of California Press.

Herscher, Andrew. 2015. "'Blight,' Spatial Racism, and the Demolition of the Housing Question in Detroit." In *Housing After the Neoliberal Turn*, edited by Rana Dasgupta. Spector Books.

Heynen, Nik, and Megan Ybarra. 2021. "On Abolition Ecologies and Making 'Freedom as a Place.'" *Antipode* 53 (1): 21–35. https://doi.org/10.1111/anti.12666.

Highsmith, Andrew R. 2015. *Demolition Means Progress: Flint, Michigan, and the Fate of the American Metropolis.* University of Chicago Press.

Hong, Andy, Lucy Baker, Rafael Prieto Curiel, James Duminy, Bhawani Buswala, ChengHe Guan, and Divya Ravindranath. 2023. "Reconciling Big Data and Thick Data to Advance the New Urban Science and Smart City Governance." *Journal of Urban Affairs* 45 (10): 1737–61. https://doi.org/10.1080/07352166.2021.2021085.

Howard, Jeffrey L., Brian R. Dubay, and W. Lee Daniels. 2013. "Artifact Weathering, Anthropogenic Microparticles and Lead Contamination in Urban Soils at Former Demolition Sites, Detroit, Michigan." *Environmental Pollution* 179 (August):1–12. https://doi.org/10.1016/j.envpol.2013.03.053.

Hu, Margaret. 2017. "Algorithmic Jim Crow." *Fordham Law Review* 86 (2): 633–96.

Hull, Matthew. 2022. "Corporations and States: A Customer-Service Corporation Inside the Punjab State Police." *Cultural Anthropology* 37 (4): 764–92. https://doi.org/10.14506/ca37.4.07.

Inwood, Joshua F. J., Anna Livia Brand, and Elise Andrea Quinn. 2021. "Racial Capital, Abolition, and a Geographic Argument for Reparations." *Antipode* 53 (4): 1083–103. https://doi.org/10.1111/anti.12704.

Jain, S. Lochlann. 2006. *Injury: The Politics of Product Design and Safety Law in the United States.* Princeton University Press.

James, C. L. R., and Grace Lee Boggs. 1974. *Facing Reality.* Edited by Pierre Chaulieu. Bewick Editions.

Jay, Jonathan, Luke W. Miratrix, Charles C. Branas, Marc A. Zimmerman, and David Hemenway. 2019. "Urban Building Demolitions, Firearm Violence and Drug Crime." *Journal of Behavioral Medicine* 42 (4): 626–34. https://doi.org/10.1007/s10865-019-00031-6.

Jefferson, Brian Jordan. 2020. *Digitize and Punish: Racial Criminalization in the Digital Age*. University of Minnesota Press.

———. 2022. "Programming Colonial Racial Capitalism: Encoding Human Value in Smart Cities." In *Colonial Racial Capitalism*, edited by Susan Koshy, Lisa Marie Cacho, Jodi A. Byrd, and Brian Jordan Jefferson, 232–54. Duke University Press. https://doi.org/10.2307/j.ctv2vr9ckn.11.

Jenkins, Destin. 2022. *The Bonds of Inequality: Debt and the Making of the American City*. University of Chicago Press.

Jenkins, Destin, and Justin Leroy, eds. 2021. *Histories of Racial Capitalism*. Columbia University Press. https://doi.org/10.7312/jenk19074.

Johnson, Gaye Theresa, and Alex Lubin, eds. 2017. *Futures of Black Radicalism*. Verso.

Johnson, Walter. 2021. *The Broken Heart of America: St. Louis and the Violent History of the United States*. Basic Books.

Johnston, Ronnie, and Arthur McIvor. 2004. "Oral History, Subjectivity and Environmental Reality: Occupational Health Histories in Twentieth-Century Scotland." In *Landscapes of Exposure : Knowledge and Illness in Modern Environments*, edited by Gregg Mitman, Michelle Murphy, and Christopher Sellers, 234–49. University of Chicago Press.

Kelley, Robin D. G. 2017a. "Births of a Nation: Surveying Trumpland with Cedric Robinson." *Boston Review*, March 6.

———. 2017b. "The Rest of Us: Rethinking Settler and Native." *American Quarterly* 69 (2): 267–76. https://doi.org/10.1353/aq.2017.0020.

Kenner, Alison. 2018. *Breathtaking: Asthma Care in a Time of Climate Change*. University of Minnesota Press.

Kimura, Aya, and Abby Kinchy. 2019. *Science by the People: Participation, Power, and the Politics of Environmental Knowledge*. Rutgers University Press.

Kinder, Kimberley. 2016. *DIY Detroit: Making Do in a City Without Services*. University of Minnesota Press.

Kinney, Rebecca. 2016. *Beautiful Wasteland: The Rise of Detroit as America's Postindustrial Frontier*. University of Minnesota Press.

Koscielniak, Michael. 2020. "Ground Forces: Dirt, Demolition, and the Geography of Decline in Detroit, Michigan." PhD diss., University of Michigan.

Koshy, Susan, Lisa Marie Cacho, Jodi A. Byrd, and Brian Jordan Jefferson, eds. 2022. *Colonial Racial Capitalism*. Duke University Press.

Krupar, Shiloh R. 2013. *Hot Spotter's Report: Military Fables of Toxic Waste*. University of Minnesota Press.

Kurashige, Scott. 2017. *The Fifty-Year Rebellion: How the US Political Crisis Began in Detroit*. University of California Press.

Kvik, Anton, Justin Rose, Frank C. Curriero, Cassandra K. Crifasi, and Craig Evan Pollack. 2022. "The Association Between Vacant Housing Demolition and Safety and Health in Baltimore, MD." *Preventive Medicine* 164 (November): 107292. https://doi.org/10.1016/j.ypmed.2022.107292.

Lea, Tess. 2020. *Wild Policy: Indigeneity and the Unruly Logics of Intervention*. Stanford University Press.

———. 2021. "Desiring Bureaucracy." *Annual Review of Anthropology* 50: 59–74. https://doi.org/10.1146/annurev-anthro-101819-110147.

Lepawsky, Josh, and Chris McNabb. 2010. "Mapping International Flows of Electronic Waste." *The Canadian Geographer / Le Géographe Canadien* 54 (2): 177–95.

Lewis, Jovan Scott. 2022. *Violent Utopia: Dispossession and Black Restoration in Tulsa*. Duke University Press.

Liboiron, Max. 2017. "Compromised Agency: The Case of BabyLegs." *Engaging Science, Technology, and Society* 3 (September):499–527. https://doi.org/10.17351/ests2017.126.

———. 2021. *Pollution Is Colonialism*. Duke University Press.

Light, Jennifer S. 2014. *The Nature of Cities: Ecological Visions and the American Urban Professions, 1920–1960*. Johns Hopkins University Press.

Lindqvist, Sven. 1979. "Dig Where You Stand." *Oral History* 7 (2): 24–30.

Lipsitz, George. 2011. *How Racism Takes Place*. Temple University Press.

———. 2024. *The Danger Zone Is Everywhere: How Housing Discrimination Harms Health and Steals Wealth*. University of California Press.

Littlejohn, Edward. 2018. "Black Before the Bar: A History of Slavery, Race Laws, and Cases in Detroit and Michigan." *Journal of Law in Society* 18 (1): 1–84.

Lorde, Audre. 1984. *Sister Outsider*. Crossing Press.

Lowe, Lisa. 2015. *The Intimacies of Four Continents*. Duke University Press.

Lyons, Kristina M. 2020. *Vital Decomposition: Soil Practitioners and Life Politics*. Duke University Press.

Madden, Mary, Michele Gilman, Karen Levy, and Alice Marwick. 2017. "Privacy, Poverty, and Big Data: A Matrix of Vulnerabilities for Poor Americans." *Washington University Law Review* 95 (1): 53–126.

Madhusoodanan, Jyoti. 2021. "A Troubled Calculus." *Science* 373 (6553): 380–83. https://doi.org/10.1126/science.373.6553.380.

Mallach, Alan. 2018. *The Divided City: Poverty and Prosperity in Urban America*. Island Press.

Mallin, Sean. 2016. "Becoming Blight: Property and Belonging in Post-Katrina New Orleans." PhD diss., University of California Irvine.

Markowitz, Gerald, and David Rosner. 2013. *Lead Wars: The Politics of Science and the Fate of America's Children*. University of California Press.

Martelle, Scott. 2012. *Detroit: A Biography*. Chicago Review Press.

Marx, Karl. 1973. *Grundrisse: Foundations of the Critique of Political Economy*. Translated by Martin Nicolaus. Penguin Classics.

Massey, Douglas S., and Nancy A. Denton. 1998. *American Apartheid: Segregation and the Making of the Underclass*. Harvard University Press.

Mattern, Shannon. 2021. *A City Is Not a Computer: Other Urban Intelligences*. Princeton University Press.

Mays, Kyle T. 2022. *City of Dispossessions: Indigenous Peoples, African Americans, and the Creation of Modern Detroit*. University of Pennsylvania Press.

McClintock, Nathan. 2015. "A Critical Physical Geography of Urban Soil Contamination." *Geoforum* 65 (October): 69–85. https://doi.org/10.1016/j.geoforum.2015.07.010.

McDonald, John. 2014. "What Happened to and in Detroit?" *Urban Studies* 51 (16): 3309–29. https://doi.org/10.1177/0042098013519505.

McGurty, Eileen. 2007. *Transforming Environmentalism: Warren County, PCBs, and the Origins of Environmental Justice*. Rutgers University Press.

McKittrick, Katherine. 2013. "Plantation Futures." *Small Axe* 17 (3): 1–15.

Menendian, Stephen, Arthur Gailes, and Samir Gambhir. 2021. "The Roots of Structural Racism: Twenty-First Century Racial Residential Segregation in the United States." Othering and Belonging Institute, University of California Berkeley, updated June 30. https://belonging.berkeley.edu/roots-structural-racism.

Metzl, Jonathan M. 2019. *Dying of Whiteness: How the Politics of Racial Resentment Is Killing America's Heartland*. Basic Books.

Miles, Tiya. 2017. *The Dawn of Detroit: A Chronicle of Slavery and Freedom in the City of the Straits*. New Press.

Millar, Kathleen M. 2017. "Toward a Critical Politics of Precarity." *Sociology Compass* 11 (6): 1–11. https://doi.org/10.1111/soc4.12483.

Miller, Karen. 2015. *Managing Inequality: Northern Racial Liberalism in Interwar Detroit*. NYU Press.

Mills, Charles W. 1997. *The Racial Contract*. Cornell University Press.

Mishel, Lawrence. 2017. *Diversity in the New York City Union and Nonunion Construction Sectors*. Economic Policy Institute. https://www.epi.org/publication/diversity-in-the-nyc-construction-union-and-nonunion-sectors/.

Mol, Annemarie. 2002. *The Body Multiple: Ontology in Medical Practice*. Duke University Press.

Montgomery, Alesia. 2020. *Greening the Black Urban Regime: The Culture and Commerce of Sustainability in Detroit*. Wayne State University Press.

Moreton-Robinson, Aileen. 2015. *The White Possessive: Property, Power, and Indigenous Sovereignty*. University of Minnesota Press.

Mueggler, Erik. 2001. *The Age of Wild Ghosts: Memory, Violence, and Place in Southwest China*. University of California Press.

Muehlebach, Andrea. 2012. *The Moral Neoliberal: Welfare and Citizenship in Italy*. University of Chicago Press.

Muehlebach, Andrea, and Nitzan Shoshan. 2012. "Post-Fordist Affect." *Anthropological Quarterly* 85 (2): 317–43.

Murphy, M. 2006. *Sick Building Syndrome and the Problem of Uncertainty: Environmental Politics, Technoscience, and Women Workers*. Duke University Press.

———. 2013. "Chemical Infrastructures of the St. Clair River." In *Toxicants, Health and Regulation since 1945*, edited by Soraya Boudia and Nathalie Jas, 103–15. Pickering & Chatto.

———. 2017a. "Alterlife and Decolonial Chemical Relations." *Cultural Anthropology* 32 (4): 494–503. https://doi.org/10.14506/ca32.4.02.

———. 2017b. *The Economization of Life*. Duke University Press.

Murray, Yxta Maya. 2015. "Detroit Looks Toward a Massive, Unconstitutional Blight Condemnation: The Optics of Eminent Domain in Motor City." *Georgetown Journal on Poverty Law and Policy* 23: 395–461.

Nguyen, Victoria. 2020. "Breathless in Beijing: Aerial Attunements and China's New Respiratory Publics." *Engaging Science, Technology, and Society* 6 (November): 439–61. https://doi.org/10.17351/ests2020.437.

Nichols, Robert. 2020. *Theft Is Property!: Dispossession and Critical Theory*. Duke University Press.

Nixon, Robert. 2011. *Slow Violence and the Environmentalism of the Poor*. Harvard University Press.

Noble, Safiya. 2018. *Algorithms of Oppression: How Search Engines Reinforce Racism*. NYU Press.

Oldenziel, Ruth. 1999. *Making Technology Masculine: Men, Women and Modern Machines in America, 1870-1945*. Amsterdam University Press.

Onuoha, Mimi. 2017. "Notes on Algorithmic Violence." GitHub. https://github.com/MimiOnuoha/On-Algorithmic-Violence.

paperson, la. 2017. *A Third University Is Possible*. University of Minnesota Press.

Pasquale, Frank. 2016. *The Black Box Society: The Secret Algorithms That Control Money and Information*. Harvard University Press.

Pattillo, Mary. 2008. *Black on the Block: The Politics of Race and Class in the City*. University of Chicago Press.

Peck, Jamie. 2014. "Pushing Austerity: State Failure, Municipal Bankruptcy and the Crises of Fiscal Federalism in the USA." *Cambridge Journal of Regions, Economy and Society* 7 (1): 17–44. https://doi.org/10.1093/cjres/rst018.

Peck, Jamie, and Heather Whiteside. 2016. "Financializing Detroit." *Economic Geography* 92 (3): 235–68. https://doi.org/10.1080/00130095.2015.1116369.

Pellow, David N. 2021. "Struggles for Environmental Justice in US Prisons and Jails." *Antipode* 53 (1): 56–73. https://doi.org/10.1111/anti.12569.

Perry, Andre, Hannah Stephens, and Mannan Dogoghoe. 2024. *Black Wealth Is Increasing, but so Is the Racial Wealth Gap*. Brookings Institution. https://www.brookings.edu/articles/black-wealth-is-increasing-but-so-is-the-racial-wealth-gap/.

Petty, Tawana Honeycomb. 2020. "Safe or Just Surveilled?" *Logic Magazine*, 10. https://logicmag.io/security/safe-or-just-surveilled-tawana-petty-on-facial-recognition/.

Pierre, Jemima. 2012. *The Predicament of Blackness: Postcolonial Ghana and the Politics of Race*. University of Chicago Press.

Pollock, Anne. 2021. *Sickening: Anti-Black Racism and Health Disparities in the United States*. University of Minnesota Press.

Puig de la Bellacasa, María. 2021. "Embracing Breakdown: Soil Ecopoethics and the Ambivalences of Remediation." In *Reactivating Elements*, edited by Dimitris Papadopoulos, María Puig de la Bellacasa, and Natasha Myers, 196–230. Duke University Press.

Pulido, Laura. 2015. "Geographies of Race and Ethnicity 1: White Supremacy vs. White Privilege in Environmental Racism Research." *Progress in Human Geography* 39 (6, January): 1–9.

———. 2016. "Flint, Environmental Racism, and Racial Capitalism." *Capitalism Nature Socialism* 27 (3): 1–16. https://doi.org/10.1080/10455752.2016.1213013.

———. 2017. "Geographies of Race and Ethnicity 2: Environmental Racism, Racial Capitalism and State-Sanctioned Violence." *Progress in Human Geography* 41 (4): 524–33. https://doi.org/10.1177/0309132516646495.

Pulido, Laura, Tianna Bruno, Cristina Faiver-Serna, and Cassandra Galentine. 2019. "Environmental Deregulation, Spectacular Racism, and White Nationalism in the Trump

Era." *Annals of the American Association of Geographers* 109 (2): 520–32. https://doi.org/10.1080/24694452.2018.1549473.

Purser, Gretchen. 2019. "Day Labor Agencies, 'Backdoor' Hires, and the Spread of Unfree Labor." *Anthropology of Work Review* 40 (1): 5–14. https://doi.org/10.1111/awr.12158.

Purser, Gretchen, and Brian Hennigan. 2018. "Disciples and Dreamers: Job Readiness and the Making of the US Working Class." *Dialectical Anthropology* 42 (2): 149–61. https://doi.org/10.1007/s10624-017-9477-2.

Quizar, Jessi. 2024. "A Logic of Care and Black Grassroots Claims to Home in Detroit." *Antipode* 56 (3): 801–20. https://doi.org/10.1111/anti.12842.

Radford, Gail. 2013. *The Rise of the Public Authority: Statebuilding and Economic Development in Twentieth-Century America*. University of Chicago Press.

Ramirez, Hernan. 2011. "Masculinity in the Workplace: The Case of Mexican Immigrant Gardeners." *Men and Masculinities* 14 (1): 97–116. https://doi.org/10.1177/1097184X10363993.

Rector, Josiah. 2022. *Toxic Debt: An Environmental Justice History of Detroit*. University of North Carolina Press.

Regan, Joshua, and David Myers. 2020. "Enhancing Community Safety Through Urban Demolition: An Exploratory Study of Detroit, Michigan." *Justice Policy Journal* 17 (1): 1–24.

Reno, Joshua. 2015. *Waste Away: Working and Living with a North American Landfill*. University of California Press.

Resnick, Elana. 2021. "The Limits of Resilience: Managing Waste in the Racialized Anthropocene." *American Anthropologist* 123 (2): 222–36. https://doi.org/10.1111/aman.13542.

Richter, Daniel, and Dan H. Yaalon. 2012. " 'The Changing Model of Soil' Revisited." *Soil Science Society of America Journal* 76 (3): 766–78. https://doi.org/10.2136/sssaj2011.0407.

Riis, Jacob A. 1996. *How the Other Half Lives: Studies Among the Tenements of New York*. Bedford Books.

Robbins, Paul. 2007. *Lawn People: How Grasses, Weeds, and Chemicals Make Us Who We Are*. Temple University Press.

Roberts, Dorothy. 1997. *Killing the Black Body: Race, Reproduction, and the Meaning of Liberty*. Knopf Doubleday.

Roberts, Elizabeth F. S. 2017. "What Gets Inside: Violent Entanglements and Toxic Boundaries in Mexico City." *Cultural Anthropology* 32 (4): 592–619. https://doi.org/10.14506/ca32.4.07.

Robinson, Cedric J. 2020. *Black Marxism: The Making of the Black Radical Tradition*. University of North Carolina Press.

Rodriguez, Akira Drake. 2021. *Diverging Space for Deviants: The Politics of Atlanta's Public Housing*. University of Georgia Press.

Roediger, David. 2020. *The Wages of Whiteness: Race and the Making of the American Working Class*. Verso.

Roediger, David R., and Elizabeth D. Esch. 2012. *The Production of Difference: Race and the Management of Labor in U.S. History*. Oxford University Press.

Rose, Arthur. 2024. *Asbestos—The Last Modernist Object*. Edinburgh University Press.

Rydin, Yvonne. 2013. "Using Actor-Network Theory to Understand Planning Practice: Exploring Relationships between Actants in Regulating Low-Carbon Commercial Development." *Planning Theory* 12 (1): 23–45. https://doi.org/10.1177/1473095212455494.

Safransky, Sara. 2020. "Geographies of Algorithmic Violence: Redlining the Smart City." *International Journal of Urban and Regional Research* 44 (2): 200–18.

———. 2023. *The City After Property: Abandonment and Repair in Postindustrial Detroit*. Duke University Press.

Schuller, Kyla. 2021. *The Trouble with White Women: A Counterhistory of Feminism*. Bold Type Books.

Schumpeter, Joseph A. 1950. *Capitalism, Socialism, and Democracy*. Harper.

Scott, David. 2018. "Preface: Evil Beyond Repair." *Small Axe: A Caribbean Journal of Criticism* 22 (1 (55)): vii–x. https://doi.org/10.1215/07990537-4378876.

Scott, James C. 1999. *Seeing Like a State: How Certain Schemes to Improve the Human Condition Have Failed*. Yale University Press.

Seidman, Herbert, and Irving J. Selikoff. 1990. "Decline in Death Rates Among Asbestos Insulation Workers 1967–1986 Associated with Diminution of Work Exposure to Asbestos." *Annals of the New York Academy of Sciences* 609 (1): 300–18. https://doi.org/10.1111/j.1749-6632.1990.tb32077.x.

Sharpe, Christina. 2016. *In the Wake: On Blackness and Being*. Duke University Press.

Shryock, Andrew. 2008. "The Moral Analogies of Race: Arab American Identity, Color Politics, and the Limits of Racialized Citizenship." In *Race and Arab Americans Before and After 9/11: From Invisible Citizens to Visible Subjects*, edited by Amaney Jamal and Nadine Naber, 81–113. Syracuse University Press.

Simone, AbdouMaliq. 2004. "People as Infrastructure: Intersecting Fragments in Johannesburg." *Public Culture* 16 (3): 407–29.

Simpson, Audra. 2018. "Sovereignty, Sympathy and Indigeneity." In *Ethnographies of U.S. Empire.*, edited by Carole McGranahan and John Collins, 72–89. Duke University Press.

Slyomovics, Susan. 2024. *Monuments Decolonized: Algeria's French Colonial Heritage*. Stanford University Press.

Smith, Neil. 1996. *The New Urban Frontier: Gentrification and the Revanchist City*. Routledge.

So, Wonyoung, Pranay Lohia, Rakesh Pimplikar, A. E. Hosoi, and Catherine D'Ignazio. 2022. "Beyond Fairness: Reparative Algorithms to Address Historical Injustices of Housing Discrimination in the US." *Proceedings of the 2022 ACM Conference on Fairness, Accountability, and Transparency*. June, 988–1004. https://doi.org/10.1145/3531146.3533160.

Sofia, Zoë. 2000. "Container Technologies." *Hypatia* 15 (2): 181–201. https://doi.org/10.1111/j.1527-2001.2000.tb00322.x.

Solomon, Marisa. 2019. "'The Ghetto Is a Gold Mine': The Racialized Temporality of Betterment." *International Labor and Working-Class History* 95 (April): 76–94. https://doi.org/10.1017/S0147547919000024.

———. 2022. "Ecologies Elsewhere: Flyness, Fill, and Black Women's Fugitive Matter(s)." *GLQ: A Journal of Lesbian and Gay Studies* 28 (4): 567–87. https://doi.org/10.1215/10642684-9991341.

Spears, Ellen Griffith. 2014. *Baptized in PCBs: Race, Pollution, and Justice in an All-American Town*. University of North Carolina Press.

Speed, Shannon. 2020. "The Persistence of White Supremacy: Indigenous Women Migrants and the Structures of Settler Capitalism." *American Anthropologist* 122 (1): 76–85. https://doi.org/10.1111/aman.13359.

Stack, Carol B. 2008. *All Our Kin: Strategies for Survival in a Black Community*. Basic Books.

Star, Susan Leigh. 1990. "Power, Technology and the Phenomenology of Conventions: On Being Allergic to Onions." *The Sociological Review* 38 (1_suppl): 26–56. https://doi.org/10.1111/j.1467-954X.1990.tb03347.x.

Stoetzer, Bettina. 2022. *Ruderal City: Ecologies of Migration, Race, and Urban Nature in Berlin*. Duke University Press.

Story, Brett. 2019. *Prison Land: Mapping Carceral Power Across Neoliberal America*. University of Minnesota Press.

Stout, Noelle. 2019. *Dispossessed: How Predatory Bureaucracy Foreclosed on the American Middle Class*. University of California Press.

Stovall, Maya. 2020. *Liquor Store Theatre*. Duke University Press.

Strangleman, Tim. 2013. "'Smokestack Nostalgia,' 'Ruin Porn' or Working-Class Obituary: The Role and Meaning of Deindustrial Representation." *International Labor and Working-Class History* 84 (October): 23–37. https://doi.org/10.1017/S0147547913000239.

Stuelke, Patricia. 2021. *The Ruse of Repair: US Neoliberal Empire and the Turn from Critique*. Duke University Press.

Sugrue, Thomas. 2005. *The Origins of the Urban Crisis: Race and Inequality in Postwar Detroit*. Princeton University Press.

———. 2020. "Livable Cities." In *We Own the Future: Democratic Socialism—American Style*, edited by Kate Aronoff, Peter Dreier, and Michael Kazin, 207–22. New Press.

Surkin, Marvin, and Dan Georgakas. 2012. *Detroit: I Do Mind Dying: A Study in Urban Revolution*. Haymarket Books.

Sze, Julie. 2020. *Environmental Justice in a Moment of Danger*. University of California Press.

Sznel, Monika. 2020. "The Games We Play: What Is Participation in Urban Planning? Insights from Warsaw." In *Life Among Urban Planners*, edited by Jennifer Mack and Michael Herzfeld, 196–215. University of Pennsylvania Press.

Táíwò, Olúfẹmi. 2022. *Reconsidering Reparations*. Oxford University Press.

Taylor, Dorceta. 2014. *Toxic Communities: Environmental Racism, Industrial Pollution, and Residential Mobility*. NYU Press.

Taylor, Keeanga-Yamahtta. 2019. *Race for Profit: How Banks and the Real Estate Industry Undermined Black Homeownership*. University of North Carolina Press.

Taylor, Keeanga-Yamahtta, and Adolph Reed. 2019. "The Reparations Debate." *Dissent*, June 24.

Team, Victoria, and Lenore Manderson. 2020. "How COVID-19 Reveals Structures of Vulnerability." *Medical Anthropology* 39 (8): 671–74. https://doi.org/10.1080/01459740.2020.1830281.

Thomas, June Manning. 2013. *Redevelopment and Race: Planning a Finer City in Postwar Detroit*. Wayne State University Press.

Thompson, Heather Ann. 2017. *Whose Detroit?: Politics, Labor, and Race in a Modern American City*. Cornell University Press.

Torkelson, Erin. 2021. "Sophia's Choice: Debt, Social Welfare, and Racial Finance Capitalism." *Environment and Planning D: Society and Space* 39 (1): 67–84. https://doi.org/10.1177/0263775820973680.

Torrejón, Camila, Dusan Paredes, and Mark Skidmore. 2023. "Impact of Demolitions on Neighboring Property Values in Detroit." *Journal of Regional Science* 63 (5): 1073–99. https://doi.org/10.1111/jors.12654.

Trouillot, Michel-Rolph. 2000. "Abortive Rituals: Historical Apologies in the Global Era." *Interventions* 2 (2): 171–86. https://doi.org/10.1080/136980100427298.

Tsing, Anna Lowenhaupt. 2015. *The Mushroom at the End of the World: On the Possibility of Life in Capitalist Ruins*. Princeton University Press.

Valverde, Mariana. 2011. "Seeing Like a City: The Dialectic of Modern and Premodern Ways of Seeing in Urban Governance." *Law & Society Review* 45 (2): 277–312.

Van Horssen, Jessica. 2016. *A Town Called Asbestos: Environmental Contamination, Health, and Resilience in a Resource Community*. UBC Press.

von Schnitzler, Antina. 2016. *Democracy's Infrastructure: Techno-Politics and Protest After Apartheid*. Princeton University Press.

Voyles, Traci Brynne. 2015. *Wastelanding: Legacies of Uranium Mining in Navajo Country*. University of Minnesota Press.

Walker, Mabel. 1938. *Urban Blight and Slums*. University of Chicago Press.

Walley, Christine J. 2013. *Exit Zero: Family and Class in Postindustrial Chicago*. University of Chicago Press.

Wang, Tricia. 2013. "Big Data Needs Thick Data." *Ethnography Matters*, May 13.

Ward, Stephen M. 2016. *In Love and Struggle: The Revolutionary Lives of James and Grace Lee Boggs*. University of North Carolina Press.

Warren, Christian. 2000. *Brush with Death: A Social History of Lead Poisoning*. Johns Hopkins University Press.

Warren, Gwendolyn C., Cindi Katz, and Nik Heynen. 2019. "Myths, Cults, Memories, and Revisions in Radical Geographic History." In *Spatial Histories of Radical Geography*, edited by Trevor Barnes and Eric Sheppard, 59–85. Wiley.

White, Hylton. 2012. "A Post-Fordist Ethnicity: Insecurity, Authority, and Identity in South Africa." *Anthropological Quarterly* 85 (2): 397–427. https://doi.org/10.1353/anq.2012.0033.

White, Monica M. 2018. *Freedom Farmers: Agricultural Resistance and the Black Freedom Movement*. University of North Carolina Press.

White, Richard. 1991. *The Middle Ground: Indians, Empires, and Republics in the Great Lakes Region, 1650–1815*. Cambridge University Press.

Willoughby-Herard, Tiffany. 2015. *Waste of a White Skin: The Carnegie Corporation and the Racial Logic of White Vulnerability*. University of California Press.

Winner, Langdon. 1980. "Do Artifacts Have Politics?" *Daedalus* 109 (1): 121–36.

Woods, Clyde. 1998. *Development Arrested: The Blues and Plantation Power in the Mississippi Delta*. Verso.

———. 2017. *Development Drowned and Reborn: The Blues and Bourbon Restorations in Post-Katrina New Orleans*. University of Georgia Press.

———. 2023. "Regional Blocs, Regional Planning, and the Blues Epistemology in the Lower Mississippi Delta." In *Making the Invisible Visible*, edited by Leonie Sandercock, 78–99. University of California Press.

Wright, Gwendolyn. 1991. *The Politics of Design in French Colonial Urbanism*. University of Chicago Press.

Ybarra, Megan. 2021. "Site Fight! Toward the Abolition of Immigrant Detention on Tacoma's Tar Pits (and Everywhere Else)." *Antipode* 53 (1): 36–55. https://doi.org/10.1111/anti.12610.

Yezbick, Julia. 2020. "Domesticating Detroit: Art Houses, Blight, and the Image of Care." *City & Society* 32 (2): 316–44. https://doi.org/10.1111/ciso.12280.

Zhang, Amy. 2024. *Circular Ecologies: Environmentalism and Waste Politics in Urban China*. Stanford University Press.

Zhang, Aurora. 2023. "Redress and Worldmaking: Differing Approaches to Algorithmic Reparations for Housing Justice." *Big Data & Society* 10 (2): 1–5. https://doi.org/10.1177/20539517231202983.

Zimring, Carl A. 2016. *Clean and White: A History of Environmental Racism in the United States*. NYU Press.

Zuboff, Shoshanna. 2019. *The Age of Surveillance Capitalism*. Profile Books.

INDEX

Page numbers in *italics* refer to figures, tables, and maps.